I'd Like to Apologize to Every Teacher I Ever Had

My Year as a Rookie Teacher at Northeast High

TONY DANZA

THREE RIVERS PRESS
NEW YORK

To my parents,
Matty and Anne Iadanza

Copyright © 2012 by Marc Anthony Productions, Inc.

All rights reserved.
Published in the United States by Three Rivers Press,
an imprint of the Crown Publishing Group,
a division of Random House, Inc., New York.
www.crownpublishing.com

THREE RIVERS PRESS and the Tugboat design
are registered trademarks of Random House, Inc.

Originally published in hardcover in the United States
by Crown Archetype, an imprint of the Crown Publishing Group,
a division of Random House, Inc., New York, in 2012.

Library of Congress Cataloging-in-Publication Data

Danza, Tony.
I'd like to apologize to every teacher I ever had/by Tony Danza.—1st ed.
p.   cm.
1. Danza, Tony.   2. High school teachers—United States.
3. Actors—United States.   4. Teaching—Anecdotes.   I. Title.
LA2317.D26A3 2012
371.10092—dc23
[B]   2012011320

ISBN 978-0-307-88787-0
eISBN 978-0-307-88788-7

PRINTED IN THE UNITED STATES OF AMERICA

Book design by Jennifer Daddio/Bookmark Design & Media Inc.
Cover design by Nupoor Gordon
Cover photograph © ThinkFactory Media/Barbara Johnston

Contents

SECOND SEMESTER

Author's Note

This is the story of my year as a tenth-grade English teacher at Northeast High, an inner-city public high school in Philadelphia. The events and conversations are as true and accurate as I can write them, using my daily diary entries, lesson plans, emails, videotape, YouTube postings, and memory as my guides. A few of the incidents in this book were recorded in the 2010 A&E television series *Teach*, which was shot in my classroom during the year I taught at Northeast, but please remember that television—even "reality" TV—has a way of altering actual events. I hope in this book I've drawn a truer picture of Northeast, my students, and my experience.

That said, some of my students and fellow teachers have requested that I use pseudonyms to protect their privacy. In a couple of cases I've changed identifying details for the same reason. All the poems, stories, letters, lyrics, and emails, however, are genuine and are published here in their original forms by permission of their authors.

FIRST SEMESTER

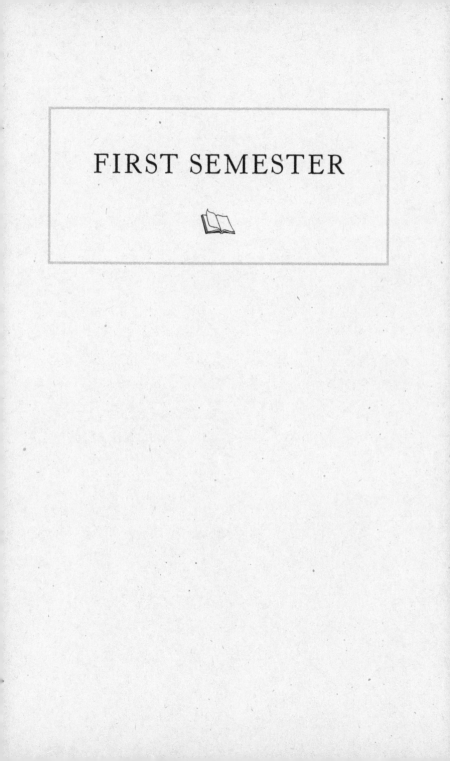

One

You're Fired, Go Teach!

ROOM 230. First day of school. I unlock the door and try to wrap my head around what's about to happen here . . . in *my* classroom . . . where I'm *Mr.* Danza. That *Mister* alone takes some getting used to—a whole different kind of Boss. At Philadelphia's Northeast High, only my fellow teachers get to call me Tony. School rules. This gig isn't acting, it's for real. Real kids, real lives, real educations at stake. And any minute now *my* students are going to walk through that door.

Engage the students. The mantra that was drilled into my head during teacher orientation starts playing like a bass drum in my chest. One of my instructors rolled her eyes when she said it, and then she added, "No one ever seems to question why the burden is all on the teacher to do the engaging, when we ask so little of the students, or for that matter, their parents."

Her vehemence startled me. "I never thought of it that way," I told her.

"No," she said, not unkindly. "But I promise, you will."

It's stifling. I turn on the AC—a luxury I'm grateful for—and double-check my room. It looks as good as I could possibly make it in my week of prep. The institutional beige cinder-block walls and the desktops are scrubbed so clean even my mother would approve. I dusted the bookshelves, squeegeed the windows, and installed dispensers of hand sanitizer by each door—an attempt to defend my students against the swine flu epidemic that's threatening the nation. This last touch, I hope, will show the kids that I sincerely care about their well-being and not that I'm a germ freak. I've also decorated the walls with fadeless blue paper and encouraging banners, which say things like THE ONLY PLACE SUCCESS COMES BEFORE WORK IS IN THE DICTIONARY and my favorite, NO MOANING, NO GROANING—if only I could follow that advice myself! Above the blackboard, I've glued big letters to spell out: TAKE PART IN YOUR OWN EDUCATION. And on the wall are listed my class rules:

1. BE here, on time and prepared
2. BE kind
3. BELIEVE

I try to shrug off the advice of a veteran teacher I met last week at Becker's, the local school supply warehouse where I bought all this signage. He was a sweet-faced guy, moonlighting as a checkout clerk to make ends meet—so much for those "outrageous" public school salaries—and he immediately marked me as a novice. His tip-off was the huge pile of educational decorations I was charging to my own credit card. Philadelphia teachers receive only a hundred dollars each for classroom supplies for the whole year; obviously I was way over budget in more ways than one. So this veteran offered a tactic to save my skin. "Never smile before Christmas," he warned. "Smiling puts you at their mercy, they'll eat you alive."

Fortunately, before I can dwell on this memory, the bell rings. Actually, it screams like an air-raid siren. But then, the strangest thing happens. Outside, the hallways are bedlam, but in my classroom dead quiet reigns, even after the first student walks in. She's small and neat, wearing jeans, a white T-shirt, and a plastic headband. She bounces a little on the balls of her feet and grins at me, but doesn't make a sound.

I HAVE A BIG MOUTH, which is how this whole thing got started.

In 2007 I was two years into my dream job—hosting a live, one-hour TV talk show in New York City. It aired from ten to eleven every weekday morning on the ABC network, right after *Live! with Regis and Kelly* and before *The View*. I felt like the king of New York. The show not only gave me a window into the true complexity of the greatest city on earth but also offered a platform for me to do some serious good. One of my favorite segments was our "School Room Makeovers." The producers would enlist charitable corporations to donate much-needed school equipment, and then we'd take a camera crew into an impoverished school and remake the science lab, gym, art room, or reading room. When we learned that the music department in one school had just six instruments for four hundred kids, we approached Casio and C. G. Conn and acquired keyboards and brass instruments. We rebuilt and reequipped the music room, and that school now has a fine jazz orchestra. Given half a chance, I'd have leveraged my show to rebuild *all* the public schools in New York. Unfortunately, my show was canceled.

Now just about every TV actor has had a show canceled—it's a basic occupational hazard. But this time, for me, was different. After the show ended, my wife and I separated. We'd been married twenty years. And only the youngest of my three kids was still living at home back in Los Angeles. Plus, I could smell sixty.

Sixty's over the speed limit. My dad only lived to be sixty-two. Suddenly, it hit me that I could be running out of time, and this realization made me begin to consider a serious change of direction. I thought about the reasons I'd been so proud of that talk show, and it occurred to me that when we made over all those schoolrooms, I wasn't only trying to address the problem of underfunded schools, but also reaching for a thread that ran all the way back to my own school days. My original career plan in college was to teach. I actually have a degree in history. After graduation I got rerouted, first into boxing, then into acting, but it was no accident that my character on *Who's the Boss?* ultimately became a teacher. I was still trying to live out my early vocational dream. But playing a teacher on television could never compare with teaching for real. Maybe now was the time to stop, regroup, and get back to the road not taken. The classroom wasn't yet closed to me. I could still make a contribution. *Sure* I could. Do something that would make my own kids truly proud of me.

What kicked me into gear was a documentary made by Teach for America, the organization that trains college graduates to teach in rural and urban public schools. The film focused on some TFA teachers in Baltimore, Maryland, and culminated with a rousing school production of *Bye Bye Birdie*. As a song-and-dance man, I can always be had for a musical, and the energy and passion of the kids in the film were truly impressive. But what throttled me was the camera's pan to the audience as the cast was taking a bow at the end of the show; there were maybe seven people there to applaud those kids. As a parent, I'd volunteered to help out on numerous theatrical productions with my own kids; in the private schools that they were fortunate enough to attend, I'd never seen a performance that did not have a packed audience of family, friends, and teachers. But in this inner-city school, no one was there to support the kids. That really got to me. I wanted to help.

I looked into TFA and learned that, technically, I qualified to apply. To be honest, though, the prospect of beginning a third-act career scared me almost as much as it attracted me. Could I really do this, after so many years? I didn't know. But if I told my friends this was what I was planning, then I wouldn't let myself back out. So I opened my big mouth.

In New York, I mentioned my youthful dream to the executive producer of my former talk show. He's young, hip, and savvy, and when I said I was thinking of giving up acting to become a teacher, he didn't miss a beat. "Ever think of doing that as a reality show?"

At first the idea repelled me. I'm no fan of reality TV in general, and the idea of a reality series about teaching immediately put me off. I wanted to teach *instead* of acting, not in combination with showbiz. Besides, this would involve actual students and their actual education. As far as TV producers are concerned, the sizzle of drama is always paramount, and that goes double—or maybe triple—for reality TV producers. A classroom reality show was bound to compromise the students at best, or at worst exploit them. Either way, I wanted nothing to do with it. "Even if it received great ratings," I told my friend, "if the students didn't get the quality of teaching they needed and deserved, then I'd consider the whole exercise a failure." And there's no way the kids would come first in a TV show. Ratings always come first. As far as I was concerned, this was a nonstarter.

A few weeks later, though, I got a call from Leslie Grief, another producer friend. Les has had a string of reality TV hits, so I should have known that when I mouthed off to him about making teaching my next act, he, too, would suggest, "That might make a good TV show." I told him that even if we could do it as a TV show, which I didn't think we could, we'd never sell it to a network. Never say never to Leslie Grief. Before hanging up, he bet me he could sell the idea to a network in the next half hour. Twenty minutes later the phone rang.

"Congratulations," Les said. "You owe me. We're meeting with A&E next week to discuss your new show about teaching."

My new show about teaching. I had to admit, I liked the sound of that. My resolve began to waver. If we actually could find a way to do this responsibly, the show had the potential to produce a win-win-win-win—for students, teachers, the network, and me. Not only would I have the chance to test myself for real in the classroom but we could showcase what teachers are really up against in public school systems today, and what kids really need that they are and aren't getting from our schools. Perhaps most important, if I succeeded, we might inspire others to join the teaching profession.

The kind of show I envisioned would be risky for the network, but I was convinced that the real lives of real kids combined with my hyperreal flop sweat as a novice teacher would make for more than enough drama. *Responsible reality.* That actually had a good ring to it.

We met with three A&E execs at Sparks Steak House in New York. It was a meeting I welcomed, but as we were seated, I remembered that a famous Mafia hit had occurred just outside. I hoped this place wasn't jinxed. A steak house for lunch would not have been my pick in any case. But Les was in high gear, and when Leslie is on, he's the reincarnation of P. T. Barnum—a consummate salesman and promoter.

I let him grease the wheels but interrupted to spell out my ground rules before he got carried away. The norm in reality TV is to soft-script the show, which means that you write the story line first, then induce the characters to make the story happen in "reality." It's easier and more cost-effective than a straight documentary approach, but I wanted nothing to do with that. "In our show," I said, "the kids have to come first, no matter what production problems we encounter. We shoot it like a documentary. No scripting. No forced or fake drama. We turn on the cameras, see what happens, then create the shows out of the footage, not the other way round."

The executives exchanged doubtful glances. My vision was by no means an easy sell, but Les made sure the execs understood we were dealing with a hot commodity. "Education is all we talk about in this country," he said. "Every presidential candidate promises to be the 'Education President,' but the problems keep getting worse. Why aren't our kids learning? That's our topic."

While slicing into our steaks, we jabbered some more about the positive takeaways from the show. The conversation was more animated than I'd expected, and when I sensed that these executives could be won over, I sprang my closing argument. "One more thing," I said. "Let's be honest. Many of us think that inner-city kids are somebody else's problem. Your kids and mine go to private schools and are doing just fine. But America's public school kids are our kids, too, and these kids are going to grow up to be the majority of America's adults. What America looks like ten, twenty years from now will depend a lot on whether these kids are educated or not, happy or not, successful or not. How do we sustain a great country without education?" I paused for a second, then felt unexpected emotion as I said, "I think we . . . could actually help."

The network execs looked at each other. Then their senior guy leaned across the table and skewered me. "Can you keep spouting that dewy-eyed passion in front of a classroom full of unruly teenagers who want to eat *you* for lunch?"

I grinned. "I'll make a bet with you. Win, lose, or draw, I'm going to be in that classroom for at least one solid school year. Cameras or no cameras, once I've got students who expect me to teach, I'll be there every day, and I'm going to try my hardest to be the best teacher they ever had. That's what I mean by *responsible reality*."

It took several more meetings and a lot more spouting, but in the end, the network executives assured me that we would do it right, and

I vowed to hold them to their word. Whether I had what it takes to actually teach was a whole other issue.

"WHAT'S YOUR NAME?" I ask the grinning young lady now standing in my classroom doorway. Learn your students' names, I remind myself as the first-day jitters take hold. It lets them know you care.

"Nakiya." She shakes my extended hand with a look that tells me I'm already violating protocol. *Nuh-kie-uh,* I repeat to myself, and decide to call her Nicky.

A big kid named Daniel saunters in next. He oozes cool, and when I direct him and Nakiya to the hand sanitizer dispensers, he raises both eyebrows as if I've just belched. "Do me a favor," I cheer him on. "Whenever you come in, sanitize your hands. Now take a seat and write your name on the card there on your desk." Then, as Daniel and Nicky reluctantly obey, I position myself at the door to welcome the rest of the class and ask them, too, to sanitize before we get started. The kids all exchange the same look: this guy is nuts, a germ freak, no less.

I try to ignore the whispering as I write my name on the board and remind myself, I'm Mr. Danza to them. But when I turn and face them, they're all different to me. Twenty-six unique tenth graders, some bored, some interested, some amused, some disdainful. Some made up, some dressed down, some looking just rolled out of bed. The room is fragrant with their perfumes, aftershaves, hair gels, and breath mints. Their names are African, Spanish, Chinese, Russian, and straightforward Anglo-American. Their skin tones run the gamut from ebony to ivory, and their hairstyles range from epic fros to Marine crew cuts—with attitudes to match. In other words, it appears to be a pretty typical Northeast High School class. Evenly split gender-wise, small ones and big ones, and if they didn't know each other before, they will soon. As I process this diversity, I try to figure out how I'm ever going to keep them all straight. I've got to learn their names.

"Umm," I stammer. "Hello. I'm Mr. Danza and I'm here to . . . I'm supposed to, uh . . . This year I'll be your, ah, English teacher." It takes so long to get that out that a kid who has the look and build of a linebacker raises his hand before I finish. His name card reads MATT. "Yes, Matt," I say.

"Does anyone else think it's weird," he asks the others, then me, "that you're teaching English?"

Busted! I take this for what it is—a good, stiff biff in the nose. "The irony has not escaped me." I'm striving for humor, but Matt's question has opened the floodgates. Hands spring up, and all at once the kids start pummeling me with questions: Who are you? Is this a stunt? Why Northeast?

I try to answer honestly that even though there's a TV crew in the back of the room shooting a reality show about what it takes to teach in a big inner-city high school, I really have trained and I really do intend to give them the education they deserve. My protests are drowned out until a beefy kid named Howard shouts, "Are you a millionaire?" Suddenly, everybody listens.

I'm old-fashioned about my finances is what I am, from a time when it was nobody else's business. But I'm so desperate to be honest with the kids that I admit, "Yes, I am a millionaire." Then I add, "But remember, a million isn't what it used to be," only afterward realizing this isn't something that inner-city kids are likely to find particularly enlightening.

So maybe I deserve it when a girl in the back pipes up. "Are you nervous?"

I breathe a sigh of relief and admit: "I'm terrified!"

Then comes her punch line: "Because your shirt is totally soaked."

I look down and realize I've sweated through the front, back, and both sides of my pressed light blue dress shirt. And we're not even fifteen minutes into the period.

"Maybe you should think about wearing another undershirt," the girl, whose name card reads CHARMAINE, adds for good measure. The class cracks up.

What am I supposed to do? I lift my arms and gaze at my stained armpits and shrug in surrender. Can it get any worse? Probably. Despite the rolling cameras, despite my lack of experience, I really am determined to give these kids the care they deserve. But by now I've forgotten every single thing I'd planned for today.

In my nervousness, I default to monologue. "You know, I'm really just like you. I come from a neighborhood just like this. My schooling began in a Catholic school in Brooklyn. Blessed Sacrament—a very strict school where the nuns and priests disciplined us physically. Every classroom had a walk-in closet. If you broke a rule, a nun would take you into the closet and hit you. Usually a good slap, or two or three. Once, in the closet with one notorious nun, I received a double ear cuff. I still remember it."

The kids give me just enough of a laugh to keep me going. "My parents never went to college. I'm not sure if they even finished high school. My father was a sanitation man, a garbageman for the city, and my mother a bookkeeper. So I've been very fortunate in my life and career, but I know what it feels like to be full of doubt about your purpose in life. You are what you do, and if you do nothing, you can feel like nothing."

I try to make eye contact, make them feel that I mean it. Some of the kids are glaring at me, some squirming, some still tittering about the nun in the closet.

"I was small for my age," I plunge on. "Four foot eleven in the tenth grade, and that added to my misery and insecurity. To be accepted and not get beat up, I tried to be funny. As for schoolwork, I know I didn't do my best."

I stop walking back and forth and implore them, "Do your best! That's all I try to do now, in everything I attempt. Why didn't I then? Why did I think doing just enough to get by was enough? You know, you can have it both ways if you try—have fun *and* do well in school."

They look at me like I've lost my mind. They're not getting it, and I so want them to get this, if nothing else. "I *wish* I'd been more interested in my studies. Why didn't I get As? I received my degree, but just barely, and now I so regret that I didn't take full advantage of my school years."

They're texting, yawning, staring at my shirt, which must be dripping on the floor by now. I switch back to why I'm here. "I planned to teach, but when I finished school, I thought I was too young and—at least I was honest with myself—too foolish to teach anyone anything. So my goal of being a teacher was put aside as I searched for what else to do with my life. This could have ended badly, as I was not really prepared for life after college. How do you earn a living with a degree in history if you're not going to teach? Well, I got lucky. I took a succession of odd jobs—in the kitchen for a caterer, at a moving company. I was a good bartender. That's where I got to work on my people skills. Then I became a professional boxer and was discovered, as they say, in the original Gleason's Gym in Manhattan. Went on to do the TV shows *Taxi* and *Who's the Boss?*" I'm tempted to ask if any of them have seen those shows but don't.

One girl raises her hand. Thank you, Chloe! Another pretty smiler, she chirps, "I'm into eighties retro stuff, so I've seen some of your reruns."

Eighties retro stuff. Ouch. "Well, so, you all weren't born yet when my shows were on. But the point is, all this time I've been thinking about teaching, and as I've gotten older I've been consumed with questions about my wasted youth. I used to do this joke where someone would ask me, 'Were you a hoodlum as a kid?' and I'd answer, 'No, I just didn't have time for team sports.' I can't believe I thought that was funny. How stupid and unaware."

I'm still losing them. I'm losing them. Nothing is worse for an actor, much less for an actor turned teacher. But I get it. Like a drowning man, I plead, "Okay, enough about me. Let's hear about you. I'd like you each to come up here and introduce yourself, tell us a little something about you." They look at me like I have two heads. "Nicky," I say. First in, first up. Also she's the only one who doesn't seem to want to vaporize me. That makes her my go-to girl.

Nakiya bounces to the front of the room. "I'm Nakiya. I play basketball, lacrosse, and drums in the school band and for my church. I like to smile." She turns on the brights, and my heart melts. This is some kid.

"Thank you, Nakiya," I say, making a real effort to get her name right. "Who's next?"

A tall, slim, handsome boy comes forward and tells us he arrived from Russia six years ago. "You can call me Russian Playboy because I *love* American girls!" he says and pretends to toss flowers to the ladies in the front row, who all turn shades of red. Russian Playboy takes a bow. "I've got to still work on my English."

"Me, too," I assure him as the girls compose themselves, and our Russian Playboy strolls back to his seat.

A skinny boy with braces and a black bowl cut comes up next. "I'm Eric Choi, and I'm kinda boring." He shuffles his feet. "My parents expect so much, and they nag me a lot."

I nod. I get that. "Mine did, too."

Chloe, the eighties fan with large chocolate eyes, tells us, "I love to shop. I love fashion, love to smile." She giggles. "Can't stop."

A kid wearing a black Korn T-shirt, his long brown hair draped over his eyes, tells us, "I'm Ben, but people call me Kyle. It's a long story." Before I can ask for the story, he tells us the obvious, "I'm a complete metal head."

Then Ben-Kyle's opposite stands up. Monte reminds me of a serious Steve Urkel, the geeky kid on *Family Matters*. Monte's short with big dark eyes, his striped polo shirt buttoned all the way up. His voice is so monotone, it sounds robotic. "I only care about two things. My family and . . ." I'm not sure what I expect, but I'm completely flummoxed when he says "tennis."

The next girl up, however, bounds to the front like a natural athlete. She has long, straight sandy hair and pretty brown eyes. "I'm Tammy Lea. I play field hockey, and I can't wait to get my braces off." She smiles wide for effect. "And I love to sing and dance."

The class's three football players introduce themselves as Howard, Matt, and Daniel, then Eric Lopez informs us that he's been "breaking for about half a year," and with that, he drops to his back, spins, and flips back up to his feet like Gumby. The class goes wild.

There are twenty-six of them, and every one is a character. But there's one whose expression spells trouble from the git-go. He's a tall, lanky, good-looking kid with cornrows and an expression of supreme skepticism. When I motion him up front, he moves like he's got years to get there. "I'm Al G," he says. "I like to joke around. I get on people's nerves. I can be pretty annoying after a while."

I feel like he's putting me on notice. "Okay then," I say as Al saunters back to his seat. "Well, I like a good joke. But one of the things I want to impress on you guys this year is to get smart early. Don't wait, like I did, until you're out of high school or even college to realize the importance of excelling at your studies. Learn from my—"

The bell shrieks, and my brain snaps. My students are getting up to leave as if I don't exist. I stop them. I really have trained for this. "The bell doesn't dismiss you," I call out. "I do." I heard that at orientation, and as it comes out of my mouth it sounds dumb even to me.

Suddenly I remember the homework assignment. "Think of a story to tell the class tomorrow. It can be a family story, or something that happened to you. Half a page, minimum."

Before I can breathe, they're gone. And I feel like I've just lost a ten-round fight by unanimous decision.

Lesson Plans

After my first class has imploded and the last student gone, David Cohn comes forward and puts a consoling hand on my shoulder. He's thin, cerebral, and young enough to be my son. He's also my supervisor, and he's been watching the whole debacle from the back of the room. I'm ready to cry.

David is a concession we had to make before the Philadelphia school board would let me teach at Northeast. On the wall of the board's meeting room in the district office building hangs a sign that reads: WHAT IS BEST FOR THE STUDENTS? When I saw that sign during our protracted negotiations over the show, I assured the board members, "I have a teenage daughter of my own. And I mean to give my students here the same quality of education that I want for her." To guarantee that promise, our producers offered to pay for a veteran teacher to observe me and ensure that my students received an effective tenth-grade English course of study.

At first this concession was grudging on my part. I wanted a real teaching experience, not one with training wheels. But during the orientation that followed, my subjects ranged from classroom management to what to do if a student spits in your face. What would I do if a kid spit in my face? Was this really a possibility? As tough as my childhood neighborhood in Brooklyn had been, no teacher in my day needed to worry about dodging loogies. Maybe having a coteacher wasn't such a bad idea after all.

Now a kid's spitting seems far less of a threat than my own performance does.

"It's not as bad as it feels," David says. "Considering it's your first attempt."

I want to ask why he didn't step in and save me, but of course, that's not his job. His job, as we agreed, is to observe, and then sit me down and review what just happened.

David reminds me that teachers prepare lesson plans to help them stay on track. Which is why he had me slave for three solid days over my plan for today. As David has explained to me more than once, lesson plans have to encompass not just what I teach but also how I teach it and how I plan to assess my students' retention of the material. Each lesson must have a goal and each class three parts: the "do-now" or warm-up exercise, the main activity, and the wrap-up.

"Unfortunately," he points out now, "lesson plans are useless unless you remember to use them." The last time I even glanced at today's lesson plan was approximately twelve minutes before Nakiya appeared in the doorway.

"I cannot believe I forgot the do-now." I check over my shoulder. Yep. "Right there on the blackboard!"

"Don't worry. It happens."

I don't believe him. Time has spun me in circles, and the kids have done me in. I blew the entire class. At this rate, how am I ever going to teach all the material I have to cover in the semester?

I take a deep, shaky breath. "I have to be better."

"Don't beat yourself up," David says. "Every first-year teacher goes through this."

He should know. David's specialty is teaching teachers, and he advises all first-year teachers at Northeast. But I can't help feeling that I'm a special—and not particularly promising—case.

Two

Ignorance Is No Excuse

NEXT MORNING the alarm starts screaming at 4:20 A.M. It's pitch dark, and I've been waking up in a panic every half hour all night long. Getting up is more relaxing than trying to sleep. At least if I do some push-ups, get the blood flowing, give myself time to review my lesson plan, maybe I'll get through today without falling on my face.

As the sun rises, I stand in front of the wall of glass that I call my magic window. It opens onto a small balcony facing east and is the best feature of the apartment I've rented for the duration of my time at Northeast. I'm in the Northern Liberties section of Philly, a neighborhood in the process of being gentrified. It's full of art galleries, bars, and restaurants, reminiscent of New York. Every few minutes I can watch the elevated train run by, and I see a certain symmetry in that. In Brooklyn, where I was born, the el ran right down the middle of Pitkin Ave. As a child, I would sit by the window and wave to the people in the train as it went by, hoping that someone would wave back. I was once a kid no different from the ones I'm now supposed to be teaching. Time to get back to school.

As far as the show's concerned, I don't have to be on campus until my class begins at ten o'clock, but I can just imagine the other teachers' reception if I moseyed in around nine-thirty when they'd been busting their butts since seven. No thanks. If teachers all over the country are dragging themselves out of bed before dawn in order to get the job done, then so will I. Besides, this second day is going to go better. I feel it.

Just after seven, I pull into one of the teachers' lots and park near the row of shrubs pruned to spell out NORTHEAST. Although the campus dates back to the 1840s, the school's current brick building was erected in 1953 and looks a bit like a postwar factory, complete with a towering smokestack. The largest high school in Philadelphia, Northeast has three stories, trailers, multiple sports fields, its own football stadium, a huge cafeteria, and several cavernous gyms. We even have our own Philadelphia police station! Now there's a comforting thought.

It wasn't easy to find a school that would have us. Our production team approached districts all over the country and formally petitioned school boards in New York, Baltimore, Chicago, Dallas, Atlanta, Washington, D.C., L.A., Pittsburgh, and Newark just to name a few. None was willing to let a "celebrity teacher" with cameras into its schools. I was almost ready to give up when the woman who heads up the film and television production office in Philadelphia phoned.

Sharon Pinkenson is a dead ringer for Meg Ryan and an incredible booster for her city. She has a direct line to Mayor Michael Nutter, and the mayor always has time for the kids of his city. So when Ms. Pinkenson told the mayor that our television show, if done right, could help the schools of Philadelphia, he was interested. Leslie Grief and I flew in and made our presentation, and Mayor Nutter encouraged us, but we still had to win over District Superintendent Dr. Arlene Ackerman and her superiors on the School Reform Commission.

This process took months, and inevitably the press latched on to us. None of the coverage was very good, and some was below low. One reporter actually wrote, "Tony Danza is pimping Philadelphia's kids to kick-start his faded and stalled career." Jeez, I thought, "faded and stalled"? And "pimping"?

Somehow, the mayor continued to stand by us. Eventually, though not without vocal reservations, the School Reform Commission approved us. I was granted one double period a day to teach one class of tenth-grade English. My "load" of twenty-six fifteen-year-old boys and girls would be just one-fifth the load that regular teachers carry, so not exactly a true reflection of the job, but this was as much as the commission was willing to risk, and they made sure I understood I was lucky to have it.

Now, as I approach the cameraman and sound engineer already waiting for me near the school entrance, *lucky* does not begin to describe how I feel. *Lost* is more like it.

This is to be our routine. Every day when I arrive on campus, I'm miked and wired so that the devices are as invisible as possible before we go inside. Then we make our way past the multiple sets of guards and metal detectors that, sadly, have become as much of a fixture in urban high schools as they are in airports. This early, only a few students are around. As I watch one boy send his backpack through the screener, I ask him what he thinks of all this security. To my surprise he says, "It's good." Then he explains that he knows more than a few knuckleheads who might try to bring "something" into school. "Even though it takes some time when everyone is on line waiting, it makes the rest of us feel safe."

Forty years ago, when I went to public high school, I always felt safe. Except for keeping an eye out for some of the bigger kids who liked to exercise their fists on us small ones, I didn't give security a second thought. I blurt this out to a young man who's checking his box as I enter the mail room. He gives me a sympathetic nod and introduces himself as Joe Connelly, a first-year math teacher.

Joe has an open, easygoing manner, and I like him right away. When I spot my mailbox, with my name on it, I do a little dance to show how thrilled I am to be a real teacher. Instead of making fun of me, Joe points to the name on his own box and gives his chest a thump. We're both pretty impressed with ourselves for just being here. Soon I'm deep into the story of my convoluted journey to Northeast.

"Hey, I hear you're doing a ninety-minute class," Joe says. "Good luck keeping their attention."

"Yeah, they figured I'd need a double period. We'll see."

"So how'd the crew in the office react the first time you signed in?"

I have no idea what he's talking about. "Teachers have to sign in?"

"They do here." His suddenly sober expression tells me this is one rule I don't want to break. And since it's the second day of classes, I've clearly already broken it. "Maybe," Joe says without much conviction, "you can use the first-day chaos to buy yourself a pass."

I hotfoot it to the office and ask the two women at the counter about signing in. They point in unison, like models on *The Price Is Right*, to a formidable-looking woman who sits with her back to me at a desk behind them. This is Ms. DeNaples, assistant principal and school disciplinarian—for both students and teachers.

Ms. DeNaples rises slowly from her desk. She wears a green business suit and sensible shoes and takes her time walking to the counter. Her brown curls quiver as she faces me. "Good morning, Mr. Danza."

My comfort level plummeting by the second, I reply, "Good morning, Ms. DeNaples."

"We missed you yesterday." She points to the clock on the wall. "And why are you late for school *today*, Mr. Danza?"

I try to explain that I was unaware of the sign-in policy and that's why I didn't sign in yesterday, but both days I've arrived on campus at 7:05, and I'm so anxious to make this work that I couldn't possibly be late. In a quietly loud, cutting voice she interrupts, "You are to sign in every day, no later than seven-thirty-eight. And remember, the sign-in sheet is a legal document. There is no room for error."

As she's talking, I notice a smudge of scarlet lipstick on her front teeth. I consider telling her but think better of it. Then I realize I'm unconsciously licking my own front teeth.

I stop licking when she says, "How do you want to be treated this year, Mr. Danza? Do you want to be treated like every other teacher, or do you have something else in mind? Northeast High School is not Hollywood, you know!"

I bow my head. "I know that, Ms. DeNaples. I want to be treated like everyone—"

She cuts me off. "Then why weren't you aware of the sign-in policy? You went through orientation. Why out of all the first-year teachers were you the only one who didn't know to sign in yesterday?"

I have no explanation. And everyone in the office seems to be relishing my discomfort. They've seen Ms. D. in action before. Chances are, at least a few of them have experienced her wrath themselves.

"Why is that?" she repeats. Then she leans so close I can smell the coffee on her breath as she growls, "I can be either your best friend in the school or a complete bitch. It's up to you."

I assure her with a smile that, given the choice, I choose the former. She doesn't think that's funny. She folds her arms and glares at me. Her glare so rattles me that when she finally does pass the sign-in roster across the counter, I try to read and sign without my glasses. I can't find my own name.

She snaps, "Stop being so vain and put on your glasses." The office audience guffaws.

I want to explain that it was terror, not vanity, that discombobu-
lated me, but instead I fish my glasses out of my shirt pocket and put
them on. "Oh, there I am," I say, trying for another laugh. Not even
a smile. O for two.

As I sign, I apologize profusely, assuring her it won't happen
again. "Ignorance is no excuse," I add for good measure.

"That's correct!" she barks. Teach me to suck up.

So much for the Welcome Wagon. I slink toward the nearest door.
But before I can reach it, Northeast's principal, Ms. Linda Carroll,
appears and beckons me into her office for a word.

I take a seat in front of the principal with the sun against me. I
try not to squint. Ms. Carroll has large dark eyes, a sweet face, and a
soft voice (when she wants it to be), but I know better than to let that
fool me. She has a reputation for being as tough and no-nonsense as
she is caring.

"I'm sorry I haven't had a chance until now to sit down with you,
Mr. Danza," she says, "because there's something I'm just not sure
I understand." I nod and wait. She's smiling coolly, and I can't help
feeling like a schoolboy called into the principal's office. Finally, she
lets me have it. "Why are you here?"

I'm nonplussed. Though this is our first time one-on-one, it isn't
our first meeting. And busy as she had to have been, what with prepping a staff of several hundred for the start of school, she did sign off
on all our arrangements for the show. Is this some sort of test?

"I have to be honest," she continues before I can answer. "I was a
little apprehensive about this whole thing. So I thought I should ask
you personally, what are your intentions for this project?"

I run through all the reasons I've given myself—the old dream,
the desire to do something I could be proud of, the chance to show
America what a big urban high school is really like. I say, "At this
moment, education is the hot-button subject that it deserves to be.

It's the right time, and this show gives us what I hope will be the right vehicle to shine a light on urban education. We want to go beyond the easy description of failing schools and bad teachers and show the true humanity of our children and of the people who work with them. There is hope. There are still good kids who genuinely want to learn, and some of them go to school in Philadelphia." Wow, I think, not bad for the spur of the moment. But it's not just a pretty speech I made up. I really believe it. "I think our show can inspire more people from other professions to go into teaching for their second act, and maybe even motivate kids still in school today to want to be teachers."

Ms. Carroll waves her pencil to cut me off. "You know," she says after a painfully long pause, "I think that's why I felt comfortable enough to take this chance. Because if I didn't get anything else, I felt your sincerity. And I'm being perfectly honest with you. It is my absolute charge to ensure that my students are educated. With that said, I want to welcome you and support you to get the job done, but know that I will not let anybody or anything compromise my children getting what they need to get out of this school year. Not you, and not this production."

"I understand!" Boy do I. "It takes a certain amount of hubris to walk in here and think I can teach, Ms. Carroll. I get that."

She isn't finished. "You have to know, Mr. Danza, that if this doesn't work, you're out of here."

I feel the corners of my eyes filling with tears again. For some reason, I feel like crying all the time! But I am most definitely on notice. Ms. Carroll *is* the boss.

DURING THE PASSING BREAK before my class begins, Monte corners me in the hallway. He barely comes up to my shoulders but somehow manages to look down on me. "I am worried I made the wrong choice," he tells me, "taking your class rather than Advanced Placement English. I intend to be the first person in my family to go to college. I intend to get a scholarship to Harvard or Princeton." He really does talk like that. It's all business.

"Really?" I mentally add college to family and tennis on the list of things Monte cares about. "That's very impressive."

He ignores me. "I should be in a more challenging class. I am not sure you are qualified to teach."

Well! The kid certainly gets right to the point, and he doesn't seem to mind stabbing me with it. Fortunately, we're right outside my classroom. "Step inside, Monte," I say.

I close the door after him and try to look him square in the eye. He stares right back. I make him a promise. "Monte, I will make sure I don't jeopardize your education. I'm sure I'll make a few mistakes, but if you give me a chance, I'll prove to you that this class will be good, and good for you. Will you just give me a little time?"

He folds his arms across his small chest. He twists his mouth into a knot. I can see that this kid *thinks* about everything, and I've yet to see him smile. However reluctant, he nods.

Then the bell rings, and we're into Round Two.

It amazes me that everybody sanitizes like they've been doing it forever, without even being told to. It's the second day! These kids really do pay attention. As they take their seats, I point to the do-now assignment on the board and tell them to get to work. No sweaty monologues from me today. The prompt: "The most important _____ in my life is . . ."

The others are hard at work when Al G deigns to appear. He's about six feet tall, and a pencil mustache has sprouted on his upper lip. He may be only fifteen, but he's handsome and cocky. Arriving late and moving like a long strand of molasses is his idea of cool.

"Take off your backpack and stay a while," I say as he slides into his seat.

"More comfortable wit' it on," he mumbles. Like many kids at Northeast, he talks as if it's a crime to be understood. As if school is an imposition and if you take school seriously, then you're trying to be smart, and being smart is also a crime. That's Al's culture. He makes it clear that he has no use for the other kids in this class. They're not his crowd; the crew he hangs with let you know they're not exactly on the honor roll. Al G is a painful reminder of my own teenage self. The difference is that now the unmotivated student is no longer the exception. Looking back, I think how much less fun school would have been if everybody was like me.

I tell Al to do the assignment that's on the board. He studies the air above my head. His stare is different from Monte's but equally disdainful. I try to ignore them both as I collect the do-nows. Al G still hasn't located his pencil. He expects me to let him slide. So as I'm about to have the students share their homework—the half page written from experience—I ask him to lead off. He doesn't have his homework, either. I really ought to know better, but I cut him some slack. "You'll hand in both assignments tomorrow," I say.

Al shoots me a look that promises to make me pay for my kindness. This flusters me, so I do what I do when I'm flustered: I talk.

My name is Tony Danza and I have ADHD. I was never diagnosed with attention deficit/hyperactivity disorder, and I certainly don't mean to make light of the condition, but as I try to capture my students' attention, I discover that I have a real problem with my own. I have a hard time staying on topic. I can't help but go off on tangents when something comes to mind that I think the kids should know about. I also can't resist telling stories that have nothing to do with the business at hand—although in my mind there's always a purpose.

"You know," I find myself saying, "a lot of us in my generation wonder why we didn't make As like the kids we picked on and wanted to beat up. Our lives might have been a whole lot different if we had. You realize, most people don't aim too high and miss—they aim too low and hit."

They doodle. Girls pick at their split ends. Guys shrink into their hoodies. They gaze through me.

I talk faster. "I gotta tell you, though, whenever I got in trouble, my parents always supported the teacher. If you got into trouble with the teacher, you got into trouble at home. I was a good student early on, got pretty good grades in elementary school, but then I became the class clown. Not terribly disruptive, but mischievous. I did silly things, like I used to shoot spitballs. You chewed a piece of paper into almost a paste, and then used your ruler to launch it and it would stick to the ceiling. The nun wouldn't notice until it dried some and fell to the floor with a splat in the middle of her lesson. Sometimes they'd land on her. None of you knuckleheads get any ideas."

Eric Choi, the most physically flexible kid I have ever seen, crumples to one side so his head nearly touches the floor. He alarms me, but then I see he just looks bored out of his skull, which only spurs me to try harder to get to the point of the story. I wish I knew what it was. "Once in sixth grade we had an elderly nun who we decided was blind. To prove it, we made a dummy student. We dressed it in a school uniform and sat it at a desk. We thought it was hilarious when the sister scolded the dummy for not taking notes. Now I realize we were just being cruel."

I look at Al G as I say this, but Al's in his own world. I need to get back to the lesson, but then I remember that their homework was about personal experience, so I console myself that I'm just demonstrating the assignment. If I tell them about an experience that they can relate to and that teaches them a lesson, I'm doing my job!

"Unfortunately, sixth grade was the end of my stint at Blessed Sacrament. I had a series of incidents that culminated in a little knife fight on the school playground. I'd been beaten up by a bigger boy, and my friend came to my defense, pulling out a small pocketknife. I called out for him to put away the knife, which he was doing when the other boy jumped him with a flying kick."

The big bruiser Matt and his buddy Howard a.k.a. Frankie (another kid with two names) are suddenly listening with their mouths open. Pretty Chloe has a hand over her eyes, anticipating the cut. I smile and shrug so it doesn't sound quite so bad. "The knife found its way into the backside of the kicker. Got him in the butt. My friend and I ran and hid until it was time to go home for dinner. In those days, kids left the house in the morning, and after school we all hung with our friends in the street until dinnertime. Hiding didn't help. I had to go home eventually and confessed in tears. The pastor told my mom to take me out of his school and he also expelled my younger brother, who was only in the second grade and hadn't done anything yet of note. Thanks to me, the priest felt compelled to purge my whole family. I felt like a real schmo. You guys know what a *schmo* is? It's a Yiddish word that literally means jerk, but it's a pretty good all-purpose put-down."

I had them; now I'm all over the place again. I've heard ADHD is a sign of intelligence, but that doesn't help when I'm supposed to be teaching a lesson. During orientation we were warned that students will try anything to get the teacher off topic and waste time. My kids will have the opposite problem: they'll beg me to stay *on* topic.

The Real Deal

"There's somebody I want you to meet," David says. As we walk downstairs, he continues, "Another first-year teacher, Philadelphia native. He built a successful local contracting business by his early thirties. Then, having saved up some money, he sold his company and became a teacher."

I understand now why David wants me to talk to this guy. He's my reality without the show. Maybe I can learn something.

As we enter a basement classroom, a young teacher in shirtsleeves looks up from erasing the blackboard. He gives me a broad grin. "Hey, Tony!"

"You guys already know each other?" David looks confused.

"Old buddies," I lie as Joe Connelly and I fist-bump. "Thanks for trying to save me from Ms. DeNaples, even if it didn't work."

Joe laughs. I'm glad to know he has this period free. Since I have only one academic class and most other teachers have as many as five, I wasn't sure I'd be able to find anyone to schmooze with—even if they were game. Joe says, "Welcome to the dungeon."

I glance at the windowless walls and feel a pang of guilt over my room's view of grass and trees—another benefit of the show. But as Joe tells David how well his first classes have gone, I wonder if his more sterile surroundings might be an advantage. At least they reduce the distractions.

David suggests we compare notes and excuses himself. I pull up one of the student chairs. "So," I ask, "what made you want to be a teacher?"

Joe perches on the corner of his desk and rubs the chalk from his palms. "Mainly because it always bugged me that I didn't finish college. I was mildly successful as a contractor, but as time progressed, I started to think about what I wanted to be when I grew up."

"Hey, me, too!" I grin.

"My wife, Sam, is a middle school English teacher," he continues. "I always thought I'd enjoy teaching math, if I ever had the time to finish school. But once I bought a house, I shelved the teaching idea and focused on what I thought of as 'real' work. I wanted a storefront, some good installers doing the work for me as I focused on sales. But then my protégé left and started his own business. This opened my eyes to how hard it is to keep good help. And, what's more important, my son was born."

"Didn't that just make you more anxious about earning a living?"

"Yes and no. Becoming a father changed my ideas about what's important in a man's life. All of a sudden, I realized that I wanted my son to view me in a better light. How would I be able to ask him to finish school when the time came if I didn't finish myself? How could I expect him to hold principles above financial gain if I chose the money route? So when Joey was one year old, I went back to school to become a father. I went back to school to become a contributing member of society. I went back to school to help influence slackers like myself to buy into their own education."

"I know just what you mean!" I exclaim. I want to hug this guy. "I was a slacker, too. If there's one thing I want to do this year, it's try to reach the kids who remind me of me and *wake them up* so they don't make the same mistakes I did."

Joe runs a hand over his crew cut. "Sometimes when I tell my story, I feel like I'm being too dramatic."

"Hell, no! You're not being dramatic, my friend, you're being *real*." And then I think again. "I take that back. It is dramatic, but it's the kind of dramatic commitment we need to turn our schools around."

"So." He glances at the cameras that, of course, are filming our every move. "You're really here for the whole year . . . teaching?"

"I really am," I say, but then I remember Ms. Carroll's warning and the two days so far. "Unless they throw me out."

Joe looks across the room as if seeing his first teaching attempts, too. "The kids don't make it easy. Sam warned me."

"I think I've got to channel more of my father. He was a knock-around guy with a saying for every occasion. 'Finish strong.' 'Two wrongs don't make a right.' 'Keep your mouth shut and mind your own business.' "

"Those would all work in the classroom," Joe agrees.

"He was a tough, honest, hardworking city sanitation man. I listened to him get up early, every morning—rain, shine, or snow—and leave for work. When it did snow, we might not see him for days. He would walk out of the house, down the snowy street, and then hitchhike to the sanitation garage in Brooklyn. On the kitchen table, he would always leave half of his egg sandwich for me. It was his way of saying good morning and letting me know he was thinking of me."

Joe smiles. "Sounds like you had a good dad."

"Any time you feel like coming up to my room for fifth period," I say, "we can eat lunch together and discuss our day, school, the kids. I'll give you half my sandwich."

"That's nice of you—" Joe begins, but the bell rings and we both bolt upright. Enough shooting the breeze. Back to work.

WHEN I GET HOME to my apartment at the end of the day, I realize that, in my haste to get to school this morning, I forgot to tear off yesterday's thought for the day from the calendar on my desk. When I remedy the situation, today's thought appears: "Encourage a good student to become a teacher." Perfect, I think, but what about not-so-good students, like me?

And with that I open an envelope that was sitting in my mailbox at school this morning. Talk about timing.

From: Harry Gilbert
To: Mr. Tony Danza
    English Dept
    Northeast HS

Dear Sir:

Here's some free advice from a retired Public School teacher with over 35 years teaching 7th to 12th graders. My last position was teaching Math for 17 years at NEHS in room 6. I taught Math at Camden HS & South Philadelphia High School in addition to subbing in all subjects, teaching summer & special programs & teaching to the Scholastic Aptitude Test at over 10 different schools in the Delaware Valley.

I loved just about every minute of it, and if I had to do it over again, my choices would be very close to what I've already done. Being a teacher is part salesman, part actor & lots of compassion. You picked a great school that has fine students and some excellent staff members. Note, not all staff members are excellent all the time, but when I left, there were plenty of great educators & then there were some I wouldn't trust walking my dog.

Some Advice, in no particular order:
- *Get last year's yearbook. Sit down with 2 or more people you feel "get it" at NEHS and page through. Let them be candid. Off the record. You will learn more about the school speaking to 2 or more staff members leafing through the yearbook over drinks than you will any other way (my opinion). Forget talking with the administration, although I am sure you will meet & interact with them more than any other teacher not related to them. Contact people like the Dean of Discipline, your best contact for outside discipline & advice.*

- *I heard you are interested in getting involved in a sport or activity. For Football there is the present Mr. NEHS, Chris Riley. Riley played at NEHS, coached in the suburbs & the Catholic League, as well as other stops in the public league including one of our archrivals, George Washington HS. He might know more about current HS football in the Delaware Valley than anyone.*

- *Wardrobe. You might be thinking suit & tie. Try it once. Put suit jacket on the back of your chair. The building is hot. Buy 6 shirts from the school store. 2 black, 2 red & 2 white. Then Monday through Friday is red, white, black, red, white, etc. You will have a different shirt every day. They can be worn with dress shoes or sneakers. Sneakers are best. No denim, except on Oct 2, which is "National Denim Day" in honor of breast cancer awareness. If possible hide the tattoos. They are very distracting, like a giant scar. As you walk around the room, you might notice some students trying to look at your tattoos instead of your nose hairs.*

- *Always carry a book, notebook or newspaper. (You don't want to pop a woody at an inappropriate time.)*

- *The last 5 years of my career I started & ended every class with tasteful music & a hotel bell (DING DING DING), the type you find on the counter of motels to get attention. When the bell rang to end a class, I started my radio with a remote that is playing oldies, mostly Temptations or instrumentals.*

  - *There are 5 minutes between classes. You hear 2 songs. The kids are not offended; sometimes they sing, dance or groan. When the start bell rings, you or a student taps your hotel bell. "Ding ding ding" means to get quiet. Wait about 15 seconds, the 2nd "ding ding ding" means, if you are still making noise you really want to get into trouble.*

- *Establish this procedure early & you will have no trouble getting started. The kids can talk & make noise before the bell rings, but after that, it's business. And the main business is order & respect for others.*

- *Seating Chart. Make one up, use pencil. Do not rearrange chairs unless you are able to put them back neatly before the bell rings every day.*

  - *(1st or 2nd day) You say: "I'm only going to ask this twice, raise your hand if you need or want a special seat." Point & give them a number. After the 2nd time, give each of those students their choice of seats, then fill in the rest alphabetically. A seating chart is like a line-up. It can be changed at any time by the coach. Students are like players, they can suggest, but Coach has final say.*

- *Homework: Always. Never more than 15 minutes a night. The good kids have too much to do.*

- *Grades. Have a test or grade at least every 2 weeks. This will give you 4 grades a marking period. Give a 5th grade for work habits—that includes HW, attendance, behavior. Example: Lateness 5 pts off, absent 5 off, no HW 5 off, bothering someone too much 5 off, impersonating an A-hole, 5 off.*

  - *Allow for extra credit to make up all transgressions. Never give anyone more than 100 for anything.*

  - *Always err on the side of the student. Example: Lowest test grade ever given is a 40. Most points off for a really bad day 15. End your grades a week before the marking period & let the students determine their grade, with you having the final say. That way they know how they got the grade & they know it weeks before their parents, which gives you another bullet if necessary.*

- *Extra Credit. Look up & give me a readable page (100 to 500 words) on either Ben Franklin or Redd Foxx.*
- *Keep your sense of humor & all that makes you the charismatic figure that you are. Your persona will carry you in the classroom just as it does in life. Be yourself. Tell a fart joke.*
- *Never embarrass a student in front of others. Embarrass yourself, often to relieve the tension, but do not paint them into a corner. It's only High School. Sure it will follow them for the rest of their lives, but so will their families, friends, talents, experiences, etc.*
- *Now here's the kiss of death. After each lesson, sit down by yourself & think, "If my son or daughter were correctly rostered to this class, would I be comfortable with the lesson & the effort I put forth today?"*
    - *If your answer is yes, you can sleep tonite. Whatever the answer, ask yourself what went well, what didn't, how could I do it better, etc. The best teachers never rest on their laurels.*
- *Other topics for the first days, the first year include:*
    - *KISS—Keep it simple stupid*
    - *FACE—To stay awake do not put your hands or any object anywhere near your face*
    - *SINCERITY—If you can fake that, the rest will flow freely*

The only kids still at NEHS that I taught are for the most part Seniors in the Magnet program. I was cited in "Who's Who in American High Schools" 3 times since it started printing. Nominations come only from Students who either made the National Honor Society or went on to get honors in the first 2 years of college.

The first kid who nominated me, Robert Williams, was smart, barely made an effort & had @ an 88 avg. I thought he hated me & the class. Turns out I gave him one of his lowest grades.

When I asked him why he nominated me, he said, "because we worked every day, you always came prepared, you always did your best & you never gave up on anyone, not even those that deserved it." Wouldn't mind that being my 1 sentence legacy.

Heard you are only teaching one 10th grade class for 13 weeks. You'll be great. You put on a talk show. What could be harder than that??? Good luck Tony, I know you will do well.

Respectfully Yours,
Harry Gilbert

Three

Do Now

MS. DENAPLES has me on truancy duty. For the first hour of the school day, I'm to circle the campus wrangling stragglers. If parents drop their kids off late, I'm supposed to tell the parents it's their job to get their children to school on time. If kids are dawdling, I'm to personally escort them. "Whatever it takes." As she says this, Ms. D. puts her hands on her hips for emphasis.

Confronting students about being late is not my idea of fun. These are probably not the honor roll kids, and they don't know me from Adam, but I don't dare try to wriggle out of it. I'll work this beat with Ms. D. every morning for the rest of the week and periodically throughout the year. "Truancy and tardiness are no laughing matter, Mr. Danza."

"Yes, Ms. DeNaples." I can't help wondering if anything *is* a laughing matter for Ms. DeNaples, but far be it from me to test her. I decide that if the kids and parents wonder who I am to be telling them to get to school, I'll say Ms. DeNaples is all over me and put the same fear in them that I feel. If some of the tough kids act up, I can always call my camera crew for backup. Yes, some of these guys truly scare me. A few have tattoos up their necks, and struts that not even Eminem could match. They make Al G look easy, which I'm still hoping he might actually be. I just have to remember that they're only kids. But as we patrol the school grounds, I see in Technicolor what America's schoolteachers and school administrators are up against.

Even though the bell has rung, way too much of the student body is still outside. A few kids are racing to class, but others are taking their sweet time. A pod of smokers hang out in a side alleyway off Algon Street. I tell them to put out their smokes and get inside, and they don't budge. Finally I plant myself in front of them and tell them to "give up that dirty habit." Then I spot a bunch of kids who are walking in a totally wrong direction, *away* from school. "Hey!" I yell. "Come back here, you guys! School's *this* way." Busted, they shuffle around and pretend not to hear me. It's disheartening in the extreme. The fact that they wind up in school today is no guarantee that they'll get there tomorrow.

Suddenly a battered VW Bug pulls to the curb, and I open the door for a redheaded boy in an Eagles sweatshirt. "You better hurry up," I tell him. "Ms. DeNaples is on the warpath." Then I lean down and say to the woman in the driver's seat, "You know you're bringing your son to school twenty minutes late? That's not acceptable."

The mother, wearing a turquoise sweat suit, fishes for a scrap of paper in her handbag and asks me for my autograph.

"Only if you get your son here on time from now on," I say. I mean it, but she just laughs.

AN HOUR LATER in class, Monte's pencil is tapping so hard I compliment him on his drum skills. Eric Choi is folding an elaborate origami object. It has moving parts, requires all the concentration he's not giving me, and will make me cry. But not yet. Not in class. I've been warned, forget about smiling, and never let them see you cry. "Gimme that," I say, pocketing Eric's little paper wreath. We both need to focus.

"All right. Who would like to read their story?"

Crickets. That's what it sounds like as the kids shift in their chairs, avoiding eye contact, secretly checking their cell phones and texting.

"Emmanuel?" I walk back to a large, quiet kid who sits beside Paige in the back row. Yesterday he told us he was on the debate team. He's got to be good. But he shakes his head. "You don't want to read it? You don't have to stand up, you can read it sitting down." No answer. "How about if I read it?" He shrugs as I pick up his paper.

" 'When I was younger,' " I read, " 'I was scared about riding on roller coasters.' You know, I was, too." That gets no smiles. I finish reading Emmanuel's piece and ask for another volunteer. Not a single hand.

I thought at least Monte would pipe up. But now I've started. Anything to stop the crickets. I ask for Paige's story and offer to read it aloud. She's written about going to South Street in a rainstorm. I break into song, " 'Where do all the hippies meet? South Street, South Street.' "

All right, they snicker. But a snicker beats a blank stare. Before long I've read out five of their stories. They're all pretty light. I understand. The kids don't know me well enough yet to unload for real, so they've written about theme parks, basketball, shopping—extensions of their introductions on Day One, which to me already seems months ago.

"Danny." I call on our sweet-faced rear tackle.

He looks up, and his expression seems to twist sideways. "You mind if we read our own stories?"

I meet David Cohn's eyes. He looks like a young Grim Reaper. I stammer, "Sh-sure, Danny. Yeah. I just thought I'd help us get started, I . . . Go ahead."

I return to my desk and sit down as Danny reads a story about scoring his first defensive touchdown. I feel like a complete schmo. This time when the bell rings I'm thankful. What if I were a real teacher and had four *more* classes like this today?

INSTEAD I'VE GOT football practice. I've never played football except in the street, but that makes no difference. I'm going to have my face rubbed in all the extra demands placed on real teachers, and just see how I like it. I'll work with the marching band, the debate team, the school paper, soccer team, drama class, and choir. I'll sub for and audit other teachers, proctor tests, do hall duty and cafeteria duty, attend weekly planning meetings and perpetual professional development seminars. I'll be so tired that I fall asleep in front of the principal, on camera. But all of that is yet to come. Right now I'm one of four assistant coaches under Head Coach Chris Riley.

Riley is an alumnus of Northeast and a member of its 1986 championship team—which unfortunately was its last championship team. A hard-nosed motivator, he welcomes me aboard and hands me a whistle to hang around my neck. I hate the feeling of not knowing what I'm doing. I try to run the kids through their drills, but I have trouble even blowing my whistle. Across the field, Riley shakes his head.

We finish practice and go into the locker room. Riley calls a meeting, and the players take a knee. As the coach stands in front of them, I'm thinking I could use a rousing speech right about now. This ought to be good.

"Coach Danza has something to say."

I blink. Coach who? I like the sound of "Coach Danza," but . . . what else did he just say?

Sixty football players wait for me to tell them something that will help when things get tough in their first game of the season. Doing my best to think fast, I merge their challenge on the field with mine in the classroom. Brilliant!

"You know," I tell them, "I'm a first-year teacher this year. I never did it before, and it's like a roller coaster. So I'm up against a lot of stuff. Like you, out on the field." Trying to relate to them, I describe my screwups in this morning's class, but the more I talk, the worse my morning seems. Before I know it, these are the words pouring out of my mouth: "It was so bad it made me doubt what I was doing. Maybe I should just go home. I mean, I live in Malibu. What the heck am I doing here?"

I catch myself, mortified. I didn't really just say "Malibu," did I? Clearly I've got stuff I need to work out, but how could I stand here at Northeast High School and talk about feeling homesick for Malibu? In front of the *football team*? Am I out of my mind?

Coach Riley looks like he'd like to drop-kick me back to Malibu and put us all out of our misery, but it's the team's respect that finally pulls me together. They're still waiting, expecting me to behave like a coach. I scramble to get back to the challenge they face as members of a team that's about to go up against fierce competition. "All I'm saying is, if you guys focus on the job, put one foot in front of the other, and depend on each other, and have some fun out there, then it's going to be a piece of cake tomorrow night."

I get out of the locker room alive, but barely. My own whining chases me. Sure, we all face adversity and sometimes wonder whether we can get the job done, but can't I even see who's in front of me?

THE NEXT NIGHT the Northeast Vikings play their first game in a driving rainstorm. We lose. The coach has his players take a knee in the end zone. I stand with the other assistant coaches as Riley paces back and forth in the downpour, trying to make sense of the game for himself and everyone else. "We have to work harder and learn our lessons. We have to think about what we did and what we didn't do, then get it out of our systems and come back and do better next time."

I know this moment is not about me, but I can't help taking his words to heart. As the lights go out in the empty stadium and the rain keeps falling on some very disappointed young men, Coach Riley is fired up and raring for more. And soon we all feel his energy stoking ours.

"We finish what we've started," Riley says as he punches the air. "We go out and try again." He waits for this to sink in. "Come on, let's get out of the rain."

Everybody Cries

I meet David Cohn in his office for my daily postmortem and show him the piece of origami that I took from Eric in class. "Impressive work," David says.

"Too bad I'm not teaching art."

We laugh. Then he gives me some valuable advice. "Think about doing more with less."

I don't get it.

"Less of you, more of them. Focus on your lesson plans, spend more time on less information, be specific, and stick to the topic. Let them read—and do—their own work. Did I really see you look up a word in the dictionary for Chloe today?"

Shamefaced, I nod. "I wanted to make sure—"

"You make sure by watching them do it."

"I'm sorry."

"Don't be sorry. Every new teacher struggles to find the right balance."

"This is harder than opening in Vegas."

"You're trying too hard to make them like you."

Bingo. "Can I teach them if they *don't* like me?"

David sighs. "You can't learn *for* them, Tony."

"But I get the feeling some just don't want to work."

"There's a difference between not wanting to work and not wanting to learn. The student has to, at the very least, be interested in learning. It might make you more interesting to them if they like you, but teaching is not a popularity contest. It's about getting them involved in their own education."

I know this. I've written and posted it in my class, remember? TAKE PART IN YOUR OWN EDUCATION.

"Get out of the way," David advises. "Let the kids do it."

"Right." I repeat, "More with less."

He likes that I've made a connection with the kids. "But I hear your voice too much and their voices too little. Teaching is different today. Teachers don't just stand at the board and lecture while the kids take notes. What we're ultimately teaching them is to teach themselves."

When I get nervous in front of the class, which is often, he says, that's when I talk too much. "You're performing the class, as opposed to teaching it. At times, it gets so bad that you ask a student a question, then answer it yourself."

This all stings, but I have no grounds to dispute him. On the contrary, the evidence is stacking heavily against me. Coach Riley said he kept hearing my voice with his team when what he wanted to hear was the kids. And my wife and kids, too, have been known to complain about my interrupting and commenting. From my perspective, that shows I'm engaged in what they're saying! But now I wonder if this habit of mine might be part of the problem in my marriage and family. Have I always been this way?

"I'm afraid to wait," I admit to David. "The silence, it scares me. When you're an entertainer, that kind of silence could mean you're bombing."

"In a classroom, when it's silent, they're thinking. You've got to give them time to think." David reminds me of some of the principles of collaborative teaching that I learned during orientation. The teacher breaks the students into small groups, then sets out the lesson and has the kids work on it themselves while the teacher moves around the room guiding them individually—and quietly. "There will be times when a whole group is silent, but that doesn't mean they're not working."

"Okay. More of that, less of this." I make the talking motion with my hand next to my mouth. David smiles.

As our conference ends, I feel better. I've taken everything he said onboard, and I think I know how I'll apply it to the section on mythology that we're to start in the morning. But then, as I'm getting up to leave, David hands me back Eric's origami wreath and offhandedly asks, "You cried yet?"

It's as if he's turned on the faucet. I can feel them coming, and I put up my hands, but it's no use. The tears begin to roll, and in seconds I'm sobbing.

I flee the office, and David follows. He stops me in the hallway, but all he does is pat my shoulder. It's hard to see through the flood. Is he surprised, or annoyed? "I'm sorry," I blubber. "I can't believe how it affects you when you try so hard and get nowhere."

He hands me a Kleenex. "I remember one of the guys I started with would close his door every day after school and cry at his desk. They can reduce the best of us to tears. It comes with the territory."

It takes me a while to compose myself. Many people—guards, janitors, kids—see me. This is bound to get around to the other teachers. Probably it will please them, like a rite of passage. "Now you know what it feels like," they might say. Silver lining time: maybe it will convince them I really am doing this for real.

I DO TAKE COMFORT from one teacher at Northeast who talks even more than I do. Lynn Dixon, a veteran English teacher, is the leader of our Small Learning Community. Because Northeast is such a huge school, it's broken into eight of these communities or SLCs, housed in the eight different sections of the school where students have their core classes. I belong to the Arts and Education SLC (this appeals to our producers, seeing as we're making our show for the A&E network), and Ms. Dixon is our guiding light. Having taught for over thirty years at some of the toughest schools in Philadelphia, she has seen it all.

The twenty teachers in our SLC meet every day during second period in a recommissioned classroom that passes for a teachers' lounge. We have teachers of English, music, drama, art, math, and social studies. Today when I walk in, Ms. Dixon is telling a story about one of our veteran art teachers, an older woman in an artist's smock who looks a little bit like my grandmother when she was younger. "So this girl bursts out in class—'You're not my mother, you can't tell me what to do!'—and instead of showing how hurt she felt, Laurie here smiles sweetly and says, 'No, but I am your art mother.'"

The others must have heard this tale dozens of times, but they still whistle and clap, and Laurie the art teacher takes a little bow.

It feels weird to be in the teachers' lounge without some sort of a pass. A couple of the other teachers have already told me they're apprehensive about our project. "I don't like those reality shows," one young teacher announces as he gets up and leaves my table. I don't, either, I want to tell him, but I'm afraid the waterworks will let loose again if I open my mouth.

Others are kinder. They offer advice and tell me what they believe it takes to be a good teacher. "You have to be prepared to play many roles," says an older woman who's been teaching for decades. "You have to be a mother, father, sister, brother, social worker, counselor, friend, and anything else they need." They tell me some heart-wrenching stories about kids who've come to school hungry, or late because gunfire outside their bedroom kept them up all night, or who don't talk in class because of abuse *inside* their bedroom. They tell me about teachers almost adopting their students to keep them from falling into the abyss of foster care or homelessness. "Adoption fantasy," one man says, "comes with the territory."

What these teachers and I have in common are memories of high school as a better time. We all remember teachers who touched us—and some who didn't. We remember fistfights after school, but no gunfights. We remember walking home from school without fear of getting mugged. We remember parents who pressed us to do well in school so that we could go on to college. In spite of the fact that many of these same parents never went to college themselves, they wanted something better for us.

"We have to make up for so much that's missing in kids' lives today," says the "art mother." "Especially in the poorer schools. But this rarely factors into the equation when politicians talk about cutting the cost of education."

She's interrupted by Ms. Dixon's high, piercing cry. "May I have your attention, please!" It's impossible not to comply. She wears a bright red blazer over a T-shirt printed with a sparkling Cowardly Lion. Her blond hair fans across her shoulders except for a clump held by an oversize polka-dot bow. But for all her love of kitsch, Ms. Dixon is the maestro of edicts from the district and the administration. She gathers up a pile of papers on the table near the door and passes them out. It's her job as head of our SLC, she informs us, to distribute notices, warn us of the deadlines to get our grades in, and tell us where to enter them on the district website. She will remind us about required seminar schedules, common planning times, technology instruction, and how to fill in graphic organizers for classes that we think might attract more students to our SLC. It's beginning to dawn on me just how much work teachers are besieged with *outside* the classroom. This, I think, is another thing that politicians and the media rarely mention.

Not everyone, however, is paying attention. One teacher nibbles on health food and reads a diet book while Ms. Dixon talks. Another noisily unwraps a large cinnamon bun and nudges his neighbors, who actually are trying to listen to Lynn's announcement about a new academic mandate that we all will be expected to fulfill. At first I'm perplexed by the man who sits by himself in the back of the room like one of the problem kids. I decide he doesn't like the others. Later he'll confide that it's just a matter of decibels.

Not only is it Ms. Dixon's job to teach, run our SLC, advocate for students and school, and mediate with problem kids, but also, critically, she knows how to repair a copy machine and keep it working. She won't let anyone else work on it. "The copy machine is essential. The copy machine has your name and password," she informs us. "You must log in before you copy anything." She goes on to explain that most teachers in the school are limited to a fifteen-thousand-copy quota for the year. Fifteen thousand copies might sound like plenty, but if you have five classes a day, then those fifteen thousand copies go fast. "So one of the perks of being a member of the A&E SLC is that we all have unlimited reproductive rights."

That gets a good laugh, which loosens things up. It actually is nice to know we can make as many copies as we need, but reproduction isn't all that's unlimited in Lynn Dixon's world. In her office, she can find just about anything you could possibly need for a lesson. She has Tootsie Pops and colored pencils, Viking helmets, subject-related movies, books, costumes, award certificates, magazines, old newspapers, even a life-size cutout of President Obama. Ms. Dixon is a Shakespeare expert, and since I'm going to teach *Julius Caesar* this year, she gives me a T-shirt with an image of old Will pumped up like an action star. "Shakespeare's *ripped*," she says, mimicking our students' slang as she hands me a stack of teaching materials.

Ms. Dixon also has tricks for teaching. "Ever hear of a six-word memoir?" she asks me.

I have no idea what she's talking about.

"Hemingway wrote the first one: 'For sale: Baby shoes, never worn.' A whole life story in six words. Try it with your students, Tony. It will make the children think. And that's what we want them to be doing, critical thinking, not just rote learning. But they'll also like this assignment because it's short, and they do like short. Best try it yourself first, though. So how about it?"

"How about what?" She makes my head spin.

"A six-word memoir. Your life in six words."

For the next five minutes I sit like a dunce, counting words on my fingers. Could she give me the night to think on it? I feel a sudden and uncomfortable kinship with Al G.

Then it comes to me. I count again on my fingers. "I've got it! 'Once a fighter now a teacher.' "

Ms. Dixon beams, looking as proud as if she just taught me to take my first steps. "That's one big story in six words, Mr. Danza." She pauses and says gently, "Now prove it."

Four

The Half-Sandwich Club

WHEN I ANNOUNCE we're going to study myths, Monte looks like he wants to die. But when I ask for a definition of the word *myth,* he's the only one who can answer.

"A myth is a story with supernatural gods or goddesses that explains why things happen, like an origin myth."

"Origin myth! Or creation myth. Very good, Monte. As a matter of fact, we're going to focus on creation myths."

We talk a little about how myths helped people in ancient civilizations make sense of natural phenomena, like the planets and the rising and falling of tides, and also helped them answer the riddle of their own existence. I tell the class that as I was reading Greek myths and getting ready for this unit, I found myself thinking about where I originally came from, where I've been living, and where I am in my life right now. Then I stand in front of my desk and shake out my hands. My plan is for them to write their own myths, but I want them to understand, this can be fun.

"So I wrote my own creation myth rap." I tap my foot. "It goes like this. One, two, three, four . . ."

In the beginning before there even was time,
the world was so quiet without even a rhyme.
Thor the God of Thunder was his name,
he wasn't happy being quiet, this god Thor had some game.
He was the first rapper, yes it's hard to conceive,
cause rappin' ain't easy when there's none to receive.
With hammer in hand he went right to a place,
where still there yet was no one there to get in his face.
He swung his hammer hard and he pounded the ground,
and up sprang an audience that followed around.
Everywhere he went he swung his hammer again,
and more and more homies found out just what was in.
His rhymes were all chill, every woman would swoon,
and just cause of that, the religion of rap saw a boon.
Not only men but women too got into the act,
it's cool to kneel and pray at the altar of rap.
God Thor was a gangster and then one day
he woke up the sun and found a brand-new way.
Still cool and tight and always chill,
he realized then someday he'd have to pay the bill.
So back to school he went and what a change he did see,
he teaches now in Philly, teaching the mantra of we.
His uniform he wears with beaucoup Viking pride,
a him he never knew, he swims against his own tide.
His students he loves he can't believe his luck,
for them his many fears he will continue to buck.
This change is for the best, he feels it deep to his core,
he bows now to teachers forevermore.
Peace out.

The kids clap along, laughing and nodding. It's fun for them to watch me make a fool of myself, but the rap also seems to have the desired effect. If I can do it, so can they.

"You know," I tell them when they've quieted down, "I wrote that line—'a him he never knew, he swims against his own tide'— but when I read it just now I realized it was actually a *him he used to know*. Coming here to Philly and teaching you guys, I've actually come back to my old self, a kid from Brooklyn just like you. It's like coming home. So thank you for that."

Chloe and Katerina exchange glances, then call out in unison, "You're welcome, Mr. Danza!" And everybody cracks up. Wiseguys.

"All right, all right," I say. "Your assignment is to write your own creation myth. Explain creation and natural phenomena, and include gods, goddesses, or spirit forces. Your myths have to contain at least three of these elements."

They moan and groan. We read and discuss the myth of Anansi, the trickster spider credited by Ashanti legend with creating the sun, the stars, and the moon. Then, remembering David's advice, I pair them up to write their own myths, which they'll perform together in front of the class. "Get creative," I urge them. I tell Eric, "Maybe you can use your paper skills."

The next day, Eric Choi and his partner, Ben-Kyle Whatever Your Name Is, which is what I call him because of his two first names, present "The Magic Button Myth." Eric has fashioned a large round paper button attached to a paper spring that he sticks to the blackboard. On the button they've printed: DO NOT PUSH. In the myth the two boys act out, one god warns the other *not* to push the magic button, which of course guarantees that the second god *does* push the button, thereby blowing the world into existence. The class cheers, and shy, gawky Eric does not know what to do with the praise.

In Matt's myth, his god is suffering from indigestion and farts the world into being. Another smart student has conjured up a god named Danzeus. I've won their enthusiastic participation, and no matter how outrageous their myths may be, this feels like a victory.

I'm still riding high at the end of class, when Katerina asks me if her mother can bring in a cake tomorrow for her birthday. Katerina is one of my two Russian students. She's soft-spoken and polite, always saying, "Good morning, Mr. Danza," "Have a good day, Mr. Danza." She's also a serious student, so I have no qualms about celebrating her birthday. Before the school year started, I hung a calendar on the wall and wrote everyone's birthday on it, and I always make some sort of fuss over each kid's day. I've even made up my own birthday song to sing them.

"Fine," I tell her, and promptly forget all about it.

The next day I make my usual birthday fuss over Katerina at the beginning of class. We all sing her "Happy Birthday," and I do a little soft shoe in her honor. Katerina blushes prettily and thanks us. Then we get back to work.

No myth is complete without a hero, and Theseus, who slayed the Minotaur, is a pretty chill hero. After we read the story of Theseus, we discuss the various characteristics that make a hero. The students' list:

- Courage
- Care for others
- A willingness to stand up for his beliefs

They also decide that a hero is a warrior, someone like Theseus who wins a great battle.

All good, but I want to extend their conception of heroes to real life. "Does anyone in your family or community qualify?"

Several students mention friends or relatives who have enlisted or are planning to fight as soldiers in Iraq and Afghanistan. They see them as heroes. Others say they consider their moms their personal heroes. Howard, who lives with his mother and sister, says his mother has kept them together and taken care of them with zero help from his father. He and the other kids agree, that is heroic.

By the end of the period, the kids are finding heroes among neighbors, grandparents, even some teachers—people they certainly never thought of as heroes before, and I like that. I ask, just as the bell rings and they're getting up from their desks, "Could you be heroic? Think about it."

Because I have the kids for two periods, I give them a brief break before we begin our second period. They stretch their legs in the hall, and after a few minutes I go out to reel them back in for our second forty-five minutes together. I've just gotten them into their seats when there's a knock on the door and a woman with a thick Russian accent enters. She's tall and attractive with long blond hair, and is dressed as if headed for a nightclub, though she's carrying a huge chocolate cake and drinks. Katerina is a pretty, young girl, and seeing her mother, I am reminded that apple trees make apples. I'm also reminded that I agreed to this.

I can't believe Katerina let me go through my whole birthday song and dance without reminding me this was coming. It's going to completely derail my lesson plan for this period. But what am I supposed to do? The kids are psyched. Besides, as I watch this loving mother lighting candles for her daughter's wish and beaming at the rare opportunity to see Katerina in her element, I think of my daughter Emily in her junior year of high school back in California without me anywhere near her. Swallowing hard, I keep my mouth shut and wait for my piece of cake.

It so happens that a friend of mine has just sent me a DVD of some of my old bouts as a professional boxer. So while everyone is eating, I slide it into my laptop and turn the projector up to the screen. "Anybody want to see some of my old fights?" We're having a fine old time when there's another tap on the door.

Assistant Principal Sharon McCloskey steps into the room, sizes up the situation, and summons me into the hall. "Mr. Danza, what exactly is going on in your class?"

I try to explain, but she doesn't need my explanation. Ms. McCloskey's not ordinarily as gruff as Ms. DeNaples, but at this moment they could be twins. "Mr. Danza, if we allowed every mother in this school to bring a cake for her child's birthday, we wouldn't get much done, would we?" Again she doesn't let me answer. "And what are you showing them along with their cake?"

I stammer something unintelligible and watch her turn away. "Don't let it happen again," she throws over her shoulder and walks down the corridor shaking her head.

Back in the classroom, the kids can't wait to hear how much trouble I'm in. So much for heroism. Katerina and her mother stand and chime in unison, "Sorry, Mr. Danza."

PARENTS ARE A FORCE in education, whether they realize it or not, for better and for worse. I prefer meeting them over a birthday cake, even if I do have to pay for it, than over the phone, but when my kids are in trouble, I don't have much choice. I delay calling Al G's mother as long as I possibly can. But he's a handful, constantly talking, joking, and—my pet peeve—he yawns loudly. I've moved him from seat to seat in hope of finding a sweet spot next to just the right person. But you move one kid, and it can start a chain reaction that messes up the whole class. I have one student, Paul, a calm, steady sweetheart who's my go-to guy. I can almost always put a problem next to him or move him next to a problem, but not even Paul works with Al G. I've finally resorted to sticking Al right in front of Mr. Cohn. That at least quiets him down, though it doesn't get him to work. Meanwhile, the rest of the kids are miffed at me for giving him so many chances. I can't tell them that I do this because Al G reminds me of myself, or that I'm afraid if I come down hard on him, I'll lose him completely. But that's why it takes me so long to make the call. Finally I have to tell his mother what's going on. I ask her to come to school so we can talk about her son.

Al G's mom is young, like many of the mothers in the neighborhood. We meet downstairs in the lobby so I can escort her to my classroom, and my first impression is that she looks a little too glamorous for the occasion. She has long, flashy fingernails and a hairdo right off the cover of *Essence*. Then I remember; we are filming a TV show. The kids and I don't even notice the cameras anymore, but that note hasn't reached Al's mother and the rest of the community.

Upstairs the walls of my room are filling with student work, and ordinarily I'm proud to show them off. However, there's nothing to show from Al G. "You know," I tell his mother, "I think I get your son. He's a kid who doesn't realize he needs school yet and at the same time thinks he knows it all. Am I right?"

She eyes me warily. I hurry up. "Because I was the same kind of kid. I thought it was uncool to act like I cared about anything the teacher said."

"Al G doesn't want anybody to know how smart he is," she says slowly.

"I know that. But you and I know that he *is* smart. He's very smart. He just doesn't do the work. When I ask him about it directly, he tells me he'll do it, then he just doesn't. We're three weeks into school, and he still hasn't handed in the assignment from the first day."

"He has a lot going on," she says.

Is she defending him? "I need your help," I tell her. "School is important to his future. It's the only chance he has. He's smart. He can have a good future if he will just do the work. I won't give up on him, but I need your help."

She listens, nods, doesn't say much more, and I can't tell if I've made a dent or not.

Al G's mother must have some power. The next day he slinks into class and drops on my desk quite a bit more than the half page I requested about his personal experience. It would be pushing my luck to ask him to read it aloud, so I read it to myself. It describes a basketball court in a park near where he lives.

The day he's writing about began normally. Al was playing in a pickup game, with winners holding the court and losers forming new teams to try to upset the winners. There were the usual altercations, disputed calls, and hard fouls of playground basketball, but this day deteriorated into an urban nightmare. One of the boys, unhappy with the outcome of the game, left the park and came back brandishing a gun. He was threatening some of the players on the winning team when another youth pulled a pistol. Both boys started shooting, and Al G hit the ground, crawled to cover, then hightailed it out of the park.

I finish reading and remember that the memory I gave the class as an example for this assignment was about the time I helped my uncle Mike lay linoleum in my mother's kitchen. Talk about a different world. My reality as a kid was a tough neighborhood, but nobody was getting shot at. I mark the paper, and when I return it I ask Al if he ever goes back to that park.

"'Course," he answers. "It's right by where I live."

The gap between my life and Al's widens even further. Maybe stories like this are what his mother meant when she said he has a lot going on. I remember now that when I called to request the conference, her first words were "Is he okay?"

"Well, you did a good job on this," I say. "It's well written. You're good at this, and I want you to keep writing."

Al G smiles to himself. It's barely detectable, but I think the praise pleases him. I know it does.

A FEW DAYS LATER Al G is given an in-school suspension by another teacher and has to sit all day with other problem kids in one of the three portable classrooms maintained for this purpose at the back of the school. I go out and knock on the door where I've been told I can find him. "Okay if I come in and see Al G?" I ask the teacher on duty.

This man is older and wears a been-there-seen-it-all expression. "Sure," he deadpans. "Come on in and join the party."

In-school suspension is for relatively low-level infractions. More grievous offenses warrant home suspensions and last longer than a day, but it strikes me that being stuck out here is the harsher of the two punishments. It's dead time. The portable is colorless, cold, and blank. There are rows of desks and about ten kids, boys and girls, drooping in various stages of boredom. Nothing is happening. Certainly, no learning is going on. When I make my way back to Al's row and ask if I can sit next to him, he just shrugs.

A few of Al's friends are here, too, and this makes it difficult to talk to him, since they're always watching and he's fronting. "Why you here?" he asks me.

"I always visit my friends in jail." He hides his smile by dropping his head low between his shoulders, but I don't mean it as a joke. I want him to make the connection. We sit in silence for a while. Then, as if there's been no break in the conversation, I say, "Look around. Do you think this is where you belong? This where you want to be?"

Al doesn't answer. I don't really expect him to, but the point's been made. Now my job is just to be here and not say anything else.

We sit in silence. Still nothing from him verbally, but I feel like he's happy I showed up. It's as if I've been suspended, too.

After a half hour or so, I get up to leave. He looks up and says, "Thanks for coming by." He speaks clearly enough that I can actually understand what he's saying. No smirk. This is a considerable concession, especially in front of the other kids.

As I return to my classroom, trying to figure my next move, I run into Al G's math teacher, Ms. Green. She's young, energetic, and generous, and I have a little crush on her. Oh, and she's also concerned about Al. She reinforces what I already know, that he can do the work but doesn't think it's cool to excel. Her seventh-period math group is especially tough for him because he has friends in the class. She describes Al G as a show-off who can also be an endearing kid. I haven't seen the endearing kid yet, but I know the show-off. We agree to work on him together.

Ms. Green's strategy for getting Al working is to have him teach her class. I ask her if I might come and observe that. We devise a game plan.

The next day I enter Ms. Green's class dressed like Al. I wear a backpack like his, a hoodie, and his brand of Nikes—shoe style being paramount to these kids. I take a student seat and put my feet up on a nearby desk, showing off those familiar sneakers. From the head of the class, Al spots them and smirks. Direct hit. I loudly unwrap a sandwich, which I proceed to eat as he watches from the teacher's spot and tries to do his job. He writes a math problem on the board. I raise my hand, and when he calls on me I ask a question about bacon, which for some reason he's always talking about. He ignores me the same way I do him when he asks dumb questions. Then I give him my Sunday punch: I yawn as loudly and demonstratively as I can. Just like him. He shakes his head.

The math class is having a good laugh at Al G's expense, but then he gets serious and really does try to teach. The kids continue to act out, and Al threatens to throw people out of the class and call the dean, all to no effect. I raise my hand and ask him to help me with the math problem sheet. Math is not my subject, and I'm not acting. He makes a real attempt to explain the problems to me, and like a real student, I struggle. He stays with it, attempting to get me to understand while trying to control the rest of the class, which is not easy. When I still don't get it, he's clearly frustrated. I know that feeling.

I ask him, "What do you think about teaching now? Not that easy, right?"

He won't admit it, but his face softens. The bell rings, and his classmates razz him as they leave. They make Ms. Green promise, no more student teachers. Al G is complaining to Ms. Green, but when I get up to go, he stops me. "Thanks for coming." That's the second time he's said that to me. Then he adds, "Keep working on that problem." He can be endearing after all.

Small victories, I think, as I make my way down the corridor in my cool sneakers.

IN ADDITION TO all their other classes, most teachers are assigned advisory—today's term for homeroom. I don't have any official advisory students, but I soon begin acquiring unofficial ones, and as soon as I do, that term, *advisory*, makes perfect sense to me. This is the period when teaching is all about advice, when you serve as part counselor, part friend, part surrogate parent. As one of the teachers in my SLC told me, counseling can be a bigger part of the job than teaching. "In poor schools, the teacher has to pick up the slack created by less involved parents and more kids with problems."

My first unofficial advisory kids are strays. I meet them in the hallways or cafeteria, or when I'm working with one of the teams or clubs. Then they start turning up and camping out in my classroom. First one, then two and more. I do have air-conditioning, and that's a lure. I also give out half sandwiches to anyone who needs one at lunchtime, but they also seem to like hanging with me, and I'm a sucker for that. Soon they're coming every day, first thing in the morning, during fifth-period lunch, or any time they can finagle a hall pass. I ask, "Where are you supposed to be?" And they all have the same answer, "My teacher knows I'm here with you."

Then I have to write a note to the teacher explaining that they've been with me and I am sorry for them getting back to class late. This strikes me as funny because when I was in high school I used to practice writing notes and signing my name in preparation for the day when I became a teacher and had to write a hall pass for real. But it's not really funny. Most of these kids have problems, and some are serious. When a good kid comes to school late and looking like hell, I'll try to go easy, couch my concern in a compliment, such as "You're never late, what happened?" But what do you say when the answer is "They turned off the electricity on us last night, and it was too cold to sleep. It was a crazy night." You offer sympathy and write him the note. You do what you can, which too often is not enough, but you have to be willing to try.

Phil is sixteen, one of a group of four boys that I call the Wanderers because they're constantly walking the hallways. They dress in black and have complexions so white and pasty I wonder if they've ever even seen the sun. Always together, they come to school every morning, swipe their student IDs to prove they're on campus, then just roam for the rest of the day. Northeast is so huge and there are so many nooks and crannies to hide in that if a student knows the school well enough and keeps moving, he can avoid going to class all day. These four are masters of avoidance.

When I first notice the Wanderers, I can't resist trying to talk them into going to class and taking school seriously. Other teachers tell me I'm wasting my breath. The Wanderers have a well-established track record for getting in trouble. But I always think that very few kids are really bad and many are just mixed up. When I catch Phil alone one day, I ask what his dad thinks about him skipping classes, and he tells me he has no father. His mother is alone, and his older brothers have all been in trouble. "So what else is new?" he asks. But instead of sounding sullen, Phil seems to be challenging me to answer. I want to try to help. That's what teachers do, right? That's what I'm here for.

The other three Wanderers refuse to see any value in changing or in anything I say. They razz Phil about me, but then he starts coming to my room at lunchtime on his own. I give him half a sandwich, and after we get to know each other a bit, I ask for his roster. I visit each of his teachers. Big surprise: he's failing all his courses because he never goes to class. One teacher tells me that Philip's cut class every day since school started. Another says he has over sixty unexcused absences and his teachers have all but given up on him.

Remembering that each of these teachers has another 149 students to worry about, I ask them to please give me the assignments he needs to make up, and I'll make sure he completes them. I know it's extra work for them, but despite their skepticism, they give Phil and me the benefit of the doubt.

I want to show Phil that his teachers do care what happens to him. I want him to see the importance of changing his behavior. I talk myself hoarse trying to get him to see the error of his ways. But just when I think I'm making some headway, he's charged with credit card fraud. It seems he and his friends used a stolen Visa card.

Phil's arrest really shakes me. I try to tell myself that I just arrived in his life too late, that there's nothing more I could have done, but the last time I see this kid he tells me he's facing a three-year jail sentence. He's also beginning the Twilight Program, a night school for kids who work or have problems and want a General Educational Development certificate. I tell him this is his last chance, but that if he gets his GED the judge will take that into consideration. "Show them you're trying," I beg.

Phil nods and says he gets it. But I can tell he doesn't really. He won't last in the program. He feels buried, thinks he's lost too much ground and will never catch up. "You can, Phil, if you want to," I plead, but I can feel him already slipping away. I want to throw him a lifeline but have no idea how. How do you help them all?

ANOTHER OF MY unofficial advisees is a senior named Courtney, who sings in the choir and acts in school plays. She used to spend her free time in the choirmaster's office, but after finding me she starts hanging out in my classroom instead. She's a popular girl, funny and bright and getting ready to go on to college, but one morning she comes to me in tears. "I'm not going to graduate."

"What are you talking about? You're a great student. I thought you were doing well."

"I am, except I'm failing physics."

Uh-oh. I can't write a definition of physics, let alone offer any real help in the subject. I stall. "Why are you failing?"

"I got behind, and I can't catch up."

"So you just haven't done the work, right?"

"Right," she says, eyes averted.

"Wait a minute. Who says you can't catch up? Who do you have?"

I recognize her physics instructor's name from orientation. "Believe me," I assure her, "there is no way a first-year teacher wants you to fail. Let's go see him."

Asking for help can work wonders. Teachers appreciate that. And like Phil's teachers, Courtney's is willing to work with her. Unfortunately, as good a student as she is, Courtney, like Phil, has let herself slip dangerously behind. It will take real commitment and work to catch up.

I give her my "mountain" speech, which I used to give my own kids when they felt overwhelmed by schoolwork. "It's like when I used to wash dishes for a Jewish caterer. We would serve seven-course dinners for over three hundred people. After each course, hundreds of plates, glasses, pots, and silverware would be piled high on the dishwasher's counter. That mountain could look so overwhelming that I didn't know where to start, but I learned that if you just get to work on one piece at a time, little by little the mountain gets smaller, and eventually it's gone."

The good news for Courtney is that there's time. And support. My assistant on the TV production crew, Kelly Gould, was a physics major in college. I enlist her help, and she and Courtney make a good team. They decide that Courtney's big project will be a Rube Goldberg contraption that turns on her hair straightener. After building it, Courtney enlists another girl from the unofficial advisory, a beautiful black girl named Farah, and together they make a video of her contraption in action. First Courtney describes all the moving parts and their purposes. Then she introduces Farah, who makes a twirling, spinning entrance and, Vanna-like, activates the machine. A ball rolls, dominoes fall, Matchbox cars slide down ramps, and finally a hammer falls and hits a switch that turns on the straightener. It takes more than a few attempts to get all this to work as designed, but eventually they're successful. Courtney earns an A on the project.

She catches up in her physics class, and the threat of not graduating is forgotten. However, the lesson is not lost. She overcame her own doubts and triumphed. Hard work paid off, and she saw that really anything is possible. I do my own little victory dance, a triple-time step with a break.

EVENTUALLY KIDS FROM my English class start joining the half-sandwich club—often when they're in some kind of trouble. Matt becomes a special project, as he's always getting in fights. I can relate to that, but in certain ways Matt tops even my own youthful self. He has an anger problem and a self-image problem. Objectively, he's a good-looking young man with a sandy brown crew cut and soulful eyes, and girls think he's cute. He reminds me of Steve McQueen. A strong athlete, he's the starting middle linebacker for the football team—where it's all right to hit people—but in class he'll nudge other students and then argue when they nudge back. He's constantly in motion, and I have to ride him to go back to his seat and pay attention. Nothing I try succeeds in settling him down, though.

By the end of October, Matt is tied for the dubious record of getting into the most fights at school. His last one was bad. A friend of his was jumped and then Matt got into it with some African-American students. And now four of these same guys have jumped Matt, working him over pretty badly. Black-eyed and bruised, his face is a mess. I phone Matt's father, who says he's worried, too. "Matt's antsy," he tells me. "He has so much energy. But he also says there are problems at school with some of the kids."

I get what his father's saying. "There's a racial element involved" is how one girl in my class puts it. Ever since he was jumped, Matt's had a different attitude, as if he's ready to blow up any second.

"Yeah, I was antsy as a kid, too," I tell his father. "But we have to straighten out his attitude, and you have to help."

He says he will, but a few days later Matt tells me he's on the verge of being expelled. This is still on my mind when I stop, on my way home from school, in front of Joe Hand's Boxing Gym at the corner of Third and Green. Joe Hand is a local boxing promoter who has a chain of these gyms around the city. Walking past this neat little storefront every day, I've noticed that it's nearly brand new, which is unusual for a city boxing gym. It has rings both front and back, and quality heavy and speed punching bags. There's a computer room, where Joe Hand lets kids in the neighborhood use the computers for schoolwork. He also drops the monthly dues and lets them train for free. There are knowledgeable trainers and some good fighters who work out here, including the undefeated welterweight Mike Jones. There are also businessmen and some women getting into shape. My bad knees have talked me out of joining, but I've been sorely tempted, and today I remember the real reason why. Boxing has a special place in my heart because it was my ticket out of trouble and into a new life when I was young.

Before learning to box, I was always in fights, in and out of school. I liked the action. I was small and thought I needed to prove I was tough. After I learned to box, I no longer felt that need to prove I was tough, because I knew I was. Also, just in terms of expended energy, boxing takes some of the fight out of a kid. Even a kid like Matt.

I enter the gym and meet the manager, Petey Pop, and one of the pro trainers, Dan Davis. As I stroll around the rings, I feel like I'm home. Petey asks why I don't come by and work out, as long as I'm living right around the corner.

"I'm getting old," I tell him, but Davis convinces me we can work around my bad knees, and with that I'm in. I agree to come by a couple of times a week to hit the mitts and the bags. I also order a cobra punching bag to be delivered to school.

The cobra is mounted on a spring that's anchored in a sand-filled pedestal. It's a speed reflex bag for combination training. The next morning I get permission to install it in one of the visitors' locker rooms across from the football coach's office. The space is small and shabby, with a row of lockers and benches on either side. My plan is to set the bag up in the open area in the middle, and during fifth period I'll teach Matt to use it.

When I tell him about this plan, Matt's excited. He's up for punching anything, and the prospect of punching something called the cobra positively sings to him. Then other kids spot us carrying the bag and two pairs of boxing gloves down the hallway, and pretty soon I'm the Pied Piper. Both boys and girls want in, nerds as well as football players. Before long I've got about a dozen kids perched on the benches taking in the lesson.

I've been practicing with a bag like this for years, so I decide to show off a little. The cobra is used to develop hand speed, hand-eye coordination, and balance, and I quickly set it dancing. The rhythm is hypnotic. Then I throw a seven-punch combination, left jab, right cross, left hook, right uppercut, left hook, right cross. The kids hang on every move. "And always finish with the left hook," I say. "Like this." Bang, the bag whiplashes.

"Wow!" The kids applaud. "Mr. Danza can still fight." Music to my ears!

Everybody then takes a turn with the gloves and the bag. A couple of the girls do better than the guys. For some reason, the girls aren't as self-conscious. They're just having fun. The boys tend to get more competitive, which can be a problem. But Matt excels. He's big and strong for a fifteen-year-old, and he throws himself fully into the workout. As I'd hoped, the exercise does seem to calm him down, a midday release for all his pent-up energy.

Over the next few weeks we go down almost every day during fifth period and trade rounds. I make Matt work harder than I do. Then we start meeting at Joe Hand's Gym, and Matt gets to train with some real pros, like Boogaloo Watts, a famous Philly fighter from my era. Matt actually has some potential and talent. My strategy seems to be working. He appears more confident, less like he needs to prove how tough he is every day. And boxing and working out with him wins me his respect and some trust, which makes life easier for both of us in class. But it's not a cure-all. The more time I spend with him, the clearer it becomes that Matt has a fire smoldering deep inside. Although it's not exploding quite as often, it's not fully under his control, either. Because we are closer now, I expect him to be less disruptive, but some days he's just too wound up; he'll roam around the room, touching objects, elbowing his friends, still way too antsy.

We're looking for a happy ending here, but this is reality. Because of his obvious anger, I ask Matt if he would be willing to talk to a counselor, and he surprises me. "Yeah," he says, not even shrugging it off.

I call his father and ask him what he thinks. He agrees that he and Matt's mother will come in for a meeting with the head of the department, the counselor, and me. At the meeting it's decided that Matt will start seeing the counselor on a regular basis. All's well until the meeting adjourns.

The bell has just rung, and the corridor's packed with students changing classes. As Matt's parents leave the office and try to thread their way to the exit, they get stuck behind a group of black girls doing what this particular group usually does: talking trash and horsing around. The language is crude, a strong brew of F-bombs and racial epithets.

Matt's father gives the girls a chance, but when they don't clean up their act, he confronts them. He points out that he's walking here with his wife, and that they are in school. He asks them to watch their language. The girls take offense. They jeer, afraid of nobody. They insult Matt's parents to their faces, and in no time flat the confrontation escalates into a screaming match.

Afterward, Matt's father calls me to defend his son. "Now I can see that everything Matt said about Northeast and the students there is true. I see what he's complaining about. I think he's right."

This is just what a kid like Matt does not need to hear. "Whatever you do," I tell his dad, "don't tell him he's right about this." I try to explain the nature of the girls he had the run-in with. "This is cultural. This is how they communicate. It's what they see at home and in the media. They're just kids."

This is enough to calm him down for the moment. He agrees to let Matt finish the year. "But next year he's going to a Catholic school."

I'm reluctant to admit it, but the discipline of parochial school may be what Matt does need.

Bobby G

One weekend I take the train up to New York to visit my friend Bobby Governale. We've known each other since college, when we both planned to be teachers. He went on to fulfill that dream and taught music for thirty-three years. If anybody can set me straight about what I'm doing this year, it's my friend Bobby.

We meet at his neighborhood bar in Long Island. Bobby wears a pressed yellow button-down shirt, gray flannels, and polished loafers. When we hug I smell Aramis. Retirement seems to be agreeing with him, but I still think it's a shame. He retired at fifty-five, at the height of his teaching prowess, because the school system began to shrink his retirement benefits. The longer he stayed, the less he would get. Another paradox of education in America. They want the experienced teachers to retire and make room for new teachers they can pay less. Talk about your penny-wise.

We settle down, and I tell Bobby about my classroom sweats, my sleepless nights, and failing Matt. I feel like I'm in confession.

Bobby listens, nodding. "What are you afraid of, Tony?"

It seems so obvious to me. "There are days when I don't have the foggiest idea how to connect with them. How do I get them excited about learning? About what I'm trying to teach them?"

He taps the tips of his fingers together. "What else?"

He knows me too well. I say, "Okay. I keep thinking they'll see through me. I know they will. You can't lie to them. They'll see me as the fraud that I am."

He laughs. "Knowing you all these years, I knew you'd be a good teacher."

"Hey, Bobby, did you even hear what I just said?"

"Sure, I heard. You remember way back in the beginning, when you were making *Taxi*, you came out to visit my class at Oregon Avenue School?"

"Do I ever. You rocked." Bobby at the time was teaching sixth, seventh, and eighth graders. He was also some dancer, and that day he was combining his talents to teach his kids to disco-dance. Disco was the rage back then, so we were all doing the hustle, and Mr. G. was demonstrating some of the more athletic moves that had made him famous in the clubs. He had the kids twirling and leaping into each other's arms, and as they did he would yell, "Smile!" The kids were having a ball, but that wasn't all. Bobby somehow turned the whole thing into a lesson about music theory and dancing as human interplay or something. He made disco dancing the key to the day's curriculum. That class confirmed for me that Bobby Governale was my hero.

"I had no idea what I was doing," he says. "I was flying by the seat of my pants. I often felt as if I was faking it. And those kids could really get to me. You caught us on a good day, but there were two boys that year that I wanted to strangle. In fact, they made me so angry I nearly quit. I thought, I just can't deal with them, and they make it impossible to teach the others, so why not just throw in the towel?"

He did? My hero? "How did you get past it?"

"Stuck with it. The first year or two, not really knowing the curriculum, is tough for every new teacher. You just keep trying. If you're motivated, you do. The kids eventually see your passion, and that's what makes them buy in."

Eventually. But that suggests time, and time is one thing teachers today don't have. I flash back to my first week at school, before classes began, when Ms. Carroll called all the teachers down to the auditorium and lectured us about Adequate Yearly Progress, or AYP. "There's always the threat of a complete takeover by the district if a school doesn't perform," she warned us. "In a takeover, many teachers and staff are likely to be fired." What she meant was that, as a result of No Child Left Behind, schools that fail to raise their test scores adequately each year can be targeted to become Renaissance Schools, a euphemism for reformed schools. This is every school administrator's worst nightmare because it means that the district will inject the troubled school with "new leadership" in the form of hired educational management consultants, teams of district advisers, or charter school management services. "Out with the old insiders, and in with the new outsiders" is how one disgruntled teacher described it to me. I realized that day that teaching is anything but a secure job. And with the constant pressure to make AYP, time is on no teacher's side.

"How long do you think it takes," I ask Bobby, "to really get good at teaching?"

He stops for a moment, like he wants his words to be just right, and then he says, "It's when they get it. It takes some time for sure, but you can tell the ones who'll be great teachers. They're the ones with the passion. The ones who try things and watch other teachers, and network with teachers even outside their subject areas." He's going now. "You've got to be motivated to be a motivator. You've got to be able to excite the kids with a story or an action and then get them to bite on what you want them to learn." He does that thing with his face that he always does when he's remembering. "My classroom was a safe zone. Nothing but a place to learn and have fun with music, but if I saw a kid with an issue, I told him or her: see me, let's talk. The kids are going to love that about you because they'll know they can talk to you."

"How do you know if you're motivated enough?"

Bobby assures me I'm motivated and a motivator. It will be the same in my classroom as in his. He's so positive. It's one of the reasons I love and respect my friend. Still, my eyes start to fill up so that I have to look away. I hope he's right, but me, I still have serious doubts.

Five

Making the Grade

How best to reach your students? That is the question.

I figure I'm off to a smart start when I assign *Of Mice and Men*. It's a thin little book, which will make the class think it's easy. When I hand out their copies, they immediately flip to the end. "It's only got 112 pages. Chill!"

I just smile. This is Steinbeck, and as they quickly discover, it's not the easiest read. There are heavy metaphors on every page. The biblical tone of the prose also puts them off, but I frame the book as a story about two friends, which appeals to them. Once we're a few chapters in, we screen the classic 1939 movie version of the novel, with Lon Chaney and Burgess Meredith. We talk about what might be wrong with Lennie and why George is so attached to the big, dumb lug. We look at how Steinbeck set up their friendship, their characters, the setting and mood. The kids start to get into it.

After every few chapters there's a quiz. One part of the quiz, courtesy of Ms. Dixon, asks them to compose "gists" of what they've read. A gist is a twenty-word explanation or summation. As you read more chapters, your gist tells more of the story, but it has to stay at twenty words. The last gist tells the whole story. I love to watch the kids trying to tell the story and counting words on their fingers. Gists also make it easy to tell who is reading and who is not.

I feel like we're sailing along when, midway through the unit, Howard comes to me after class to complain. Howard is the biggest kid in the class and plays on the football, soccer, and baseball teams. He also has no father in his life. He likes to goof around, but at my desk he seems earnest when he tells me, "I don't get this story. Doesn't matter how hard I try, nothing sticks."

I really care about this kid, so I spring into teacher mode. "Here, Howard, let me show you." I open the book and demonstrate how to underline important passages and make notes in the margin as he reads. I assure him it's okay to go back and reread sections that he forgets or that don't make sense the first time. "I do it all the time myself."

He says, "I read the same page over and over. I just can't remember it. I'm not good at it."

I have an idea. "It's just practice, like anything else. How much do you practice soccer?"

He answers, "A lot."

"How much you practice reading?"

"Not at all."

"I'm telling you, this is the only difference."

"But I just don't enjoy it—at all."

"Practice reading, and you'll get better at it. Eventually you'll enjoy doing it, just like you enjoy soccer. You didn't enjoy soccer when you first started, right?"

He won't go there. Soccer, he insists, was fun for him from the very first kick, even when he was bad at it. We throw that back and forth a little. Then I say, "Yeah, but you like it more now that you're really good at it, right?" He shrugs. "It's like the ukulele," I say.

"Hunh?" Howard's eyebrows shoot up to his buzz cut. "Ukah-what?"

"I've been using thought-for-the-day calendars for years," I tell him. "Every morning, the calendar gives me an idea or piece of advice. Well, on April 24, 2006, the thought for the day was 'Get a ukulele and a chord book, practice thirty minutes a day for thirty days, and you'll entertain your family, friends, and yourself for the rest of your life.' I was like you. I barely knew what a uke was back then, but I kind of liked the idea, so I got myself a ukulele and a chord book and started practicing. It wasn't much fun until I got better at it, but now I've been playing for almost five years, and that uke is like my third arm. I love it."

Howard clearly thinks I'm insane, but I persist. "I want you to apply that same advice to your reading. Try it. Read for thirty minutes every day—anything you enjoy—practice and you'll get good at it, I promise." He squinches up his face and goes out shaking his head.

I track down David Cohn and tell him about my little conference with Howard. I'm seeking guidance and, as always, sympathy. David frowns and says, "Let me show you something."

He pulls a printout from his desk. "This is a list of kids in the school who've been identified as gifted." He points. There, near the top of the list, is Howard's name.

David's expression puts me on the hot seat. There are only two possibilities here. Is this reading issue something serious that's been going on with Howard for a long time, something that I really do have to figure out? Or am I getting played? I try not to judge people as I judge myself, but if I do, I think this kid is playing me.

Nevertheless, Howard has made me realize that I need to find more ways to make my students *want* to read. The so-called literacy initiative that threads throughout our curriculum does not help. In addition to teaching our main literary units, every few weeks I'm required to give my students directed reading assignments from preselected articles and short stories, followed by assigned tests on these readings. We also sample data from informational texts and textbooks, with tests that direct the students to retrieve pertinent facts. The goals of the literacy initiative are to help students better interpret what they read, and to give them practice in different types of reading. But these scripted exercises consume entire periods, interrupting our focus on the core curriculum, and let's just say the students don't love the material. Obviously, kids—like all of us—will learn to read better and faster when reading material that interests them. The students in my class who have the most difficulty reading are not illiterate but aliterate. Like Howard, they can read, but don't.

I'm haunted by one particular research finding I learned during orientation, that students who don't read over summer vacation can lose as much as a whole grade's reading level. How can I make sure this doesn't happen to my kids? The only way I can think of is to make them want to read on their own, and the only way to do that is to convince them that they enjoy reading. A tall order. I decide to get as creative with our reading drills as Northeast's athletic coaches are on the practice field. If Howard can have fun kicking a ball, he can have fun with reading.

First I find short stories for them about sports and celebrities. Then one day I hear the kids talking about the movie version of *Twilight*. It dawns on me: teen romance and vampires. Irresistible. These books are written in the vernacular of their age group. They might not be great literature, but if I can get my students excited about reading vampire romances, that excitement just might spark a reading habit that continues even when they're out of school. I get a deal on thirty copies of the first book in the Twilight series and plunk one down on every desk.

The volume's door-stopper thickness is a shocker. "It's four hundred ninety-eight pages!" Howard yelps in disbelief. But most of the girls are game and help me convince the boys. We'll go slow. I have them read just three chapters a week, with quizzes on Fridays. I make study work sheets for *Twilight* just as I do for the regular books in the curriculum. The work sheets help to focus their attention on plotlines and help them understand what they're reading, although no one except a few of the boys is having trouble with this book. The work sheets also help them prepare for my quizzes.

The point that *Twilight* helps me drive home is that books are more than boring print, more than strings of letters and pages to turn. "Books are stories," I tell the class over and over. And *Twilight* is proof positive. This particular story, of forbidden and dangerous love between the sweet and innocent Bella and the bloodsucking but gentlemanly Edward, resonates with kids who are both attracted to and terrified by the opposite sex. As far-fetched as I find the story, I see why the kids get into it: they can relate. Even the boys start coming around. Eric Lopez breaks the ice and makes me look good when he openly admits he likes the book. Howard laughs at the love scenes, but he has no trouble with the quizzes. And he's no longer complaining about Steinbeck as much.

Meanwhile, I'm also getting creative with our "real" work. On Halloween, I devote the entire class to my own special edition of Pictionary. Competing in teams, the kids have to draw scenes from everything we've read since the beginning of school, from creation myths to *Of Mice and Men*. Nakiya proves to be our virtuoso artist, illustrating "Theseus leaving Ariadne on the island" with a full-color cartoon. For fun, and to give them something to really lampoon, I throw in a few prompts from class, including "Eric Choi's head lean" and "Mr. Danza." For some mysterious reason, their drawings of me all have very big mouths.

When we finish reading *Of Mice and Men*, I'm faced with the prospect of my first major exam. As my quizzes have taught me, writing a test can be even more challenging for the teacher than taking it is for the students. My very first quiz, second week of school, asked the kids to name the elements of plot, to draw a plot diagram, to identify the hallmarks of a myth, and to write a twenty-word gist of a short story we had read. That day I was so proud of myself for working all this out that I practically skipped down the corridor, telling the other teachers, "I'm giving my first quiz." They nodded or gave me a thumbs-up while not so subtly shaking their heads at the new guy. Since then my quizzes have taught me that accuracy counts long before the student gets anywhere near the test, and woe be to any teacher who misspells Theseus or confuses Anansi with Ashanti. The kids may not be able to answer every question correctly, but they're sure to find every punctuation or spelling mistake *you* make on a question and rag on you about it for weeks. Also, the test can't be too easy, and you can't just "teach to the test." The questions have to cover all the information you've been stressing in class, but they also have to require higher-level thinking. The test might ask them to discuss the concept of irony, for example, or to explain how a situation in a story gives them some insight into their own lives. Oh, and a little humor woven through the questions is always a plus, because the kids like it and it makes you feel clever. Tests, like every other aspect of the classroom, have to *engage the students*.

But a comprehensive exam is like a quiz on steroids. Because my Steinbeck exam is my first attempt at a unit test, I study quizzes and tests from the Internet and from my teachers' textbooks as if I'm the one being tested. I ask some of the other English instructors what exactly they would include on the test. Their consensus is that students in the tenth grade should know the story, the characters, and vocabulary used in the book. But I also want my students to understand tone and mood, imagery, and all the figurative language. I have to make this test my own.

The first section ends up being twenty questions on story points and background information. In the vocabulary section I use each target word in a sentence and ask for a choice of a corresponding word. To test command of figurative language, I pull passages from the book for the students to read and decide which literary term applies to each one. The final section asks them to describe the tone and mood of five different passages and decide which words appeal to which senses.

When the test is finally written, I feel good about it. Now to prepare the class. Again, *engage the students*. Creativity counts.

"Tomorrow," I announce, "we're going to do a final review for your *Of Mice and Men* exam." As usual, groans and moans. I hold up my hand like a policeman. "Relax, the bunch of you. The review will be a scavenger hunt."

They look at each other. Not everyone knows what a scavenger hunt is. I don't explain, just break them into six teams and tell everybody to meet for class the next morning at the baseball bleachers behind school. After class I fill one paper bag for each team with a map of the school showing the test station locations, a passport with a picture of everyone on the team, a page for each challenge, a pack of Post-its, and two Sharpies. I fill burlap bags with sand and lean on Dr. G., the science teacher, to loan me a couple of his live hamsters to stand in for dead mice. I recruit teachers, guards, and anyone else I can nab to serve as "station monitors."

The next morning rewards me with beautiful crisp October weather. Everybody's present, and when they've assembled on the bleachers, I read out the basic rules. "At six different locations throughout the school you will meet challenges related to *Of Mice and Men*. When your team has passed each challenge, the station monitor will stamp your passport and give you the clue to your next location. There is to be absolutely *no* running in the hallways, no loud or disruptive noise, and no leaving campus. Your team has to stay together, and all team members must be at the station when you complete the task in order to receive your stamp. Finally, each team must show integrity. You know what that means? That's your word of the day."

I've never seen these kids so energized by a class. As I hand each team their closed bag of equipment, they taunt each other. "You goin' down!" "I got this one. The rest of you losers might as well quit now." "Just you wait, man. I've got *skills*." Competition is a drug, and when I blow the whistle for them to open the bags, read their first location clue, and get going, they're like ponies out of the gate at Belmont. The rule against running is a lost cause.

Here are their first five challenges:

- "Pet Lenny's Dead Mouse," a.k.a. hamsters
- "Name That Character," based on a list of personality descriptions and quotes
- "Buck Some Barley" by lugging the sandbags from one side of the courtyard to the other and back again
- "More Than a Feeling," give the mood and tone of these passages
- "What Nice Figurative Language You Have," match passages from the book to the appropriate literary device

And while my students are tearing around the school, I stay on the baseball field and set up the final challenge—a game of horseshoes to play, just like the characters do in the book. Having worked up one of my best teacher sweats setting up the hunt, using a rolling desk chair as a dolly to move all the stuff around the school, I'm still wet when the first team of scavengers comes screaming out the gym door.

"We won! We won!" You'd think there was a million-dollar purse attached to this victory. And much to my surprise, one of the members of this winning team is none other than I-can't-remember and I-don't-like-to-read Howard.

I could be a schmo about it and give him a hard time, but I raise a high five, and Howard meets it with a big grin. "Game's not over yet," I tell his team. "There's still one more challenge, and the others aren't far behind."

We start playing horseshoes and don't stop until the bell rings, by which time everybody, I most of all, feels like a winner. Tired, but a winner.

The next morning is test time, and another thing giving quizzes has taught me is that administering tests is its own art. As I patrol the class, I recall that when I was in school the nuns seemed to grow extra eyes in the backs of their heads for test days. Cheating was an exercise in futility. We could write the answers on our palms, slip cheat sheets up our sleeves, read our neighbors' answers horizontally or upside down, but we always got caught. Those nuns had what teachers at my orientation called "with-it-ness." However, being with it takes a few extra skills in the twenty-first century, when virtually every student carries a portable electronic device capable of instant messaging, texting, and data storage. Every classroom today is unofficially wired. Students will look you straight in the eye and pretend to be listening to you while texting blindly with the devices in their pockets. On regular days I have to punctuate every lesson with reminders, requests, and demands that kids take out their earbuds and put away cell phones. On test day, I have to be hypervigilant.

Still, I believe that my students really have absorbed their Steinbeck, and after class I'm elated to discover that almost everyone—

including Howard—has passed the test with flying colors. In between the fake dead mice and barley bags, it appears they've actually figured out the irony of George killing his best friend, Lennie, and why Steinbeck used that biblical tone. The biggest thrill for me is Al G, who pulls a ninety-one. When I give him back his results next morning, he smirks at me, and it's definitely one of his best smirks.

FOR THE PAST two years the school has been planning to switch from free dress to uniforms this November. It's Ms. Carroll's decision, but the kids and some of the parents have fought her, and as the day of the switch approaches, they're still up in arms. The kids see it as an infringement of their rights, and the parents are riled up over the expense of the uniforms. Now add to this a strong and unfair suspicion that the new policy has something to do with our show. I hear the grumbling: "Only reason we have to wear uniforms is because Tony Danza's here." That's not true, but it is a sentiment that will linger all year.

I tell my class that, in solidarity with them, I will wear the same outfit every day, too. "I actually like the idea of uniforms, since it takes the worry out of what to wear," I say. What I don't tell my kids is that my uniform set me at odds with my production team, just as theirs sets them at odds with the school administration. When I went out to shop for my teacher clothes, the producers sent along an assistant who would phone back to the production office with my choices, which amounted to black shoes, gray pants and a belt, blue dress shirt, and a Northeast High School tie. Neat, easy, and classic, just like the kids' uniforms. To get me through the year, I bought five pairs of identical slacks and six shirts, all of which passed muster. But then we came to the tie. A showdown over a tie! The producers were dead set against the neckwear, said it made me look stodgy and old-fashioned. I wouldn't budge. To me the tie signifies respect for the job of teaching and the students. It's the way a teacher is supposed to dress. I won, which turned out to be a very good thing, since the boys' uniform includes the same school tie.

"Viking pride, everybody!" I point at my uniform as kids pass me in the hall. "We're all in this together." This doesn't even make a dent in their grumbling, but I feel good and I think I look good, too.

On the day the policy takes effect, any student not in uniform is directed to the auditorium, where I've been given monitor duty, thank you very much. I appear in the doorway, and more than a thousand kids boo me so loudly that I have to leave to make them stop.

Outside, I spot my student Pepper stopped at the security gate for a uniform violation. Pepper's a small, quirky kid called by his last name because it describes his personality, but he's not usually a troublemaker, so I go over to see what's up. He's wearing the khaki pants, white shirt, striped school tie, and dark sweater the code requires, but he has on the wrong color shoes. His tough luck that Ms. DeNaples happens to be monitoring that entrance. She points him toward the auditorium.

Pepper grins and tells her, "I have the right shoes in my backpack."

"If you have the right shoes, why aren't you wearing them?" Ms. D. demands.

Pepper doesn't answer, but after he changes his shoes, he hands a small object to Ms. DeNaples saying, "This is for your trouble."

She looks in her hand to see what he's given her, and her face turns scarlet, then purple. Before he has time to blink, she's on him, hauling him down to the office. I trail them at a safe distance, but they disappear into the principal's office. No telling how long this will take, so I head back to the auditorium. A few minutes later I'm flagged down by a teacher who takes particular pleasure whenever administration has a "problem."

"You hear what your kid Pepper did?" He can hardly contain himself.

"No, I couldn't figure it out. What did he do?"

"He gave Ms. DeNaples a dog biscuit." The corners of his mouth bubble with laughter, and a second later he's chortling so hard he has to go into the hall.

I'm stumped. Why a dog biscuit? And what's so funny? I hope Ms. D. has a dog, but I have a sneaking suspicion she doesn't.

David Cohn's in the roster room when I track him down, and he just gives my befuddled look right back to me after I tell him the story. Then Ms. DeNaples herself comes in, still bristling. She takes one look at us and must see our bewilderment, or maybe because Pepper's my student she thinks I should take some responsibility. "Don't you know what his little *gift* means?" she snarls.

"I'm sorry," I say as humbly as possible. "I really don't."

She looks at me like I'm too dumb to live, let alone teach this monstrous kid. "It means I'm a bitch."

I can feel David stifling a laugh while I'm still fumbling for the connection. "Dog-bitch, get it?" she says, now seeming really hurt.

David offers, "At least he's creative."

"*Mister* Cohn." She jumps down his throat. "If that's your idea of creativity, maybe you should consider a different profession."

David swallows hard, his mouth still twitching, and escapes to the hall with me right behind him. I'll see Mr. Pepper in class.

Opportunity comes in all shapes and sizes. The whole class has heard about Pepper's stunt and is already lionizing him, so rather than make this a group exercise, I invite him to see me after class, fifth period. He gets that this is an invitation he can't refuse and looks a little sheepish as he agrees, uncertain what I have in store for him. I leave him wondering as I wrangle the class to attention.

My lesson plan calls for a do-now about physical fitness and nutrition. I do want my kids to begin thinking about their health as a component of their educational and intellectual fitness, but today is clearly not the day. Eric Lopez and Matt start ranting about the uniforms. They ask me what I think, and as I'm about to answer, Monte announces that he likes the new policy because it makes everybody look as serious as he is about school. Eric Choi agrees: "Now I don't have to wear the dorky shirts my mother always buys for me." But Chloe and Katerina groan. They're already in mourning over the shopping they'll be deprived of for the rest of the year. Ileana and Ben-Kyle grouse about free expression.

How about this? Disagreement! Strong opinions! I erase the fitness do-now from the board and write a new prompt: "How do you feel about the uniform policy? Explain why."

The kids eat it up. They get right to work and, minutes later, are eager to read their opinions out loud. The compositions have more energy and conviction than almost anything they've written so far this year. So I divide them into teams to debate the issue. In one of my first professional development seminars, I learned that students retain ideas best through discussion, especially debates. And the uniform policy seems ready-made for this. I can just sit back and let the sparks fly.

Charmaine speaks first. Because of her eclectic fashion sense, I have a feeling she is in the con column, and I am so right. "I know I am still a minor, but this is America and I should be allowed to dress any way I want to." I love when kids play the America card. Patriotism, the last refuge of a scoundrel.

White Nick (so named because Nakiya is our Black Nick) counters with a question. "What if what you're wearing is distracting?"

Al G chimes in. "Yeah, some of these girls wear crazy stuff. I like it, but it's crazy."

Paige begs to differ. "Why should I be punished because some girls dress like sluts?"

"I thought you were talking about my two different socks," complains Charmaine. The class laughs hard at that.

"What about the cost?" I ask to stir the flames.

"My mom is worried about that," Daniel says, and several other kids say theirs are, too.

"How much does it cost to buy your school clothes now?" I ask.

Monte jumps on this. "I would suggest that we will save money in the long run, and just think about the energy you save by not having to worry about your clothing selection." I picture Monte in front of a closet agonizing over the selection of outfits that will make him look neat, smart, and college-bound.

The discussion goes back and forth for the whole period, and the kids are so *engaged* that I decide to make debates a weekly feature in my class. We may not resolve the uniform issue, but when we take a final vote, the pros actually edge out the cons. Even Pepper seems more thoughtful about the policy by the time the bell rings. Nevertheless, as he's leaving I remind him about our date. We still have business to attend to.

When Pepper arrives at the start of fifth period, I'm sitting at my desk. I ask, "You ever write an apology note?" He shrugs and looks down at his shoes. I hand him a piece of stationery and an envelope. "Well, you're going to write one now."

I sit him down and tell him to pull out his pen, to use his best handwriting. To do it right I probably should let him choose his own words, but I don't want to take any chances. I dictate: " 'Dear Ms. DeNaples,' comma."

He puts his head down and writes exactly what I tell him to. Not even a whimper. He knows he has to do it. And when it's done, he delivers the note to Ms. D. in person. I watch from outside the office as she reads it in front of him. All is clearly not forgiven, but she sighs and dismisses him with a warning. "Disrespect is no laughing matter."

When Pepper comes out of the office, we stand there for several seconds looking at each other. Then I ask, "You going to lunch?"

"Yeah." He turns and heads for the cafeteria, looking as disheveled and hangdog as always. But as he enters the stairwell, he gives me a little backward wave over his shoulder. We're off the hook, and at least some modicum of Ms. D.'s dignity is restored. I call that even.

No Fear Shakespeare

"Why do we teach tenth graders Shakespeare?"

David Cohn must hear the anguish in my voice, but he still insists on answering my question, as teachers will do, with another question. "Why do *you* think we teach Shakespeare?"

"No way! You're not going to pull that one on me." Tomorrow I'm supposed to start the unit on *Julius Caesar,* and I'm as intimidated as my students by the Elizabethan verbiage and just the thought of teaching Shakespeare. I need to know why we're doing this. "Seriously."

"Mental gymnastics," he says.

I don't get it.

"The work Shakespeare puts them through will serve them when they're older."

"Come on. That's a hard sell for me, forget the kids. David, I have to convince them and myself this is worth the effort." The truth is, I'm not sure I know enough to teach Shakespeare.

"Front-load the unit."

"What's that mean?"

"Get them to think about who Shakespeare was, and his historical context."

It occurs to me that David Cohn himself, with his pale features, sad eyes, and well-trimmed brown beard, would make a good stand-in for old Will. The Shakespeare of Northeast High. "You mean," I say, "find a way to feel connected to him, like having them do a research project on his neighborhood?"

"That's one approach. It's okay to get creative."

"Maybe have them draw the playwright at work, or the Old

Globe? Poster board displays?" I think of all the class projects I wish I'd taken seriously in my day. "I bet Eric Choi could make an origami Shakespeare."

"How about library exercise? They can use the computers," David suggests.

"Yeah. Rotten kids get to use the Internet. All we had was the encyclopedia."

"Just make sure they don't discover No Fear Shakespeare," David deadpans.

"What's No Fear Shakespeare?"

He lets out a laugh and shakes his head. Gotcha! "Translates the old English to modern English."

"Really? *I love it.*" I make a beeline for my laptop.

"And you, too, Brutus?" doesn't have quite the ring of "Et tu, Brute?" but No Fear Shakespeare immediately makes my life easier. For the zillionth time since school began, I give thanks for the World Wide Web.

I'll admit it: I have help. I'm determined to do as much of what a teacher does as I can without extra assistance, but there are times when having the production company behind me does make my life easier. Unlike other classes, we have our own ultrafast Wi-Fi connection, which gives me access to the whole Internet, including YouTube, to enhance my lessons. I've found that YouTube is loaded with videos on every great work of literature. Some comic, some serious, but all certainly interesting to the kids. I think this gives my students an advantage over other classes, which have only limited access and certainly can't tap YouTube, but I've heard teachers argue the opposite.

"David," I ask, "do you think all these electronics are changing the way kids learn? They do seem to have a shrinking attention span, and a lot of them couldn't stay on task if their lives depended on it. We're supposed to integrate technology into the classroom, but what if this technology is causing the shrinking? How do you use something that inhibits learning to aid education?"

David finishes signing the form on his desk—another teacher's evaluation, fortunately, not mine. "I don't think we have a choice," he says. "Technology is a fact of life. The kids are used to having constant stimulation. Advertisers, software companies, Facebook, television shows—" He throws a sidelong glance at our ever-present production crew. "Practically from the moment they're born, kids have all these forces clamoring for their attention, begging to entertain them and sell them something. Then they come to school, where they and their parents tell administrators that it's the teachers' job to engage them and break through all that other stuff. As far as the kids are concerned, they've done their part if they show up. They sit in front of the teacher the same way they sit in front of a computer screen, waiting for that instant message."

"But sometimes I can stand on my head and do somersaults. Nothing."

"The mistake many new teachers make is to confuse engagement with passive entertainment."

I grimace. "Kind of an irony for an entertainer like me to be here, then."

David looks at the ceiling. "You said it, I didn't."

"Ouch. Well, you can't say I'm not trying. What *does* it take to really engage them, then?"

"Two words. *Active participation.* Look what happened when you got them involved in that scavenger hunt for *Of Mice and Men.* When they're making it happen, they're learning. When all that's happening is you talking, chances are much lower that they're learning. They tune out and look for their BlackBerries. Of course, it could be worse."

"How?"

"You could be teaching math."

"Hah! Fat chance."

David pushes back from his desk and looks out the window at the football field, where Nakiya is conducting the Northeast marching band on the fifty-yard line. "They haven't really changed that much, you know. If you can connect them emotionally to a moment in a book or a poem, the differences will melt away." He sighs and brings his attention back to me. "But *they* have to feel it, Tony. No matter how much you may want to, you can't feel it *for* them."

"I just asked about technology in the classroom." I put my laptop away. "You don't have to get all heavy on me."

Six

Never Smile Before Christmas

LIKE IT OR NOT, we're on to Shakespeare, and I'm now excited
about the challenge. I ask each student to create a project demonstrating the Bard's importance and influence, and the kids actually come
through. Eric Choi constructs a detailed model of the Old Globe
Theatre entirely out of little pieces of paper. Others draw posters and
dioramas. Daniel's portrait of Shakespeare looks surprisingly like Mr.
Cohn. Laura devises an ingenious board game tracing Shakespeare's
life and career, which everybody wants to play. But despite the fun
they have with the projects, they're still moaning and groaning over
the language every time I tell them to read a scene, and we haven't
even gotten to the Ides of March yet—let alone Thanksgiving. Good
thing David turned me on to No Fear Shakespeare, my inspiration
for an exercise I call Shakespeare to Street.

The idea is to have the kids rephrase *Julius Caesar* in their own
lingo. "You know that language you kids all speak that drives me
crazy," I tell them. "Like 'you be and I be.' Well, here's your chance
to let it loose. I want you to do that to Shakespeare. Take a scene and
act it out in street language. You'll each perform a scene, and we'll
vote for the winners."

Success! Not that I always understand their translations. At one point in her performance, Paige says, "Caesar, don't you be draulin'." After she finishes, I ask what *draulin'* means. Her reply: "It means when someone is acting completely off the chain."

"Oh." I nod as if she makes perfect sense. Shakespeare would have liked that.

Fortunately, it matters less that I understand my students' translations than that they understand the play. I have high hopes when I test them on the first three acts. Everyone except Howard is present, and nobody just turns over the paper in defeat and stares at the ceiling. I give them our whole first period and collect their answers before the break. My plan is to review their answers as a group during our second period, but then Howard saunters in.

He has an approved excuse—a morning doctor's appointment—but now I have to figure out a place for him to make up the test. I've seen other teachers put a student's desk in the hall for a makeup, and that seems like a reasonable plan. As long as the door is closed he won't hear a word inside, and we can go ahead with our review. Howard gives me his usual goofy grin and shrugs. "Okay with me."

The test review doesn't disappoint. The kids are able to identify the date of the Ides of March and the first man to stab Caesar, and they're into the story. I tell them we'll wrap up the last two acts by watching the movie with James Mason as Brutus and Marlon Brando as Antony. We're having a good discussion when I notice Matt has his phone out. "Matt, put the phone away."

He ignores me. He's texting.

"Matt, put your phone away."

"Uh-oh, Matt," the others cry.

I don't see or suspect a thing until that night, when I grade the individual tests.

Matt and Howard are good friends. They're both solid athletes, and by some outrageous fortune, their *Julius Caesar* tests contain almost identical right and wrong answers. I begin to think they cheated several hours before I figure out how they did it. Matt was texting Howard in the hall when I was telling him to put away his phone. Clearly, you can't be a Luddite and also be with it as a teacher today.

In the morning I ask our production office to show me yesterday's tapes. We had two cameras going, one inside the classroom and one to shoot Howard taking his test. The camera outside was positioned at the end of the hall, to be unobtrusive and get a long shot. "I knew he was up to something," the cameraman says as he racks up the shot.

There it is. Howard is dropping the phone from his pocket, checking the screen, then writing on his test. Phone from the pocket, checking, and writing. Over and over again. Worse, he's got that Cheshire cat grin on his face, like he's pulling off a heist. They really did forget there were cameras.

When I get to David Cohn's office, I'm steamed. "Matt and Howard cheated on the test."

David closes his laptop and leans back in his chair. His face betrays nothing. "How do you know?"

"Well, their answers match up exactly. Matt was texting him the answers from inside the class. We've got it on tape." I'm pacing.

David takes his time answering. "Did you personally see anything?"

"No. I can't believe it, but I totally missed it."

"In a real-life situation without cameras, if you didn't see it, there's nothing you can do about it."

I feel my mouth fall open. "So what do I do?"

He folds his arms and doesn't answer. It's clear that he has no intention of using the taped evidence against the boys. His deal is teaching for real. And he's right. I wanted it this way.

I confront Howard after class alone and ask him baldly, "You cheat on the test?"

Just as brazenly, he denies it. "What?" he sputters, with a look of offended innocence. "No!"

"How do you explain the fact that your answers and Matt's are identical?"

He shrugs. "Coincidence."

I keep it up for a while, but he doesn't give an inch.

I corner Matt. "You think you were doing your friend a favor? Cheating is no favor and just gets you in trouble."

Matt won't meet my eyes. He shifts his feet. His hands dig deep into his pockets, but he won't cop to it, either. Finally I let him go.

One of the girls in the class later lets me in on the boys' conversation after Matt's meeting with me:

Matt, all over Howard: "Didn't you know they had a camera on you? What were you thinking?"

Howard, genuinely shocked: "No way. They were all the way at the other end of the hall."

I have enough evidence to put it behind me. I've learned a valuable lesson about the downside of technology in the classroom. After this, I'm much more vigilant about turning off cell phones in class, and no one is allowed to bring any electronic devices into the hallway when taking a makeup test. Unfortunately, my kids have also just proven that cameras in schools aren't always a bad idea.

FROM THE BEGINNING, I've planned to fly home to be with my family for the Thanksgiving holiday. I love Thanksgiving—no gifts, just great food, family, and friends. Plus, I miss my daughters and my wife, and I need to find out if they miss me. Back in September, Thanksgiving promised to be a natural break, an automatic trip, a no-brainer. But student events have a way of overtaking the calendar. As November arrives, I realize we have a big football game scheduled for Thanksgiving Day against our archenemy, Central High. This is the oldest public high school rivalry in the country, and I really should be there for the three boys in my class who are playing, as well as for the rest of the team. Also, if the marching band keeps winning, they'll be competing in state championships that weekend, and Nakiya has made me promise to come. Simple logistics don't help, either. Even if the school calendar were empty over the break, it's a long trip for a short holiday. To get to California, I'll have to leave late Wednesday, after school. It's a six-hour flight. Then I'm home three days, and early Sunday morning back on another long return flight. And that four o'clock wake-up on Monday won't adjust for three hours of jet lag.

There's another problem. I'm so wrapped up in my responsibilities here that at home I'll probably spend the whole time talking and thinking about my students. At this moment that might not go over too well with my wife and my real kids. I don't know how other teachers do it, even without the distance. Maybe this explains the clichéd image of teachers as spinsters. With everything you have to do for school, who's got anything left for a marriage or family?

When I phone my elder daughter early in November, I confess that I still haven't bought my plane tickets because "I'm not sure yet when I can get home." It doesn't help at all when she says, "Oh, that's okay, Dad." It is? Is she telling me it's okay because I've already missed so much of her life that it really makes no difference to her anymore whether I'm there or not? Does she have a new boyfriend I don't even know about? Or does she mean it really is okay because she thinks I'm doing something important, giving my all to kids who don't have the advantages she has? I'm trying hard to teach my students to read, yet I can't even read my own daughter anymore.

I'm standing alone at the window fifth period, mulling all this over and watching the fall leaves fly by, when my student Gwen slouches in. It's completely slipped my mind that I asked her to come for a conference, but I try to look smart.

Gwen doesn't seem to like me much. In class, for no reason, she shoots me dirty looks that rival Al G's yawns. The camera has caught those looks, and the show will play them in a montage for laughs. But she's a good student. Until recently her work was solid. It's her new tendency to slack off that we need to discuss.

She slumps behind her desk and glowers, rubbing her chronically sweaty palms on her jeans. Like most girls at fifteen, Gwen has body and appearance issues, and sweaty palms are a particular source of embarrassment for her. In other respects, though, she's bold. One of the few open lesbians in the school, she's a member of ALLY, the school's Gay-Straight Alliance club. Unfortunately, her senior girlfriend just ended their relationship. Gwen is angry, and not just at me.

"I'm concerned, Gwen," I tell her. "You're a good student, but suddenly the work's not showing it. I don't think you're doing the reading."

She tucks her hands up under her armpits and says nothing.

"Is something going on? Something bothering you?" I'm thinking, How do I talk to a girl about girlfriend problems? I guess it's the same as talking to a guy about girlfriend problems. Gwen mumbles, so low I can barely hear her, "There's some stuff at home."

"Ohhhh." I'm so relieved I'm afraid she can hear it. Home I can handle. As long as it's not my own home. "What's going on?"

She shrugs. Her father just lost his job and is acting very different. He can't find work, and has pretty much stopped looking, which pisses off her mother because it means *she* has to do double shifts as a nurse. So then her parents fight.

"How's your relationship with your dad?" I ask, imagining what my daughter would tell her teacher if he asked about her home life right now.

She shrugs again. "Like I said, he's different now, kind of a creep." She tells me they used to be close. "Now, not so much."

Wow, that sounds familiar. I take the seat next to Gwen's and think about what I'm going to say. I don't know the first thing about Gwen's father, but I know what it's like to lose a job and worry that you won't be able to provide for your family. To worry about what being out of work says about you and what your daughter might think of you. "You know," I say, "I got fired last year."

She rolls her eyes. What could Tony Danza possibly know about what *her* family is going through?

"No, really. I got fired and I thought I was finished. Done. Too old to work on TV, who'd want me anymore?"

She gives me a long, cold stare. "So you came here."

"Heh, yeah well, maybe a little bit, but no, that's not where I'm going. Listen, I . . ." But where am I going with this? I've dragged this kid here and asked her to pour out her troubles. Now what exactly do I have to offer her? I say, "What I mean is, losing your job is major. Especially for a guy. At least *to* a guy. When I lost my job, it took a toll on my family life, too. I'm not sure my wife knows if she even wants to be married to me anymore, and things are not so great with my daughters, either. You know what they say in the television business when they fire someone?"

She's not letting up. The fish eye says, Where is this going?

"They say, 'You're canceled.' And that's just how I felt, like I'd been canceled. Erased. And I brought that home. I felt sorry for myself. I lost my temper. I'm pretty sure if you asked them, my wife and daughters would say I acted like a creep, too."

Her chin sinks to her chest. I can almost hear her thinking, What does any of this BS have to do with me?

"Look," I try again. "I can't speak for your father, and I'm not defending him. But you need to understand a couple of things, Gwen.

First, you can't let the stress at home interfere with your studies. I know it's not easy, but this is important. No excuses, not even good ones." She wipes her hands on her jeans again and won't make eye contact.

"Second," I continue, "I don't know your father, but remember when we talked in class about walking in someone else's shoes before you judge them, and the meaning of empathy? Well, I think this situation calls for a little bit of that from you. I'm not excusing your father's behavior, just like I don't excuse my own, but this is hard all around, on everyone, not just on you. Try to keep that in mind. You know, when I came home after being fired, I wanted my family to understand how much I hurt. The more I didn't get that from them the more I needed it and the harder I tried to get it. That's when it got bad. And don't forget I have my New York Italian way of discussing things. I can be loud. I have been known to yell. I call it passion, but especially not enamored with my passion is my youngest, Emily. She calls it temper. She's right."

I sneak a peek. Gwen's tracking now. I continue. "I'm not crazy about my temper, either, and I have tried to work on it, but I grew up in a family that was the opposite of my wife's. No one in her family ever raised their voice, and I grew up in a family where if people weren't yelling, they didn't care."

Gwen almost laughs. I wait for her to say something. She doesn't. "The problem with men," I blurt out, "is that they are what they do."

Gwen lifts her head. "What?" She looks at me.

"Men feel worthless if they're not working. At least most of the guys I know do. Women are tougher. They put more stock in relationships and other activities. But for men, the job defines them. So when they lose it, they don't know who they are. I know about that."

I feel an ugly hole in the pit of my stomach, but Gwen is studying me with new eyes. She's not about to tell me, but I sense her black mood has lifted. It never ceases to amaze me how quickly the young can shift emotional gears.

The door opens, and Joe Connelly pokes his head in, asking, "You having lunch?"

I start to beg off, but Gwen stops me. "I think we're good." She gets up and hugs her backpack to her chest. "Thanks, Mr. Danza."

"Keep me posted, and do your reading, Gwen."

She gives me a little thumbs-up as she leaves, and when she's gone, Joe jokes, "Another small step for mankind?"

"I don't know," I tell him. "But I think, maybe."

That evening I phone my wife and tell her about Gwen. I apologize for acting like a creep. We agree that it doesn't make sense for me to fly home for the few days I'll have off for Thanksgiving. I hate that she agrees so easily.

The next week Gwen's work improves, though the hard looks continue. It's just her, I guess. She does let me know, "Things are getting better at home." I tell her I'm proud of her.

Still, the prospect of missing Thanksgiving, my favorite holiday, leaves me feeling a little too sorry for myself. I need a change of pace, a break from Philly. Maybe I can't go home to L.A., but why not go home to New York? Even better, why not take the kids with me? I've always admired teachers who take their classes on major field trips, and what could be more major than the greatest city on earth?

The good news is that the production team likes the idea of a field trip segment. The bad news is that the network wants us to go to Washington, D.C., instead of Manhattan. They have several reasons for this preference, not the least of which is expense. And it's true that D.C. is the nation's capital, and none of the kids have ever been, and we can visit the Folger Shakespeare Library there, so even if I did have any say in the decision, I can't really justify my objection. But I vow to find a way to get the kids to New York later in the year.

Meanwhile, the school administration approves our Washington trip for November 16, and I hand out permission slips to be signed by every student's parents. The class is jazzed, but as the trip gets closer, I start sweating. Among many Northeast students the rule seems to be, Rules are made to be broken. And for all the manuals, books, policies, and programs that have been written and announced about school discipline—despite the presence of a Philadelphia police station on campus!—only students who get into physical fights face serious consequences. Behavior codes are clearly posted, and teachers remind students of them every day. Everyone knows the policies on uniforms, hoodies, iPods, running, shouting, and the rest, but no one is consistently and actively enforcing these policies. Even in my own classroom, I have no real framework for disciplining my kids. If they wear hoodies or have their earbuds in, the teacher is supposed to make them take them off, but if the students don't listen, the teacher is stuck. The only recourse is to make a thing out of it, involve the dean's office, and probably lose precious class time, and not many teachers are willing to trade their all-important "momentum" for discipline. The kids know this, and some push as far as they can. If they're like this in class, I don't want to think what the bus will be like.

As if to drive the point home, the day before our trip I get an alert from Assistant Principal McCloskey during fifth period that Pepper, my dog biscuit kid, was just assaulted in the hallway. Downstairs, sitting in the school police station, Pepper looks pitiful. His eye is bruised and swollen and his cheek discolored.

"I was standing in the hallway, just talking to a friend, when this kid came by and punched me in the face," he explains. He's close to tears.

Having absorbed my share of punches, I can see that Pepper's taken quite a shot. He's not a bad kid. He can be a slacker and sometimes an instigator, but he's never mean. And he's small, so I immediately identify and sympathize with him. "Did you see who did it?" I ask. "Do you know why he hit you?"

"I don't know why. It almost knocked me down. I looked up and saw him running away, but I'm not sure who it was."

We sit together for a few minutes, just waiting. The station, adjacent to the cafeteria and the teachers' lounge, is not much of a police facility. There are three or four desks and computers, benches for offending students, a holding room for extreme cases, and a viewing station linked to all the surveillance cameras around the school. Right now there are three guards—two men and a woman—present, two boys being processed at the desks, and another in the holding cell. The phones ring every couple of minutes.

"Is it always this busy?" I ask the female guard, who appears to be the toughest of the three officers.

"This is nothing. You should've been here half an hour ago." She jerks a thumb over her shoulder at one of the kids at the desk. I know him, so I ask him why he's here.

"I got in a fight with him," he answers, pointing to the holding cell, where another boy is pacing and yelling. Fighting still has some kind of magnetic draw for me, and I'm on the verge of involving myself in this case, too, when Officer Anderson calls Pepper and me over to view some of the surveillance tapes from the time and area of his incident.

Anderson is a big man, a veteran school guard, and his tone with Pepper is both optimistic and comforting. "Let's see if we can find your guy."

We face the bank of video monitors. "Do you have cameras covering the whole school?" I ask.

"Just about. Definitely where your student was assaulted." Officer Anderson runs some tape back and forth, switching from hallway to hallway. He zeroes in on the location, searches the time code for the reported time of the incident.

Suddenly, we're there. The hallway fills with bodies during the period change, and there's Pepper. Just standing, talking. Although we can't see the actual punch, there's no evidence that he's doing anything to invite trouble. Then, a second later, he recoils, and there's the student running away—down the hallway, into the stairwell. And, on the next monitor, up the stairs he comes, facing right into another camera.

Officer Anderson knows him. "Mr. Danza, there's over three thousand kids in this school and about two hundred knuckleheads, and this is one of 'em. I'll pull his schedule."

Pepper and I go back to the bench outside. I tell him it's good that we know who hit him, but Pepper still looks miserable. Officer Anderson comes back with a photograph and a schedule. "I was right, a real knucklehead."

When I look at the picture, I mutter under my breath. So that's the jerk who punched my kid. I feel like a protective father, and I want to give this bully a beating he'll remember.

Officer Anderson calls on his walkie-talkie for Officer Morton, who appears almost immediately. "Bill, go up to 238 and get Elvis Jones and bring him down here. He assaulted another student." Officer Anderson hands Morton the paperwork and returns to his desk. "Never a dull moment."

Officer Morton sends Pepper back to class but asks me to accompany him to get Elvis. It's not the best idea I've heard. My emotions are running high. I remember what it felt like to be small and picked on, what it took in my day to make bullies back down. You can't fight fighting with fighting now. I know that. But this Elvis creep messed with one of my kids, and my blood is boiling.

When we get to room 238, Officer Morton knocks on the door. Mr. Florio, the basketball coach, is teaching his English class. Morton explains the situation, and Mr. Florio calls Elvis out of the class. I wait in the hallway, and when Elvis emerges I'm stunned at his size. He easily has fifty pounds and more than a foot of height over Pepper. As we start down the corridor, Officer Morton says nothing, but I can't hold back. "Why'd you hit that little kid?"

Elvis acts as if he hasn't a clue what I'm talking about. "I didn't hit nobody, and I don't have to talk to you, you ain't my teacher."

"Why'd you run? Is that what you do, punch kids half your size, then run away?" He doesn't answer, which just steams me more. "You afraid to pick on somebody your own size?"

He turns then. "You're my size."

"Why, you want to try me?" I say.

He looks at Officer Morton, who's facing straight ahead, saying nothing but walking in lockstep beside him. Elvis turns back to me. "You're only talking like that because you know I can't do nothing."

The steam keeps building. The days of kids backing down just because you're a teacher are clearly over. Elvis wants to fight me, and the feeling is so mutual that it's all I can do to haul myself back from the brink. Fortunately, Officer Morton has a cooler head, and he wears the uniform of authority. As we get to the stairwell, he says, "I'll take it from here, Mr. Danza."

I stop. The stairwell door shuts in my face. Through the glass I see the kid throw a final glare at me over his shoulder. That was close. Almost too close. He still might try to retaliate against me, either personally or through his friends. It's the code: if pushed, you have to push back. As Coolio says in "Gangsta's Paradise," "Me be treated like a punk, you know that's unheard of."

Elvis's code may be my old code, but it's wrong. I'm going to have to watch myself.

"You can't let them see that they get to you," David Cohn advises when I tell him about my near altercation.

"How do I do that? Don't smile before Christmas?"

"Show them you're in charge by acting like their leader. Watch them and listen, and learn from what you see and hear. Show them how you expect them to behave. And don't ever let them pull you down into the fray."

"Easier said than done."

"Sometimes," he admits. "Have the courage to be calm."

"Hah!" I hold my head in mock agony. "I'm the wrong casting for that! I do like that, though, 'the courage to be calm.' I only wish I had it."

"Give it a try on the trip to D.C. I'll be there to back you up."

"Well, at least Elvis won't be."

CALM IS NOT in the cards. At six o'clock on the morning of November 16, I'm pacing on the corner outside school. It's freezing cold. The chartered bus is late. We're supposed to be on the road by six-thirty, and I'm the only one here. The other chaperones show up over the next fifteen minutes. They include Al G's math teacher, Ms. Green; David Cohn; and Kelly Barton, Northeast's past principal, retired now, who serves as our production's liaison to the school district. Kelly's a big easygoing guy who's done more than a few field trips in his day. He tells me to stop worrying.

Fat chance. I'm taking this crew well out of my comfort zone, and I'm scared. "Our production team's not even here," I wail. But then they are. And my twenty-six students all magically appear right about when the bus does, at 6:28. Kelly's right; I need to get a grip.

Because we're shooting every minute of this excursion, it's not as typical a field trip as I'd like. But in a few ways it's better. The show has provided lunch for everyone on the bus, and the box lunches are quality, with a variety of sandwiches on what is the most important part, a great roll. Well-fed kids tend to be happier kids, and the same goes for teachers. Also, because activity looks better on camera than kids sleeping or staring out the window, I've planned some group fun. The road spotter game using an iPhone app morphs into an energetic competition between the kids and the teachers. And I've brought my trusty ukulele so we can have a sing-along—special for Howard. I mess with them a little, playing old songs the kids don't know, then surprise them with Rihanna's "Umbrella." I learned it from a video on the Internet especially for the trip, and it's a hit. Even Fred the bus driver sings a few choruses. By the time we get to the capital, the sun is gleaming, and we're all pretty chill. Even me.

When the kids point out the windows, recognizing buildings they've seen only in books, their oohs and aahs thrill me. Then Fred gets on the loudspeaker and starts playing tour guide. He charms the kids and really knows Washington, D.C. We don't have time to stop everywhere, but he drives us as close as possible to the White House and the Washington Monument. I tell Nakiya, who's sitting next to me, about the time I came to Washington with my Boy Scout troop when I was thirteen and won our race to the top of the monument. "Back then, people were allowed to climb the stairs to the top. It was different then," I'm sorry to say. "I remember the hit song playing on the radio that day was 'Can't Get Used to Losing You' by Andy Williams."

"The things you remember, Mr. Danza," Nakiya says, tuning up her dazzling grin. I couldn't agree more.

The Folger Shakespeare Library turns out to be close to the Capitol, which makes it seem as if every inch of D.C. has historical significance. I'm pleased that the kids get this and that they're uncharacteristically polite to the curator who greets us and escorts us into the library's Great Hall, where vintage texts and illustrations of Shakespearean works are displayed.

"Look, Mr. Danza," Katerina calls out. "Julius Caesar *is dying!*"

The other kids crowd around the exhibit, showing the kind of enthusiasm they normally reserve for a new Jay-Z single.

"I wonder why they wore bedsheets in Rome."

"They called 'togas,' schmo."

"Isn't Rome in Italy?" Nakiya's voice climbs over the others. "Mr. Danza, why didn't Shakespeare write *Julius Caesar* in Latin? I'd rather read *Julius Caesar* in Mr. Smith's class than those stupid grammar lessons."

Many of the kids, including Nakiya, have a running battle with their Latin teacher, but I'm not going there. "Okay, gang," I call, trying to subdue my surprise and ecstasy at their *engagement*. "It's showtime!"

We file into the Elizabethan replica theater, where an acting troupe called Bill's Buddies begin to act out scenes from several of Shakespeare's plays and then invite the kids up onstage to become part of the performance. Nakiya, Chloe, and Eric Lopez are all natural hams, but even Monte and Eric Choi get into the act. Onstage and not afraid to make fools of themselves, they're laughing so hard I'm not sure they realize they're learning. The kids' knowledge of *Julius Caesar* when quizzed by the acting troupe gives me a whole new sense of my students' involvement. The educators at the Folger who put together this program are no slouches, and even by their standards, the kids know the play. My students make me look good.

After the Folger Library we move on to the National Archives for more interactive exercises, this time focusing on the Constitution. The students take on the role of archivists, selecting and analyzing primary sources—ordinary diaries, letters, and memoirs—for historic examples of constitutional issues, such as separation of church and state, and checks and balances. Then they find where in the Constitution these concepts are supported. The idea is to demonstrate what the Constitution means in people's real, everyday lives. Even my most unmotivated students are working, which illustrates how, when learning is fun and collaborative, kids do respond.

As they divide into teams, each researching a different set of records, the kids look so good in their uniforms, like authentic archivists pulling documents and poring over them. White Nick and Ben-Kyle take charge of making a video of the class at work, with Nakiya narrating. This is recorded on a DVD for us to take back to school with us.

By the time we get to the Lincoln Memorial, everybody's so steeped in the aura of history that the kids act downright reverent as they gaze up at the huge stone likeness of Abraham Lincoln. We take some group pictures with the Washington Monument in the background, which I will copy and frame for each kid, and they let off a little steam chasing geese around the Reflecting Pool. All in all, it seems to me, this day is as good as they come—a day I hope these kids will remember the way I remember my day here as a young Boy Scout.

On the way home, Russian Playboy cements his image as the class ladies' man. In the back of the bus, I catch him making out with his girlfriend, so I move him. By the time we reach Philly, he's kissing the girl next to him in his new seat. This Russian boy just can't keep his hands off American girls, but I don't dare laugh. To the kids it's a big scandal. Teen breakup in the making. "You wanted drama," I tell our director.

But as far as he's concerned, it's all just too normal—no use to the show. He pulls his cap down over his eyes and pretends I don't exist. Sometimes that's his way of dealing with me.

The next day my production partner Leslie Grief calls to tell me we have a boring show. "You got nothing yesterday," he complains.

"What, nothing?" I can't believe him. "Washington was beautiful. The kids were beautiful. They were learning, engaged. They loved it! I loved it."

"Tony." Les sounds like he's reasoning with a two-year-old. "Nothing happened. There's no drama. We're going to have to start setting things up if you expect to have a show that people will watch."

"Setting things up" is code for rigging the show, manipulating the story line—and the kids. "Over my dead body," I tell him.

"Then maybe we should pull the plug right now. Not one second of the trip to Washington is usable. There's nothing to watch." He sounds defeated.

I try to pump him up. "Les, this is exactly the show we wanted to make. It's the *reality* of education today. And I think there was plenty to watch on the trip."

"We have a commitment to film until the end of the semester," he says. "Let's try to get something we can use, all right?"

I pull the phone away from my ear, almost but not quite hanging up on my partner. He's a man who knows what it takes to make a successful TV show, a man I like and respect and whose opinion I simply can't accept.

No sooner have I hung up than I'm called down to the office by my buddy Ms. DeNaples. "Mr. Danza, did you notify your students' other teachers that they would be missing class yesterday for your little field trip?"

"I—I thought the kids would tell them."

"Mr. Danza, what you think and what they do are two entirely different issues. Notifying the other faculty was your responsibility. Many of the teachers had no idea why your students were absent. As you know, momentum in the classroom is important, and when a student misses a day, the teacher can lose that momentum. Do you understand what I'm saying, Mr. Danza?"

"I do, Ms. DeNaples. I absolutely do, and I'm very sorry."

"You need to apologize personally to those teachers, and you need to make sure this never happens again."

"You have my word, Ms. DeNaples."

I don't even look at our cameraman as we leave the office. That dress down is all on tape, but not even my being worked over by the likes of Ms. D. will give Leslie the drama he's looking for.

As PREDICTED, I spend almost all Thanksgiving Day on the football field, and I'm not really sorry, since we win big against our number one rival, Central. I spend most of the weekend on the bus with Nakiya and the marching band riding to and from their state competition, where they're pretty ecstatic to place third. And I have to admit I'm glad not to be fighting jet lag as I sign in on Monday. I even think it's a compliment when Assistant Principal Byron Ryan strides over and informs me, "Ms. DeNaples suggested you as a chaperone for the Winter Formal."

I look up, having heard only the words *Winter Formal,* which immediately trigger memories of my own school prom in 1967. We held it in a gym decorated with silver snowflakes, and "Good Lovin' " by the Young Rascals was the hit of the evening. I remember everybody doing the Monkey and the Jerk. I took a girl named Darlene but really wanted to be with her friend Gina, who was with my friend Mike. "Sure," I tell Mr. Ryan. "Sounds like fun."

He gives me a lopsided smile, and I wonder what's up, but he's taking a phone call before I can ask. By lunch, word's gotten around, and I'm seeing that same lopsided smile on a lot of faculty faces. "What exactly happens at this dance?" I ask.

"Oh, it's not that bad."

"They're just kids."

What is this? *West Side Story?* What goes on? What? Finally I decide to go to the source and ask one of the seniors on the football team. He says, "It's chill."

"That doesn't answer my question."

He looks at the ceiling as if it's the Sistine Chapel. "It's the dancing."

"What do you mean, it's the dancing?"

Shrug. "You'll see."

All right. If my pal Ms. DeNaples can put me up to this, she can tell me what "this" is.

Good ol' Ms. D. "They dirty-dance."

I liked that movie! "You mean, like Patrick Swayze and Jennifer Grey?"

"If that means the girls bend over and back up against the boys and grind in a sexually explicit manner, then yes."

"Oh." I don't quite remember the movie that way. But I'm beginning to get the picture.

"It's not allowed, but that doesn't stop them. So it will be your job to keep an eye on all the action everywhere in the gym. And stop it when you see it."

"How?"

She tips her head and gives me her own special smirk. "Oh, Mr. Danza. I'm sure you have your ways."

THE NIGHT OF the formal I show up in a suit and tie, with no idea what to expect. The gym is decorated with stars and colored lights. Some of the boys are actually trussed up in tuxedos, and lots of the girls are wearing corsages, just like in the olden days. There's nothing old about the music, though. The bass makes the floor bounce. I plug my ears with little wads of paper napkin. Whatever happened to melody?

The usual teachers are here, by which I mean the ones who always seem to work the after-school activities. The young dean of students,

Rob Caroselli, wears a Cheshire cat smile as the others welcome me. "If it's simulated sex," Coach Riley tells me, "that's no good."

"And how am I supposed to break up simulated sex?"

"You ask them if they'd like their mothers to see them do that."

"Oh, the old mother trick." I wince.

Coach Riley and Mr. Caroselli laugh and wish me luck as they walk away, but for the most part the kids seem happy to see me. Students generally love it when their teachers show up at their events, and some feel let down if you don't show. That makes me feel as if I always have to be there, and when I'm not, I feel guilty. On the plus side, when you do come out for them, they usually work a little harder for you in the classroom. But it can make for very long days and weeks, including weekends.

The kids congregate at the edges of the dance floor. Most of the football team hangs together—Howard and Matt inexplicably wearing their uniform jerseys. And many of the girls dance in small, loose clusters. Others merge into crowds so thick I can't see who's inside. Those clumps spell trouble. I have no choice but to wade in, however reluctantly. If the tall boys are all looking down, chances are they're watching a bump and grind. Some girls back up against the boy and push and rub in an upright version of lap dancing. Other girls *are* sitting on guys' laps in the bleachers.

"Okay, okay!" In comes Cop Danza, trying to be cool and looking at everybody but the girl and guy in question. "Break it up, you guys. That's enough! Would you want your mother to see you do that? Get a room!" I kid them. Then everybody laughs and dances away to find another dark corner. They act like it's all fun. I'm not sure how I feel about it.

"I hate being the party pooper," I tell Katerina and Chloe, who sympathize with my embarrassment. They've come to the dance together, without dates, and both look and act like high-fashion models.

I tell myself *they* would never dance dirty. I need to tell myself that, or else I'll start thinking about my daughter at her winter formal, and no telling what I'll do then.

"No, you're cool, Mr. Danza," Chloe assures me. "We're glad you're here. Wanna dance?"

I can feel myself blushing right down to my toes. I raise my hands. "Oh, I don't think so." But they're talking about line dancing. Pretty soon we've got a conga line stretching across the gym. The football team and even some of the dirty dancers join in. It's different, being a kid today, but still, they really are all just kids.

Northeast's Got Talent

All teachers bring extracurricular skills and passions to the job. That's why some volunteer to coach tennis or softball, others supervise the school paper or literary magazine, and still others organize field trips to botanical gardens or planetariums. I happen to have some skills and connections in the theatrical department, so arranging a school talent show seems a natural for me. At first I'm thinking a student show, but I ask around and learn that the students already have an annual talent show. The teachers, however, have never done anything like this. Making Viking history is right up my alley.

Putting on a show together also seems like a good way for me to get to know and connect with teachers beyond my SLC. And it will be for a good cause: we'll charge a buck a ticket and distribute the earnings among the band, the choir, and the school newspaper. Enough teachers like the idea to give me momentum. They're not above a little fun and camaraderie, and since we'll film the entire enterprise, they might just wind up on television. That said, I don't pitch the talent show to the production company ahead of time. I want this to be real, and I want to organize it on my own terms.

The catch is, it has to be a rush job. The school calendar doesn't have a lot of breathing room before Christmas, and the auditorium is overbooked, especially right after school, when it's easiest to get a good student audience. So when the date is set, I have just two weeks to pull it all together. No small feat.

I reach out first to the choirmaster, Mr. Flaherty, for sound equipment, and I enlist Mr. Dyson, a math teacher who can play the piano, to accompany the acts. I recruit Nakiya and Katerina, both talented artists, to help me print up and distribute flyers inviting teachers to show off their hidden talents. We call the show *Northeast's Got Talent*, after the TV show. The first- and second-place finishers will receive gift certificates, which helps attract contestants.

About a week before the show, I hold auditions in my classroom. Mr. Dyson is on hand to play an electronic keyboard from the band room, and the turnout is good. One teacher wants to play the guitar and sing an original song he's written for his wife, who's due with their first child any minute now. We figure he'll open the show; if his wife goes into labor that day, it will add a little suspense. Ms. Deltoro, who works in the counselor's office, wants to sing a duet with Mr. Cooper of "If I Loved You," from *Carousel*. Five other male teachers sign on with me to harmonize a medley of dance songs in the style of the Mills Brothers; we call ourselves Tuxedo Junction. (We practice in the stairwell, where the acoustics are fantastic.) Various other teachers will sing solos or recite poetry. Mr. Dyson will play the "Minute Waltz" on the piano, and we'll close the show with Voltron, a lip-synching boy band made up of five first-year male teachers led by Joe Connelly, who reportedly can moonwalk.

Nakiya is thrilled when I ask her to be the MC. I try to set it up as we would in Hollywood, scripting her introductions with jokes based on the acts, then writing out the script on cards that she can discard after each segment. Her job is to move the show along. During our lone rehearsal, we stand in the wings and work on being funny while listening to each act, coming up with asides that might get a laugh, help cover the transitions, and calm the teachers who seem anxious.

I have my work cut out for me with Ms. Solomon, a social science teacher who has raging stage fright. She keeps warning me, "I've never done anything like this."

I tell her, "You can do it. I sing in public all the time now, but the first time you have to get up and sing like you do in the shower, it's tough." Then I tell her a story. "I used to go to the great songwriter

Sammy Cahn's home for parties. At these soirees would be all sorts of famous people, like Gregory Peck and Sean Connery, even Jackie Collins. Inevitably, everyone would gravitate to the piano. Sammy would play and make people sing. The first time he asked me to sing I was so nervous, especially given the audience, I could feel my heart pounding. I sat next to him on the piano bench, and he whispered, 'You can do it, have some fun.' I swallowed and I started rough, but once I got through it, I couldn't wait until the next party."

Ms. Solomon chews her lip all the way through my story, and I can tell I've done little to reassure her. So I have a couple of students bring the choirmaster's keyboard up to my room and ask Mr. Dyson to work with her. Once she gets going, Ms. Solomon turns out to have a strong gospel voice. "You have to keep practicing," I tell her, "but my money's on you for the contest."

The morning of the performance Ms. DeNaples stops me as I'm signing in. "Mr. Danza," she says in her inimitable way.

"Yes, Ms. DeNaples."

"I assume you would like everyone in this school to know about the talent show this afternoon."

After nearly four months, I still cannot read this woman. We've hung posters all over the school to advertise the show, so she has to know the answer. "Yes, Ms. DeNaples."

"Would you like to make an announcement to that effect over the intercom?"

"Now?" I just about leap over the counter. "You mean, this morning?" The intercom is Ms. D.'s private domain. She, and only she, makes all school announcements herself—ad nauseam. But now she steps aside and makes a grand sweep of her arm to indicate that I am to step to her microphone. It feels like the parting of the Red Sea.

Making an announcement, however, is a nerve-racking experience. Everyone is watching me, no mistakes allowed. I flash back to high school and just know that if I mess up, I'll hear about it all day, maybe all year. I get through, but afterward I cut Ms. DeNaples's announcements some slack. Performing in Vegas is easier.

As planned, our opening act on the day of the show is Mr. Cerelli, whose very pregnant wife is in the audience to hear him perform the song he's written for her. He manages to finish his act, but they leave right afterward, and shortly thereafter head for the hospital. (It's a boy!)

Next Mr. Cooper and his duet partner, whose first name appropriately is Joy, warble through "If I Loved You." Much to our surprise, they then segue into "My Way"—all five verses. On and on and on they sing. I tell Nicky to go out onstage and give them the hook, but she shakes her head and draws back into the wings. "I can't!"

"Why not?"

"I have Mr. Cooper for math," she whispers. "I can't risk my grade." Turns out there are limitations to student MCs, even when they're as enthusiastic as Nakiya.

But she has her skills as well. Just as Voltron is about to come on, there's a glitch with their music, and the audience gets restless as we struggle to fix it. "Go out there with your uke and cover for them," she suggests.

Why didn't I think of that? I go out and play "Umbrella" with Nakiya holding the mike for me so the audience can hear the ukulele. The kids all sing along, and somehow on a sunny day in the middle of the auditorium up springs an umbrella. Bedlam, but in a good way.

Voltron closes the show, a funny performance with Mr. Connelly moonwalking across the stage. Then the audience votes. Nakiya lines the performers across the stage, raising her hand over each contestant as she asks the audience to applaud for their favorite. Voltron takes first, and Ms. Solomon, our nervous social science soprano, winds up with second place. The crowd goes wild, and I think, This beats the response to any show I've played in Hollywood. Seven hundred kids have shown up to see their teachers try to entertain them. Kids like to see their teachers doing something different. Really different.

As we're packing up, Mr. Dyson pauses and thanks me. "I've been at this school for six years," he says. "This is the most I've ever had to do with the other teachers here. And it was a great show, thanks."

A few days later, I find this note in my mailbox:

Dear Danza,

I contemplated whether or not to write this note. After all, I don't have any fancy schmancy letterhead (I'm trying to make it on a teacher's salary, you know). Then I remembered what my mom always said, "One good/kind act deserves another." There is a thin line between giving a compliment and "brown nosing." Make no mistake, I don't do the latter. I can't help but admit I had my doubts about you. I thought please, this guy couldn't be a teacher, he smiles too much . . . no one can be that joyful with a bunch of cameras around and not lose their cool sometimes. Well, after working with you on the Talent Show, I can say with certainty that Mr. Danza is a nice guy and a teacher. Thanks for all of your support, and the gift certificate wasn't bad, either. Welcome to Northeast and good luck with your project.

V. Solomon.

I return to California for Christmas vacation ready to take on the world.

SECOND SEMESTER

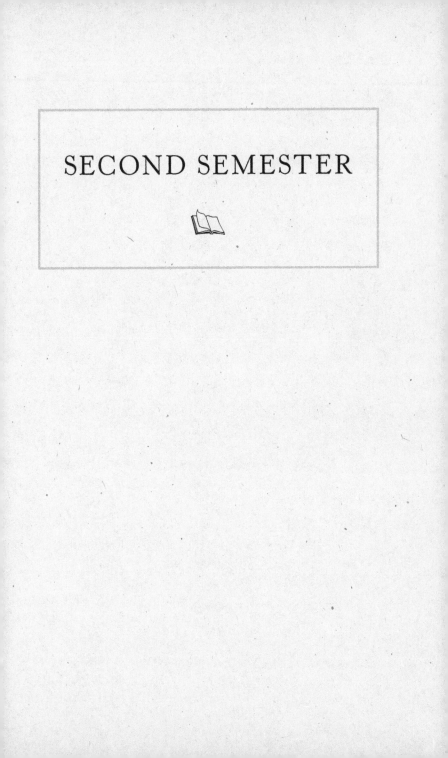

Seven

Field Tripping

AFTER CHRISTMAS, we take off with a thud. Our new academic focus, the five-paragraph essay, is alien territory for most of the class. They're intimidated by writing to begin with, and they can't understand why anyone would need a thesis statement or topic sentence. At times during this unit, we'd all rather be digging ditches, and to add to the stress, Emmanuel and Monte are prepping for statewide debate club tournament finals. Also, a big home basketball game is looming.

Three days after we come back I give the class a do-now to write a short story using six of these vocabulary words: *arrogant, mollified, anguished, complacently, ominously, metaphor, hyperbole, hero, ironic, imagery, formidable.* These words were in a story we read before Christmas. I want to see how much they remember and get them thinking before we press ahead.

Multiple reading levels within a class are a challenge that every teacher faces. Everyone learns differently, and my class of tenth graders includes a few who started the year at a third-grade reading level. Three of my girls have Individualized Education Programs, or IEPs. This means that they have some sort of learning disability or difficulty and are entitled to request help with their work from other teachers and resources in the school. If they're having trouble with an assignment or a test, they can ask to go to the school's Resource Center, and I'm required to send them. But I'd rather include them, work with them personally, give them the confidence that they're as smart and capable as anyone else. The challenge is always to move through the material fast enough to keep the advanced students interested without the others demanding more time. As if to drive the dilemma home, Monte now sits directly in front of my desk, his story already written and his face twitching with impatience. He might as well be screaming, "Come on, already!"

Charmaine, meanwhile, is a constant challenge. She is often late and disdainful, but every once in a while she's into it. Not today. Still, I can see she's written something. I coax her to stand up and read it. She refuses. I insist. Finally she hauls herself to her feet as if I've asked her to do my laundry.

"My *arrogant* teacher told me to write a story using the words *anguished, complacently, ominously, metaphor, hyperbole, hero, ironic, imagery,* and *formidable,* so I mollified him and did the work."

"Clever," I admit. "Unfortunately, that is not a story. I can't accept it."

"So?" she asks.

"So rewrite it into a story."

She folds her arms.

"Like the Nike ad says"—I'm attempting levity—"'Just do it.'" I tap another student to read, and leave Charmaine standing there. Eventually she sits down, turns her paper over, and starts writing.

A few students later I return to Charmaine, who now reads, "My arrogant teacher told me to write a story, so I mollified him and wrote the darn thing. I was anguished because my first story wasn't acceptable, so I had to complacently write this one. He ominously stood over me until I started to write, which is really annoying. He is a donkey when he does stuff like that. He will talk about it nonstop if you don't do what he says. He is not a hero of the school. It was ironic because the word I was thinking he is, is the first word on the list of words you have to use for this story. Use imagery to imagine that. This is not a formidable challenge."

I have to give it to her. It's not flattering, but it's good. The class applauds, and she nods, satisfied. Welcome to second semester.

AS IF THE CURRICULUM isn't enough of a headache, we have less than two weeks to rehearse a student variety show that the kids insisted on naming *Extravadanza* (I swear I had nothing to do with that bit of witty wordplay). With the money we raise from ticket sales, the school will at last air-condition the library, but the show isn't only for kids from Northeast. I've invited students from two other area high schools to make it an even bigger event and garner a larger audience. They'll join the cast and share our proceeds, so it's now a theatrical production involving some two hundred cast members.

Meanwhile, a massive earthquake has struck Haiti. The news of this natural catastrophe and the suffering of the Haitian people seems to touch my students in a way I haven't seen before. Thanks to the Internet and the immediacy of Web and televised images, we watch the disaster unfold in real time, and the scenes of collapsed schools, dazed orphans, and homeless families bogged down in rain and mud and heat affect my kids profoundly. They can't wrap their minds around the scale of the tragedy, and I try to build on their horror to teach a lesson on empathy. "When you do a good deed for others, it always ends up being good for you," I tell them. "Nobody can force you to lift a finger to help someone else, but when you choose to make that effort, it also makes you feel more connected and less helpless. And let's be honest; you feel good about yourself."

It's the kids' idea to piggyback on *Extravadanza* to raise money for the earthquake victims. Students who aren't working on the show form a kind of Salvation Army, making signs and donation buckets to collect Haitian relief donations before, during, and after the performance. Even Al G and Matt get in on this act, especially after I tell them I'll match whatever the group raises. They take that as a dare. *We're gonna cost you a lot of money, Mr. D.*

The night of the performance, the kids onstage sing and dance their hearts out. We do a great show, teachers and students working together in huge musical numbers. It really is an Extravadanza! And the kids offstage work the auditorium and lobby equally hard. When they discover they've collected more than four hundred dollars, which totals eight hundred with the matching funds, they're so excited they do an automatic recount. As I watch the pride with which they count, pack, and deliver their donation in person to the local Red Cross office, I wish everyone who despairs about America's "inner-city youth" could witness this. Who's a lost cause now? It gives me hope.

I want so badly to reward my kids, and taking them to New York seems the perfect way to do it. I keep thinking about my own tenth-grade English teacher, Charles "Chick" Messinger, who directed and produced Malverne High's annual musical theater productions, in three of which I was a cast member. Unlike most of my high school classes, Mr. Messinger's was fun. He loved the arts and would tell us about all the great performances he'd seen in "the city," at the Belasco, the Lyceum, the Majestic, or Lincoln Center. He talked about Manhattan as if it were an emerald city, and to us it was. Despite our proximity, as kids we rarely made the short trip from Brooklyn or Long Island; Broadway was another world. So Mr. Messinger was introducing us to something beyond our imagination, and his love of that world was contagious. He'd seen *Gypsy* with Ethel Merman so many times, he could tell whenever she made a change in her performance, right down to the slightest new hand gesture. We felt as if Mr. Messinger was just stopping by our school; his real life was on Broadway and in Manhattan. And his excitement hooked me. I once told him that because of him I wanted to be a teacher. He thanked me for the compliment but countered that I should think about acting. So I owe a lot to Mr. Messinger, and now I want more than anything to give my students some of the gift he gave me.

When I tell the class that I've gotten approval for a trip to New York from both the network and the school, there's an explosion of excitement. *We're going to New York City!* They dance around the room high-fiving and hugging each other. You'd think we'd hit the lottery. For some of them, we might as well have.

"We'll go up by bus next Wednesday," I tell them. "That way we can see a Broadway matinee." They ask what we're going to see. *West Side Story.* Blank faces. "*West Side Story* is like a Shakespeare to Street version of *Romeo and Juliet.*" Shakespeare to Street is our thing, so they get that, and they all studied *Romeo and Juliet* last year in ninth grade. "The street, in this case, is on the Upper West Side of New York City in the 1950s. Romeo and Juliet are two star-crossed lovers named Tony and Maria. He's a member of this white gang, the Jets, and she's Puerto Rican with a brother who belongs to a gang called the Sharks. The Jets and the Sharks are rival gangs, just like the Montagues and Capulets were in Shakespeare's version."

"So do Tony and Maria die like Romeo and Juliet?" Chloe and Katerina ask in unison.

I wag my finger. "No, no, no. Never give away the ending."

In class we do a quick review of *Romeo and Juliet,* and I make an effort to excite them about seeing the play. None of my students has ever been to a Broadway show. I can hardly wait for them to experience that first thrill of the overture and then the anticipation as the stage comes to life.

The kids want to know about the dinner I also have planned for us at Patsy's, my friend Sal's Italian restaurant. *Is the food good there? Is it near the Empire State Building? Where else are we gonna go? Can we see where you live?* I have to do some heavy lifting to get them back to that five-paragraph-essay lesson.

By Monday, everything's set. Our driver will be Fred, the same friendly guy who showed us the sights in D.C., and our chaperones—initially—are also recast from the first field trip. The adults are almost as eager as the kids, especially when they learn that Patsy's is a really great restaurant, so great that Frank Sinatra used to hang out there. Word escapes, and pretty soon our chaperone list has expanded to include Joe Connelly, Assistant Principal McCloskey, and Ms. Smotries, a special ed teacher who specializes in dealing with problem kids and who covers for David Cohn when he's unavailable to observe my classes. We now have enough chaperones to cover two trips.

And then Ms. Carroll informs me that she's decided to come. Nothing against Ms. Carroll, but she's the school principal. When I break this to the kids, they respond with a predictable chorus. *NOOOOO! It's our trip. The principal can't come. It's not fair, we won't have any fun with Ms. Carroll along. She's the* principal!

You just never know when you'll get a teachable moment. As a teacher, I've learned to look for them because, as a student, I so often failed to see how school could possibly relate to my life—and that disconnect allowed me to rationalize that school didn't matter. I know that some of my students think the same thing: So what if I've read *Of Mice and Men*? What does it mean to me? One of my jobs as a teacher is to open their eyes to the life lessons contained in the tenth-grade English curriculum. Lessons about friendship and heroism, treating people as you want to be treated, and walking in another man's shoes before you judge him. The teachable lesson today is one that we will read about, in various stories, all year long.

I quiet them down. "The following lesson will serve you well your whole life," I tell them. "I want you to say it along with me now: 'Make the best of a baaaaad situation.' Come on, say it with me."

We begin to chant. Pretty soon it sounds like a classroom of sheep as they bleat *baaaaaad* at each other for laughs. It takes their mind off the principal, anyway. Then I go for the lesson. "What's a baaaad situation?"

When the principal comes on your trip!

I hold up my hand. "A baaaad situation is when you don't like what's going down but you have limited options. When you run into these kinds of situations—and trust me, they come along often— you should try to make the best of things and even look for a way to turn them to your advantage. I want you all to understand something here: she's coming, and we can handle it in one of two ways. That's what I mean by limited options. We can tell her we don't want her on our trip, and hurt her feelings—I hear she has a great memory. Or, we can write her and say we don't want to go to New York without her. Maybe then we'll have a friend in the principal's office, and you just never know when we might need her help."

They toss this back and forth, grumbling and protesting. For- tunately, most of them actually like Ms. Carroll. It's not personal; it's just the idea of the principal on their trip that gets them. It takes a while, but eventually they come around. We write the note, and Emmanuel volunteers to play ambassador and deliver it to the office.

Principal Carroll is no fool; she knows a suck-up when she sees one, but she does smile at the invitation. Later she tells me she's look- ing forward to spending this time with my kids. That, however, is before the trip.

On Wednesday we assemble in the school lobby at nine, and this time we're by the book. I've instructed my kids to excuse themselves from their first-period classes, having notified all their other teachers that they'll be gone on a field trip the rest of the day. The ratio of students to chaperones is just over three to one, not including the camera crew, and when the kids realize this, some of them say they're not so sure they can still make the best of this baaaad situation, but I counsel them to just enjoy the adventure, and as soon as the bus arrives they cheer up. Fred the driver greets the kids like they're his own, and the kids give him fist bumps and hugs as they scramble onboard and find seats. The premium seats are way in back, since the front belongs to the chaperones.

We luck out on traffic and weather, and reach the city around eleven, giving us time to sightsee before the play. The kids' noses are glued to the windows as we ride up the West Side Highway and across town on Fifty-seventh Street. Philly's historic towers are no match for Manhattan's skyscrapers, and as my students gasp and point, I marvel all over again that so few of them have ever been here. I cannot wait to show them Central Park on this picture-perfect winter day.

We leave the bus at Sixty-seventh Street and walk into the park from the west side, strolling around the small loop, stopping at the fountain by the pond to snap photos. The kids climb on anything that doesn't move, and I'm absolutely loving it—for about five minutes. Then the usual suspects start acting up. Al G wanders away from the group. Matt is getting physical with some of the other guys. I take both Matt and Al aside and remind them that we've all got to work together here, that I don't want to waste everybody's time chasing after the two of them. In truth, I'm a little angry with them both for threatening a day that I badly want to be a highlight of my students' year. This is my city, and I want to show it off to them. The last thing I need is for these two students to spoil the experience for everyone else—or for me. Yeah, me!

After the kids burn off a little energy in the park, we take a group picture by the Angel of the Waters fountain, then ride the bus down to Times Square. The kids are climbing the TKTS bleachers and checking out the huge digital billboards when I notice Al G slinking away again. I call after him, but he ignores me.

Suddenly I realize why his behavior makes me so angry—and anxious. I remember something that I hadn't thought about in a long time. When I was a little boy, about seven years old, I got lost in the city right near here. My grandmother, a short, roundish woman who hardly spoke any English, had brought me with my brother and my two cousins, Patty and Vivian, to see the Christmas show at Radio City Music Hall. I think now how brave my grandmother was. The streets were jammed, and the Christmas season was in full swing. On the way into the show, Patty tapped me on the shoulder. He'd noticed the Automat across the street. When the show let out, we slipped through the crowd to see this marvelous place, like a cafeteria except that all the food was served from vending machines. Ah, the future. To us, the Automat seemed like the giant toy of tomorrow. But our delight evaporated when we turned around and couldn't find Grandma. We stood there petrified, the Christmas throng swirling around us, my older cousin trying unsuccessfully to stop me from crying. Finally a kindly NYC cop spotted us. He took us back to the theater, where we found Grandma—beside herself. First she acted about as furious as a person of her stature could be. Then she burst into tears as she hugged me.

Right now I feel only the fury as Al G forces me to chase him down in Times Square. "You've got to stay with the group," I tell him. "I don't want to lose you in these crowds."

Damned if he doesn't keep walking! I reach for his arm. When I touch it, Al turns as if I've scalded him. He yanks his elbow away and pivots to confront me. "Don't put your hands on me!"

Now what do I do? For months I've tried with this kid, putting up with his behavior, his missed assignments, his showing up late and not participating, and worst of all his loud and exaggerated yawns. I am sorely tempted to show him he's not so tough.

Fortunately, the impulse passes. I back down, and he turns and keeps walking. I stand and watch. He knows and I know this won't be good if I lose sight of him and have to chase him again. He strays just far enough to feel he's sufficiently won the round, then he slowly comes back on his own. But I'm on notice: it's going to be a long day with young Al.

Finally we make our way across Broadway to the Palace Theatre. The seats in the second balcony are not the best, but the Palace is one of those old showboat playhouses, all polished brass and gold leaf, red velvet curtain, plush carpet, and the sizzle of preshow energy that seems somehow unique to Broadway. The kids are already looking impressed when our usher leans over and reminds me that she worked at the St. James Theater when I played Max Bialystock in *The Producers.*

Katerina asks, a little breathless, "Was that a theater like this one?"

The usher nods and says, "Your teacher was the star of the show."

The kids seem awed. I could kiss this woman for giving me this extra and badly needed street cred, but all I can do is thank her.

Al G, who's sitting with me at my insistence, lets out one of his exaggerated yawns. Then, without looking at me, he says, "You did a play like this?"

"No," I say, without looking at *him,* "I planted that usher and told her to say that."

He turns and takes me in for a second, not sure if I'm on the level, then he laughs and turns away. I can't read him, either.

"Yes, Al," I tell him after a beat. "I did a big Broadway musical." I wait for a response, but before either of us can say anything else, the lights go down.

My irritation with Al compounds my annoyance at being up in

the nosebleed seats, but once the play begins I appreciate that we have a great overview of the action. The gang members in the show don't look like the ones my kids are used to. The Jets and Sharks are old school, no dreadlocks, rags, saggy pants, ball caps, or tattoos. Nevertheless, the kids can identify with the love story, and the music and dancing quickly enthrall them. They're so caught up in the play that when Tony is shot at the end, half of them scream and jump out of their seats.

It's as dark as it can be in Times Square when we emerge from the theater. My friend Sal's restaurant is only nine blocks north, theoretically an easy walk, but the streets are packed and not altogether savory. Times Square is the land of the come-on, and the kids are soft targets. Sidewalk salesmen shove flyers for girlie shows into the boys' hands, and too-eager merchants try to lure the girls into souvenir shops. Making sure that everyone's safe and together in this evil carnival atmosphere is nerve-racking, even with the extra chaperones.

One particularly friendly homeless person, who smells like he's made of marijuana, pleads with the girls to donate money for his "college tuition." A couple of the kids give him some change before I can pull them away. By the time we arrive at the restaurant, I could really use a drink.

Patsy's is a family-owned white-tablecloth restaurant that's been in operation for almost seventy years. My friend Sal's father and mother still work there with him, and his cousin Frankie is the maî-tre d'. A statue of Frank Sinatra is on the bar, he ate there so often. Sinatra had a special table upstairs where he sat when he didn't want to be bothered by fans, and that's where Sal sets us up, the kids to-gether at tables along the wall and us adults at a large round table toward the front of the room. Since I go back a long way with Sal and his staff, and I want them to know how proud I am to be a teacher, I make a big deal of introducing them to Northeast's present and past principals, Ms. Carroll and Mr. Barton. Also, since I've talked a lot about Sal to my class in the days leading up to this trip, I want him to meet the kids. After Nakiya shakes his hand I say, "Now you know Sal."

Nakiya decides to get cute about it. "I know Sal," she says as if it's a Marx Brothers routine. "Hey, you know Sal?" Sal and I laugh, but my principal thinks that Nakiya's being disrespectful and also that I'm favoring her. Ms. Carroll warns me to treat all my students the same. I decide it's time for that drink and sneak off to the bar for a quick one.

When I get back, everybody's happy. The kids have a short discussion about what happened in the play and why, but literary considerations are short-circuited when Nakiya breaks into "I Feel Pretty." Two other girls join in. Then Howard, too, starts singing. Everybody applauds as he pretends to curtsy.

Sal has put out a beautiful spread for us, and good food always soothes the spirit. Inevitably though, as dinner wears on, the kids get restless. Nakiya, Matt, and a few others initiate a hot sauce eating contest. I find it funny, but once again, my principal fails to see the humor. After dinner, when we take a group picture in front of the restaurant, Ms. Carroll looks anything but relaxed. As we board the bus, I wonder if the kids were right to object to her coming. But surely, I tell myself, everyone must be exhausted, so the worst has to be over and I can hope they'll sleep all the way home.

An hour into the trip home, someone lights a match. I can't see it, but I smell it. One of the kids must have taken a matchbook from Patsy's. I have my suspicions, and when Matt locks one of the girls in the bathroom, I go back to confront him. "Let her out now," I warn him under my breath, "and give me the matchbook."

Matt looks a little sheepish and a little defiant, but he obeys me on both counts. Back up front, Ms. Carroll is seething. She wants to hang whoever lit that match, and I wouldn't wish her on my worst enemy right now. I keep Matt's tacit confession to myself.

It's around ten when we pull up in front of school. None of the teachers can leave until all the kids have been picked up. While we're waiting, the principal pulls me aside. "I should have said something earlier, Mr. Danza."

Uh-oh. What did I do now?

"If any of the kids says anything, you know, we could both be fired."

A mental slide show begins to play: the homeless pot guy getting too close to Chloe, Al G pulling his arm away, Matt lighting a match, Nakiya teasing Sal. "Complains about what?" What did I miss?

Ms. Carroll lowers her voice. "Alcohol."

Is she kidding me? It was a long day, and I had only one drink. I am legal, and I wasn't even in the same room with the kids. How'd she know, anyway? All this explodes in my head along with a burst of frustration like I haven't felt since I was sixteen years old. Again, I'm one of the principal's misbehaving students—that's exactly how it feels.

I mutter something about being sorry. At least I knew enough to sneak off to the bar. But then, once I get ahold of myself, I have to wonder, What was I *thinking* when I did that? The truth is, I wasn't thinking. And because my principal let me get away with it, her head could be on a plate now, too. Teachers and administrators are always worried about being fired. One complaint from a child or parent can be the end of a career.

I apologize again. Ms. Carroll just stares. After a second she says, "Good night, Mr. Danza."

After the last charge is picked up, I go home, but I have a hard time sleeping. I tried to speak to Al G after the play and again in Patsy's, but he would have none of it. What if he saw me at the bar?

What if he sees my slipup as an opportunity to give me a really hard time?

When I arrive at school the next morning, Kelly Barton is waiting for me. He calls me into the office where David Cohn and I meet every day, and very casually thanks me for the great trip. Kelly's a big blond guy, always genial, the kind of guy who can fire you without hurting your feelings. I brace myself for what's coming. "By the way," he adds, "I hear Sal's bartender makes a wicked virgin martini. Amazing what you can do without alcohol. Get me his recipe next time you're up there, will you?"

I've caught a break. Problem solved. Count on Kelly to remind me that some things are just that simple.

But other problems loom, as I discover when my cell phone rings. It's Leslie Grief. "It wasn't cheap to charter that bus, you know," he launches in. "We had to take out extra insurance, pay the crew overtime, cover all those theater tickets." None of this is news to me. Cost was the main reason I had to work so hard to persuade the producers to green-light the trip. Les reminds me, "Something was supposed to happen, Tony. Something, as in drama."

I know then that Les has seen yesterday's footage and is not happy. The camera missed my confrontations with Al and Matt, and the rest of the kids were too well behaved, having too good a time. "The network's going to pull the plug on the show," Les warns me. "And I can't blame them." He hangs up.

Good riddance is my first thought. I hate constantly being miked and on camera, and I'm sick of these production battles. With every passing day I become more convinced that the kind of drama the network wants is exactly the kind that my students and I *don't* need. I'm here to teach, and the kids are here to learn, and that's all that really matters.

On the other hand, I do like being paid, especially given that this is by far the most difficult job I've ever had. I'd never bail on my class, but without the production I'll be working as a volunteer. How do you act, feel, and function like a professional if you're not being compensated? I feel a pang of solidarity with the millions of real teachers who must ask themselves this question every day. And then it hits me. I wanted reality? Well, I'm about to get my wish, big-time. Say goodbye to your Hollywood safety net, Tony. This is truly the real deal.

With all this on my mind, it's not easy to wrap my thoughts around the day's lesson plan, but I can't put off sonnets any longer. Iambic pentameter, here we come.

"It's like a heartbeat," I tell the class, and lead them in pounding our chests. *Boom BOOM, boom BOOM.* "Sonnets have fourteen lines." I draw them on the board. "Three four-line quatrains followed by a couplet. The rhyme scheme is *ABAB, CDCD, EFEF,* and the couplet is *GG.* Each line has ten syllables, and the accent is on every second syllable." I'm on a roll now. "The quatrains develop an idea, and the couplet sums it up or gives a take on what's come before."

Then I pass out copies of Shakespeare's *Sonnet Eighteen.* We read out loud as we pound our chests, "Shall I compare thee to a summer's day . . ." The love stuff gets them, and the couplet kills, but they shriek when I tell them old Will wrote this to a young man.

What!

"Yes, and some of his other sonnets are to this sexy black woman."

"Once you go black . . . ," cracks Al G.

This begins a spirited discussion of sexual preferences, both in Olde England and today. Gay rights comes up, and before I know it, the class veers from a Shakespearean sonnet to the headline issues of today. I'm thrilled as they connect the world's most famous writer to their own world.

To make sure they grasp the structure and have some fun, I have them compose a sonnet about our New York trip. They suggest lines, which I edit on the blackboard, then we read them out loud and revise together. The room rocks and rolls, everyone counting syllables as they make up phrases.

When our New York sonnet finally comes together, I am more convinced than ever that what matters most are these kids. The fate of the show and my paycheck are incidental compared to what I'm doing right here, right now.

Notice the iambic pentameter, and try pounding the beat out on your chest:

Our class was hand-selected for a show
They picked us for our personality.
This is the best class you will ever know,
We raised eight hundred dollars for Haiti.

You have to sanitize when you enter,
We used to be afraid of the swine flu.
You get sick easily in the winter
Cover your mouth before you say achoo.

We went to New York and we met pal Sal,
And also went to Washington, D.C.
The only one who had no fun was Al,
These field trips are so memorable, you see.

We saw a bum who smelled a lot like pot,
But in the end we sure did learn a lot.

Gone Bowling

The network delivers on Leslie's threat at the end of January. We've shot enough footage for about six one-hour episodes, and based on that footage, A&E decides six is enough. This means that the crew will come back a few times later in the year for some final pickup footage and interviews with the kids, but basically, I'll be on my own here now.

As the filming quietly winds down, a rumor of a different scenario fans through school. Having heard that the production is ending, both students and teachers ask me repeatedly when I'm leaving. A few of the teachers might be hoping for a different answer, but I assure them I'm not going anywhere. When I said at the outset that they were stuck with me for a full year, I meant it. Brave words. And it's true that I won't miss the camera's constant seeing eye in my classroom, or the daily wiring and unwiring of microphones. Still, I don't do well with abandonment, especially when it carries the taint of failure. Will I lose my authority now that I've lost my cameras? What if I find I need all those props? I certainly don't feel like celebrating.

Yet celebrate we must. Without coming right out and telling anybody that the series has been capped, the production company decides to throw a wrap party in a cool art deco bowling alley near my apartment. In addition to our crew, my students and all the teachers who appear in the show are invited, and we take over an upstairs room that has a square bar and its own six-alley bowling area, pool tables, and TV screens. It's a spectacular place for a party, but not for the speeches and a screening that are central to our event. Downstairs, the main bowling alley is full of people whooping it up, and the sound reverberates through the walls. Every time someone bowls a strike the cheers explode up the stairwell, drowning out our festivities. The venue seems a perfect metaphor for our whole production, I think.

The A&E executive who has just decided to cut us off at the knees hardly notices the noise barrier. But the students, parents, and teachers have to strain to hear him over the din. They've been promised that we'll view the first episode tonight, and they're eager to get on with it. Ms. Carroll, the only one allowed to see the footage as it was cut, is so happy with the results that she's brought along Assistant Principals Sharon McCloskey and Peggy DeNaples. They're almost as excited as the kids to see themselves on TV.

As the executive drones on, I look around and notice our show runner in the corner talking with another exec. The show runner is the director who sets a series' tone and is responsible for the day-to-day shooting and flow of the production. I had a hand in hiring him back in August, and he seemed perfect, but then we began to pull in opposite directions. When there were problems in school, I could never be sure if they were real, or if he was just trying to crank up conflict. Once, when David Cohn was reviewing my day in the classroom, the director wanted us to leave the office and walk down the hall as we talked. His rationale was that the shot would be more interesting than our standard static shot in David's office. This is not the way David would normally work; he doesn't evaluate a new teacher while strolling down the hallway, but he complied. Then, as we were walking, the director, off camera and out of my sight, began to make stabbing motions to urge David to really lay into me. Drama! That did it as far as David was concerned. "I didn't sign up to be an actor," he told me. Not only did he refuse to play along but he later threatened to quit if the production didn't lay off. I confronted Leslie on this and managed to keep David onboard, but from then on David understood what we were up against, and it kept us both on our toes. If the principal summoned me to her office, I had to ask myself, was there a real issue, or had the show runner put her up to it? Katerina's mother bringing in her illicit birthday cake was exactly the kind of thing he'd set up—hoping to get me in trouble. Of course, in that instance I managed to get myself into trouble without any help from him. But the worst of it was that every time a student had a crisis, I was afraid the conflict had been nudged by the production team. I never could trust them not to try. Suddenly it dawns on me: maybe teaching will actually be *easier* without them!

The executive passes the hand mike to Leslie Grief, who says all the right things. "This show is groundbreaking," he tells us. "It shines a bright light on what is happening in our schools. You guys have done something very special."

A loud crash shakes the building. Another team of players downstairs has bowled a lucky strike. What are we *doing* here?

"And now the moment you've all been waiting for," Les says with his usual showman's flair. He lifts his arm with a circular motion and directs everyone's attention to the overhead monitors normally used to broadcast football games and bowling scores during league championships. The show's opening rolls, dead silent. No sound.

I watch in disbelief as the sound techs duct-tape the same hand microphone we just used for the speeches to one end of a pool cue. Then a young production assistant holds the cue stick up to the speaker on the TV and the sound plays through the bowling alley's public address system. All this jerry-rigging strikes me as another perfect metaphor for the production. And all the anger and frustration that's been building up over the last months gets to me.

I walk over to the network executive standing at the top of the stairs, the same man who just showered us with saccharine. My voice sounds weirdly calm as I tell him, "This is no way to show something you're proud of."

Clueless, he tries to placate me. "It's not so bad, Tony. Look, they like it." He gestures with his arm at the kids, their parents and teachers, Ms. DeNaples, and David Cohn, who all are straining to follow the footage on the overhead monitors.

The executive's patronizing gesture and tone push me into a state of rage. Goodbye, maturity; hello, something more primal. It's as if all the violence I've restrained myself from unleashing at school comes charging through me now. I get in this suit's face and ask how proud he'd be to watch *himself* in a bowling alley with lousy sound. Then, for emphasis, I nose-butt him. It's not a hard hit, but it catches him by surprise. A little trick from my street-fighting days: nobody's ever prepared for you to use your face as a weapon. It scares people.

The executive reels a little and takes off down the stairs without another word. Probably for the best. Everyone else is so absorbed in the show that this particular episode is just between us.

I return to the main event not proud of myself, exactly, but not sorry, either. And somehow, the screening is well received despite the awful conditions. When it's over I detect a fair amount of relief along with enthusiasm. No one seems to realize that the coming attractions for future shows cover only the first semester. As far as the students, teachers, and administration are concerned, this is just the beginning. And it is, though not the beginning they're expecting.

Later, when I get back to my apartment, I stand for a long time staring out the magic window. The night is clear and cold, and the city lights gradually flicker out until just the streetlights are left. If only they could light my way forward. I think about losing my temper again. What would my daughter Emily say? I think of my home in L.A., the life I've left to come here. For a second I waver. It's never too late to throw in the towel. *Sorry, class, the experiment with your school year didn't work, so I'm outta here.*

I wince. No way. Goodbye is not an option. For better or worse, I'm here for the duration. I really am a teacher now.

Eight

Poetic Justice

SO HERE WE ARE. "It's just you and me, kids," I tell my class. "We've got five months until the end of school. Let's make the most of it."

Katerina and Chloe smile, and Nakiya gives me a thumbs-up, but Monte and Al G shift in their seats, looking even more suspicious today than they did in September. I can practically hear them thinking, Why's he still here? And I can't blame them.

Without the distraction of the production, I notice something enormous that I've missed until now: second semester is different. In some ways it's better than first semester because everyone is more comfortable—the ninth graders more at home, seniors more in control, and most of the teachers in their groove—but that comfort comes with a definite downside. Familiarity breeds contempt, and contempt breeds something else. The kids are louder, the horseplay rougher. Fights break out between both boys and girls. It's ever more difficult to enforce the cell phone and uniform policies. And the kids now feel freer not only to joke around with me but also to confront me. The irony is that second semester would make for a livelier TV show. Now, just when I have no use for drama, it comes at me in waves. Call it poetic justice.

FROM THE START, Paige has been an enigma to me. She can do the work but chooses not to, and I cannot figure out why. A junior beauty contest winner, she gets more than her fair share of attention from the boys, but she's moody and volatile, one minute sweet and engaged, and the next tough and ready to scream and fight. When she speaks, she fires out a rapid combination of slang and bad grammar that's impossible to comprehend. I often have to stop her and ask her to speak like she wants me to understand. But there also seems to be some affluence in her family. Like many of the students, Paige has a single mom, yet over Christmas her family went to Paris. Not many kids in our school go to Paris. Paige brought me back an Eiffel Tower key chain that I treasure. Suffice it to say, I'm completely befuddled by this kid and how to get to her—until midway through our poetry unit.

My bright method to *engage* the students in poetry is to throw a contest patterned after *American Idol*. To prepare, each student has to select and memorize a poem by a notable poet and create a poster that includes the historical context of the work, a biography of the poet, and anything else that might elucidate the poem. Figurative language, mood, structure, imagery, the works. On the day of the contest, students will present one at a time, introducing themselves and the poems they are reciting, in front of the class and a panel of teacher judges. Each poem must be at least ten lines long, and the judges must be able to verify its publication and author. Basically we have to be able to Google it.

"And to get those competitive juices flowing," I tell them, "I've made a little investment in your success. The first-place winner will receive a flip cam"—a small digital video camera that everybody in the class is hot to get—"and ten dollars. Second prize is eight dollars."

For the prizes, the kids go crazy. For the prospect of memorizing poetry, not so much.

To prove that they can do it, I promise to learn a poem myself in one night. We go online, Google "famous poetry," and up comes Rudyard Kipling's "If."

Go for it, Mr. D.!

So I do. It's thirty-two lines of pure inspiration and takes me all night to learn, but I opened my big mouth, so there's no going back.

The next morning, I prove the point. "If" belongs to me now.

"Learning a poem is a great way to get in touch with your emotions," I tell the kids. "I mean, reading a poem is wonderful, but when you learn it by heart you experience it. It's the difference between a pianist playing while reading the sheet music and a pianist playing a piece he has memorized. If you know it, you feel it in your body as if it's part of you. What's more, you already get this. The rap music you all listen to is a kind of poetry. And I know some of you can recite rap. Come on, now. Anybody?"

Al G pipes up with "Gangsta's Paradise," by Coolio. Figures. I make him stand, backpack and all, and raise his voice above his usual mutter.

> As I walk through the valley of the shadow of death,
> I take a look at myself and realize that there's nothing left.
> Cause I been blastin' and laughin' so long
> that even my momma thinks my mind is gone.
> But I ain't never crossed a man who didn't deserve it,
> me be treated like a punk you know that's unheard of.
> You better watch how you talkin' or where you walkin',
> or you and your homies might be lined in chalk.

I really hate to trip but I gotta loc,
as it clears I see myself in the pistol smoke,
I'm the kinda G all the little homies want to be like,
on my knees in the night saying prayers in the street light.

I wonder what effect this kind of music will have on these kids as they grow older. My generation grew up on love songs, only love songs, and look how we turned out. It worries me to think what rap is teaching today's children—certainly not melody! Unfortunately, my students do identify with these lyrics, and this song makes my point about poetry being all around them. Even Matt and Howard get it.

Coolio also gives me an opportunity to tie our study of poetry to their lives and to the theme of social justice that has threaded through our whole year's curriculum. Starting with *Of Mice and Men,* we've returned over and over to the issue of equal opportunity and how people react when they're not given a fair chance to succeed. This theme resonates with my students because the culture makes sure they know they're disadvantaged. It resonates with me because I know that if I hadn't gotten very, very lucky, I wouldn't have had a shot, either.

"Why do you think this gangsta feels as if anybody who disrespects him deserves to die?" I ask.

He's gotta defend his honor. Cause they'll get him if he lets them.

"Do you think this gangsta feels good about himself? You think he feels better for all this gangbanging than he would, say, if he owned his own company or designed those Nike shoes you like so much?" I point to Al G's big feet, propped up as usual on the chair in front of him. More shrugs.

Then Monte answers, "If he had his own company, people would have to respect him to keep their jobs. If he felt disrespected, he could fire them instead of killing them."

I nod. "So you think maybe there are other ways to defend your self-respect? Maybe even, if you earn your way up to a good job and do something in *society* that earns respect, then you don't feel like you need to pull the trigger whenever somebody looks at you the wrong way?"

Katerina says, "I think Coolio means that killing does no good, like when he says this guy looks at himself and realizes there is nothing left."

The others jump on that point, arguing loudly for and against. It's a solid conversation that motivates me to look at other raps for inspiration. I hit pay dirt with a YouTube video by the group Figureheads that touches on Harriet Tubman, Rosa Parks, Harriet Beecher Stowe, and *Uncle Tom's Cabin*. The lyrics deliver a call to action aimed squarely at my students:

Whatcha know about social justice
The ones who fought the ones who suffered
For basic rights like suffrage
But knowin about it ain't enough kid
It's time for you to rise up
It's time for you to lead us

I use this song to teach the class that they have to make their own opportunity but also that we should all work toward a more just society. "What you know about social justice?" becomes another of Nakiya's standard greetings to me, right up there with "Hey, you know Sal?"

TWO DAYS BEFORE the contest, I give the class the last twenty minutes of the period to practice their poems, alone or with a partner. As they work, I stroll around the room sneaking looks to find out what poems they've chosen. I work my way down the first row and stop behind the girl in the last seat. Paige. She's working solo. I peek over her shoulder. The poem is about a deadbeat dad. A missing father.

Suddenly this girl's moodiness starts to make sense. This insight by no means absolves her for her behavior and her lack of effort, but it does give me a clue to work with. Figuring out what's going on in a kid's life is at least half the battle for every teacher.

I can't help it. I'm crying. I try to cover and get to the front of the room, but Paige looks up. I hear her behind me. "You *crying*?"

I stall, not turning around. "No."

"Yes, you are," she says. Then Nakiya joins in. "You're a crybaby, Mr. Danza!" And the whole class makes it a chorus. "You're a crybaby, Mr. Danza."

Okaay. Teachable moment. I take a deep breath and spin around, wet cheeks and all. "So what if I am?" I lift my arms, full wingspan. See? No shame. "That's what poetry does to us. That's why we read poems, to get in touch with our feelings and emotions." I give it a beat. "And to win the flip cam."

They laugh at me, but they also get back to work.

Two days later, it's showtime. To enhance the *Idol* effect, I set up a table in the back of the room and make signs with scores for the judges to hold up for each contestant. Our judges include David Cohn, Ms. Smotries, Mr. Kelly Barton, Ms. Green, and Mr. Gill, a dean of discipline who channels Simon Cowell. I'm nervous about the other teachers. They're bound to judge me as well as the students, especially if this experiment goes wrong, but it makes the contest more legit to have them, and their presence raises the competitive bar; the kids like having other teachers see them perform.

Before class, when I return to my room from my morning SLC

meeting, I find that someone has scrawled across the blackboard WIN THE FLIP. I leave it as an incentive. Soon the judges arrive and the contestants file in, each picking a number from a jug to set the order of performance. We have twenty-six recitations to get through, and Al G is missing—late as usual. I've got a plan for him, though.

First up, Matt recites Carl Sandburg's "Among the Red Guns." Why this poem? "I just liked it," he says. "I think it means even if you die in war, your dreams still go on." His answer reminds me that the kids fighting in Afghanistan and Iraq are not much older than Matt. They were nine and ten when this war started and are now on the front lines. I ask if he's thinking about joining the military, and he says, to my relief, "No, I want to play football." He scores two eights and a seven, and we cut him some slack because it's tough to go first, especially for Matt.

Next up is Pepper. The kids clap encouragement, but he looks as if he's struggling not to pull his hoodie down over his eyes and go to sleep. "We've got to understand every word," I tell him. "Speak up and out."

As instructed, Pepper introduces himself. "My poem is 'Hurrah for the South!' a Civil War poem by G. W. Hopkins." I swallow hard and exchange helpless glances with David Cohn. A white kid chooses to recite a pro-Confederacy poem in a majority nonwhite class in Philadelphia in 2010? David shuts his eyes and shakes his head: don't ask.

The judges give Pepper two nines and an eight just as Al G slinks in the door. "Hey, just the man we've been waiting for," I greet him. "Guess what. You're up."

If I've won this one, Al's not about to show it. He stands up front with his backpack on and gets through Langston Hughes's "The Negro Speaks of Rivers." He hasn't made the required poster, but he only stalls a couple of times, and with Al I'll take any victories

I can get. When I ask why he's chosen Langston Hughes, he says, "Because he didn't have a good relationship with his father, like me."

When Al sits down and Paige gets up, she doesn't even look at him. She wears a big smile and moves with a glide in her step, and Emmanuel, whose seat is next to hers and who's always happy to help her, joins her up front to hold her poster. Paige routinely torments Emmanuel, and her swagger seems to dwarf him. But her artwork is not so bold. The black poster board features a vintage photograph of a black man and two little girls.

"All right, Paige!" The class buoys her. "Yeah, Paige!" I give her the go sign.

"Hi, my name is Paige and the poem I'm doing is 'Unwanted' by Marvin Bell."

She begins to recite a poem about a missing father. Her body shifts from side to side. As she races through the next six or seven lines, her smile starts to look fixed. Her hands swing as if clutching batons. Then she hits a line about the father missing his daughter's graduation.

She stops so abruptly that I assume she's lost her place. Her hand flies to her mouth. Her eyes fill with tears, and she flees to the hall.

Emmanuel's bewildered expression reflects back through the class. Nobody's ever seen Paige cry. She's the toughest girl in class. Isn't she?

When it dawns on me what's going on, I follow her outside with a box of tissues. Teachers can never have enough tissues. Paige makes a stabbing motion at the tears, but they keep coming. "Paige," I say, "this is great. Remember what I told you, this is why we read poetry, to get in touch with and express our feelings. Isn't it wonderful that you found a poem that touches you so?"

She makes a squeaking sound and nods. I give her another tissue. "You want to go back in and try again?"

She takes a shaky breath. "Yes." Then she squares her shoulders and talks to herself. "I gotta get gangsta." This seems to me a unique approach to reciting poetry, but then again, this is Philly.

Back inside, Paige takes it from the top, and the rest of us hang on every word. She makes it to the word *despair.* Then, as the tears again gather and roll, Paige lifts her arms and begs the ceiling, "Why can't I say this freakin' poem?" And she runs out into the hall again!

I go back out, and we do the whole scene over. More tissues.

"Hey, Paige," someone calls when we come back in, "just picture everybody naked." That gets a laugh out of her and everyone else, and the third time's a charm. She's so keyed up now she practically spits out the end of the poem.

The judges hold up a ten, nine, and eight, and the cheering shakes the windows as Paige pumps her fist and starts back to her seat. I stop her. "What do we know about this poet?"

"His name is Marvin Bell," Paige says. "He was in the army, but he's known for his poetry. He had two daughters and he promised to be in their lives forever, like they were his princesses, and he had their pictures and names tattooed on each of his arms."

I glance back at David, whose left eyebrow has shot up into a question mark. Has she made this stuff up? Or is she confusing her own father with the poet? I thank Paige and let it go. She's been through enough for the moment, and Monte has already taken the stage for his full, flawless six-minute rendition of Longfellow's "The Midnight Ride of Paul Revere."

Only later, when I do a little Internet research, do I discover that the poet Marvin Bell has two sons, no daughters, and never wrote a poem called "Unwanted." The poem Paige recited is online, but it was written by a blogger named Bel. I consider telling her she had this wrong but then decide against it. This was a cathartic experience, and I don't want to undermine it. Seeing Paige so moved by

a poem that she actually cried made the contest much more powerful for everyone. She faced an emotional challenge that turned into a
personal victory. I couldn't have set it up better if I had tried. There
are times when teachers have to let some things go in the pursuit of
a greater good.

WE END CLASS on Friday with ten contestants left to hear on Monday, but by midnight the Blizzard of 2010 has begun. Over seventy
inches of snow will drop on the city in the next week and a half,
breaking all records. There goes my momentum.

There was a time when I thought snow days were the best deal
going. I remember lying awake winter nights as a kid, counting the
inches piling up on my windowsill and hoping against hope that
there'd be enough by morning to cancel school. If the schools closed,
it was big news, worthy of a radio or television announcement, and as
much a surprise to our teachers as to us, which meant that we almost
never had homework over these breaks. So SNOW spelled FREEDOM.
All the kids on the block would turn out to take on the mountains
of soft pack that the plows piled high on every corner. We'd build
igloos and forts and tunnels, and I was especially good at knocking
everyone else off the hill when we played King of the Mountain. Our
snowball fights usually ended with us whiting out cars and running
like hell when the drivers stopped. Good times, but that was then.

Now, as I watch day after day of whiteout through my magic window, all I can think is, How will we make up this lost time? Every
teacher feels the ever-present tick-tock of the curriculum clock. You
have only so much time to cover so much. You sit home and worry
about losing the momentum that you painstakingly gained before the
storm. You wonder what the kids are doing with their free time, but
you know full well they're not catching up on schoolwork. So you won't

just be delayed when the storm is over; you'll be behind where you left off. You'll need to backtrack at least one day before moving on.

Which is just what we do when we finally reconvene after a full week of snow days. The remaining students recite their poems, and then, because the scores are so close, I ask those who read before the storm to run through their poems again. Only Al G refuses. "I'm not winning anyway," he says. "I'll take the score I got." I don't fight him.

The judges boil the finalists down to Emmanuel with Poe's "Annabel Lee," Janae with Maya Angelou's "Still I Rise," and Daniel with Sandra Tolson's "He Sits Alone." Because it's a three-way tie, we bring in the ultimate arbiter—the principal—to make the final call.

Before we hear the three finalists, however, I invite Al G to recite his poem for the principal. If his look could kill, I'd be down for the count, but this is an offer Al knows he cannot refuse. He stands up, comes forward, and performs his poem well. For once, I smirk at him.

Daniel is the last of the finalists to read. "He Sits Alone" describes an old man left in a nursing home to die, and Daniel recites it slowly, quietly, accompanied by a piece of low, sad instrumental music. Beside him rests a colorful portrait he's painted of a bearded man weeping by a window. By the time he finishes, Ms. Carroll, too, is crying.

After Daniel takes his bow, I ask, "What line in the poem stands out to you?"

He answers without hesitation. " 'I can't imagine what he thinks as he wipes away his tears.' "

"And why did you choose this poem?"

"I have a grandmother who lives far away, and I don't get to see her that often. She's healthy but so far away."

It's unanimous. The judges all hold up tens. The kids cheer, and Daniel gives us the kind of sweet smile that I usually associate with saints and wise men.

Ms. Carroll is still drying her eyes as she congratulates Daniel. Then I surprise the other finalists by bringing out three flip cams, so they each receive one. When the excitement of that presentation dies down, Ms. Carroll addresses the whole class. "I've had a rough week," she tells them. "The kind of week that makes me question why I'm even here. Thank you. You reminded me why I do this work."

The kids have made me look good in front of the principal and turned the poetry contest into a highlight of my year. I would even venture a guess that some of the kids remember their poems. I remember "If."

Happy Hour

Ever since the teachers' talent show, I've been trying to figure out why teachers at Northeast don't socialize. Outside of the twenty or so teachers in their Small Learning Communities, some barely know each other's names. The only time they see each other is when signing in each morning, and even within the SLC, there's little real opportunity to interact. Policy announcements and paperwork dominate the daily meetings, and after school everybody just scatters.

I understand that with two hundred overworked teachers, there are bound to be some who don't have the time or energy to spend with colleagues outside of school. But by the same token, there are probably many who'd welcome the chance to connect. Freshman teachers, especially, need to get to know veterans who can help them through the rigors of Year One. I decide to try an experiment.

If the teachers at Northeast worked at an office, chances are good that at least a few of them would get together over drinks at the end of the week, so why shouldn't a Friday happy hour work for teachers, too? Just down Cottman Avenue, a few blocks from school, there's a blue-collar bar called Nick's Roast Beef. It has a side room that always seems to be empty and would be perfect for our purposes. Before I get too carried away, though, I decide to check with Kelly Barton to make sure my plan won't violate any administration policy. After my nearly catastrophic vodka at Patsy's in New York, I'm not taking any chances. But now Kelly tells me sure, as long as no students are present and we're off school grounds and on our own time, a teachers' happy hour sounds like a fine idea.

"I take that back," he says. "It sounds like an *excellent* idea. Give people a chance to relax and get acquainted." On second and third thought, Kelly likes the idea so much that he offers to come himself and pay for a spread of food each week. "Encourage folks."

I reserve the side room for Friday afternoon, invite a few teachers from my SLC, and enlist Crystal Green and Joe Connelly to recruit some of the other new teachers. When we arrive, we find a small contingent of Teach for America teachers from our school who've discovered Nick's on their own. I pull these young women in, and pretty soon we've got the makings of a regular party.

The conversations run the gamut. Politics, city government, and the Phillies are all fair game. However, the talk always seems to circle back to work. The more beer that's poured, the more candid the comments get, and it soon becomes clear to me that the number one concern among these teachers is job security.

"You're at the mercy of the administration and the district," Tim Flaherty, an old hand, tells one of the new teachers. "That's not so scary when you have a strong principal like ours, but if you have a weak one, watch out." Mr. Flaherty, Northeast's choirmaster, has one of the highest teacher ratings in the school, so it startles me to hear his blunt warning. "Some administrations operate like a personality contest, and if the principal doesn't like you or you make some rookie blunder, then if it weren't for the union, you'd be gone."

Now I happen to be a union man. My father was in the public employees' union and I've been a member of the Screen Actors Guild for almost thirty-five years. But I'm curious what this group thinks about the political knocks on the teachers' union. What about the charge that the union protects bad teachers? That it supports giving tenure to teachers who don't deserve it, and then makes it virtually impossible to fire tenured teachers? "I mean," I say, "everybody here is giving two hundred percent in the classroom, but what about the teachers who don't?"

A pall falls over the group. Nobody wants to admit it, but we can all point to several teachers who ought to find another profession. Once when I asked David Cohn what percentage of teachers at our school he'd rate as really good, he surprised me by answering "A small percentage."

Joe Connelly volunteers a story about his wife, Sam. When she started teaching middle school, she used to tutor students during lunch. One day an older teacher objected to Sam's decision to give up her lunch break. He said he'd stood in a picket line to ensure that teachers had time to eat lunch without any additional duties. He felt as if Sam was disrespecting all the people who were involved in that fight. He even accused her of compromising the gains that were made as a result of collective bargaining. "Sam said she was willing to donate her time for the sake of the students who needed additional support," Joe concludes, "but she got his point and is still wrestling with it years later."

One of the Teach for America recruits, who looks like a schoolgirl herself, gets pretty worked up as she says to Joe, "I'm with your wife. What about those kids? With all the layoffs and cutbacks, it's the students who get screwed. To stop her from volunteering her time seems just wrongheaded—as wrongheaded as packing classrooms with fifty kids to save money."

I know what she means. Concessions have to be made on all sides to get us through the financial crisis, but how do we cut back on costs while still attracting and retaining good teachers and helping them do what it really takes to educate these kids?

Joe nurses his beer. "I think the union's more vital now than ever. We need them to outline what aspects of the contracts are necessary and what aspects are negotiable. I feel like certain police and fire locals have set a good example. They agreed collectively to take a hit on individual salaries to keep all of their members employed and their neighborhoods safe."

Everybody seems to be onboard with that, though Mr. Flaherty warns, "Sometimes when you give an inch, they demand a mile." This unleashes a wave of grousing about all the district mandates that are intended to keep bad teachers in line but make good teachers feel like their wings are clipped. Crystal Green mentions the phrase *charter schools,* and the older teachers explode. "Private schools for the masses!" It's not meant as a compliment.

Charter schools are nonunion, but they also run the gamut from good to just as bad as and worse than low-performing public schools. Tim Flaherty shakes his head. "It's criminal the way charter schools are being held up as if they're some sort of educational panacea."

Kelly Barton changes the subject to the latest outrage on the Philadelphia education scene: a scandal in a suburban school district, Lower Merion, where a family is suing the district for using a webcam in a school-issued laptop to spy on their son. Science teacher Russell Gregory, a.k.a. Dr. G., lets out a gallows laugh. "This gives a whole new meaning to the term *technology initiative.* They gave out twenty-three hundred laptops—one to every single high school kid in Lower Merion. That's quite a peep show."

"Well, it's not a total loss for English teachers," Lynn Dixon says with a laugh. "Anybody who teaches Orwell's *1984* in Philadelphia now has a 2010 example of Big Brother."

Kelly says, "Even Orwell wouldn't come up with an assistant principal dumb enough to *show* the parents a photo from the webcam." He tells us that the photo was supposed to prove their son was using drugs, but when the parents went ballistic the principal had to admit that the district had activated the camera remotely. This meant that they could watch whatever was going on in the boy's bedroom—or wherever any of the school-issued laptops happened to be sitting. "It seems they captured some four hundred shots of this kid, and who knows how many of all the other students, and their families."

"You gotta wonder what those Merion school officials were on," somebody says.

"That's easy," Dr. G. answers. "Money." He means the money in Lower Merion, which is as affluent as the area around Northeast is poor. "What I could do for my science lab with the cash it took to buy those laptops—not to mention the dough they're going to have to shell out to settle this thing."

I think back to the first day of school, when Dr. G. stopped by my classroom pushing a cart with a giant aloe plant in a large pot. With his long, crazy hair, white lab coat, and rapid talk, he struck me as the epitome of a weird science teacher, and I'd come to admire him as one of the most inspiring in the school. "For your room." He nodded at the plant. Touched by the gesture, I set the pot in a place of honor by the window and thanked him effusively. I told him that my mother always kept an aloe plant on hand and used the gel inside the leaves as a salve for cuts and sunburns. Now I'd think of her every day because of him and his gift. Dr. G. listened with his arms folded. "That's sweet," he said. "But this isn't a gift. You're just taking care of it till the end of the year. Then I'll take it back." His message was clear. At Northeast, everything was shared. It had to be; there was no surplus for extra gestures.

Nine

Our Atticus

ONE MORNING a few days after the poetry contest, a tenth grader who's not in my class wanders into my room before school and starts strolling along the wall where I've hung my students' poetry posters. This boy is slight and pale, with dark buzzed hair and shadows where he'll soon have sideburns. A widow's peak shapes his face into a heart. Some kids have trouble written all over them, but not this one. He's quiet as he takes in the biographies of poets on the wall and the images that illustrate their poems. I sit at my desk and pretend not to be watching.

Although I don't know his name, I know this boy has most of his classes near my room. First semester, when I was walking down the hall with my cameras in tow, he and I would often nod to each other. One day as I passed, he extended his hand to shake mine. Always looking to be friendly, I reached out, and just as I did, he pulled his hand away, stuck his thumb up, and got me. He laughed. Since then we've been on fist-bump terms.

Finally he turns to me. "Had a poetry contest, huh?"

I glance up, low-key. "Yeah."

Silence. He continues his perusing. "You know, I write poetry."

"No kidding." I give him my attention. "Hey, what's your name?"

"Name's Alex."

"And what do you write about?"

"Mostly about my dad. He was killed in a car accident."

The sound of kids in the hall gets louder. I want to get up and go to this boy, but I stay put. "Alex, I'm so sorry. I lost my dad, too. I was older than you, but I know how you feel."

He shrugs, as if it's no big deal, and I let a few seconds pass. Then I ask, "Do you write about anything else?"

His face goes blank. "Now I write about my mother."

I'm afraid to ask. "What do you write about her?"

"She was stabbed to death."

Well, that catapults me out of my chair. I'm across the room in two steps. Alex accepts my bear hug. I can't tell if he welcomes it, or tolerates it, but he doesn't push me away. After a minute I stand back. My heart is hammering and I'm fighting tears. What was it that teacher in SLC warned me about at the beginning of the year? "Adoption fantasy," he called it.

I screw up my courage. "Who do you live with now?"

"Me and my sister live in a foster home with my stepuncle."

Stepuncle takes me a while to figure out. It's clear that this boy's life is beyond anything I can imagine. I ask him if he'd let me read some of his writing.

He looks at his feet. "Sure."

The next day Alex brings me an overstuffed binder of his work. Not only is he prolific but the poems are good. He writes about bullying and sorrow and teen suicide and helplessness. One long poem, "I'm an Oxymoron," speaks to his own inner conflicts and really shakes me up, but it's hopeful as well, which is what kills me about this boy. The last lines read:

I'm the bright part of life even though it's dark
And at last I can be myself
I have the ability to give up
The choice of wealth
I have the advantage to win
I'm the sickness to my health
Overwhelmed with thoughts they start to talk
Worried about myself so I forget about this world and everything
  in it,
I'm an oxymoron of death
I'm life without breath
I'm that dead person living
That lost soul I struggle to find
I'm nothing just words that were spoken
I am
Poetry.

Alex wants to compete in poetry slams, and I urge him to go for it. We discuss the confidence you need to be a good performer, and I show him how to improve his enunciation and stage presence. Pretty soon Alex is a regular in the half-sandwich club.

On Earth Day he turns up in my room again before school starts. This time he clutches a poem he's written about the environment. "You think Ms. DeNaples would let me recite it over the school intercom?" he asks me.

Fat chance is what I think. Ms. DeNaples is as jealous with that intercom as if she'd won it at the Oscars. But I don't tell Alex that. After all, she did let me use it to promote the teachers' talent show. "Can't hurt to ask!" I say, and down to the office we go.

Ms. DeNaples seems to have a special on good humor going for Earth Day. Against all odds, she not only accepts Alex's offer but also invites *him* to make the morning announcements. This is un-precedented.

Alex clears his throat, and I remind him to stand straight and breathe. He takes the mike in hand. "Good morning," he announces gravely. "This is Alex, and here are today's announcements."

The office staff is mesmerized. I imagine the entire school staring at the loudspeakers in disbelief. Ms. DeNaples yielded the intercom to a *student*? A *tenth* grader, no less? Who is this kid?

Finally, after the announcements of the day's events, Alex says, "Today is Earth Day. This is a poem I've written in honor of the earth:

"If mother nature had a favorite color,
it would be deep sea blue like Poseidon's bones,
Or maybe earth brown
on days when the sun gives her enough power so she can breathe
*   again.*
Beauty has always been one garbage can short of perfection,
On most days my peers pay no attention to mother nature.
Throw away beauty with no thought.
I can only ask the people to treat the earth like their dreams.
See what beauty really is and create a rainbow.
Recycle the things that don't matter and finally make a
*   difference."*

A cheer erupts in the office after Alex signs off. Teachers congratulate and praise him. They ask to make copies of the poem so they can read it to their classes. Best of all for Alex, as we leave the office a girl he likes walks up and gives him a hug. "Alex, that was great!" she says, turning her big brown brights on him. The moment is sweet.

From then on Alex is effectively the poet laureate of Northeast.

He goes on to compete in the Philly Youth Poetry contest and earns a trip with the team to Los Angeles to compete against street poets from all around the country. He writes poetry to encourage Philadelphians to clean up their city as part of UnLitter Us, a local public service campaign against litter. Alex's poetry lifts him like a life preserver.

Whenever I hear politicians try to justify cutting the arts in public education, I think of this extraordinary boy. Although he can do a backflip off the stage to the auditorium floor, he's not a jock, or a math or science whiz, nor is he a candidate for class president or yearbook editor. But with his poetry, he's a rock star. It's what gets him to—and through—school.

ALAS, THE POETRY contest has no such rosy afterglow for my other students. As the weather starts to warm up and the pace of testing quickens, they grumble and wiggle and snicker and yawn more than ever. I'm excited about Ms. Harper Lee's novel *To Kill a Mockingbird*. I've reread it and loved it and can't wait to turn the kids on to it. Funny, the kids don't quite see it that way. After we've been working our way through the book for a week, David Cohn not so gently reminds me that I'm supposed to *engage the students*.

All right. It's time for the big guns, technology-wise. I decide to hook the projector up to my computer and plug in my SlingPlayer. That way I can screen for my students anything I can watch on TV. But what's the best media material to enhance *To Kill a Mockingbird*? I'm coming up short until about two in the morning, when I give up trying to sleep and turn the TV on to a rerun of the movie *Mean Girls*, which I later find out was inspired by Rosalind Wiseman's bestseller *Queen Bees and the Wannabes*, about adolescent girls. In one scene, the mean girls are introducing the new girl to the different cliques in the school cafeteria. Preppy blonds sit at one table, smart Asians at another. The jocks have their section, the nerds are there, the arty kids in the corner—just like every school cafeteria. Just like Northeast.

Suddenly *Mean Girls* suggests a lesson on the class structure of our school—which my students can compare to the structure of Maycomb, Alabama, in *Mockingbird*. I download the movie on iTunes and the next morning in class we screen the cafeteria scene. Then I break the students into groups to work out the parallels between characters and groups in the book, the movie, and the school. They make diagrams and illustrations, and finally present their findings to the class. There's some disagreement about who belongs to which clique in the stories and in life, but the lesson works because it connects to their own lives. And it's fun.

Games, I remind myself, are another great way to *engage* the students. We've already done versions of bingo, a.k.a. Danzo; *Jeopardy!* and Pictionary in this class. Now I find a YouTube video of myself appearing in a 1985 episode of *Hollywood Squares*. My students, who have never heard of the game show, will watch the video to see how it's played. Then, before our next class, I'll set up two rows of chairs at the front of the room to face the class. Three kids equipped with homemade paper X and O signs will sit in the first row of chairs, three more will stand behind them, and another three will stand on the back row of chairs. These nine positions are the squares, and the kids who occupy them will have to answer game questions that come from *To Kill a Mockingbird*.

When my students see the video, they make predictably embarrassing comments. *Look how young you are, Mr. Danza! Hey, you look like that guy from* Jersey Shore. I stick it out just long enough for them to get the game. "Now it's your turn," I warn them. "First nine volunteers get to be in the squares. I'll ask the questions, and the rest of you break into two teams to decide whether the person in the square is giving you a true or false answer. It works like Tic-Tac-Toe. First team to win a whole row of squares wins the round."

After the nine squares are filled, I divide the remaining students into two teams of eight—the Xs and the Os. The teams immediately start razzing each other, and the kids in the squares get into the act as well. The required preparation time is putting me at a disadvantage, so to get them started I hand the players in the squares the bluff answers I've written for the first round. When answering a question, the square players can either bluff or answer the question for real, if they know the answer. Their goal is to try to fool the teams.

We begin with team X, which chooses Nakiya in a middle square to answer the question "In what time and place is the novel set?" Nicky doesn't even take a breath before stating categorically, "The novel is set in the west during the Depression." A few team members blurt out "True," but then Gwen objects. "It's the south, not the west. False!"

Nakiya smiles and puts on her paper sign, which hangs like a bib, giving the team their X. The team goes wild, and she eggs them on by clapping. I shush them, and the Os pick Monte. Perfect, I think. Monte's poker face and deadpan delivery will give nothing away.

"On what writer did Harper Lee base the character of Dill?"

Monte pauses, motionless, and when he answers, he doesn't speak so much as he articulates: "Ernest Hemingway." The Os buy it because Monte is never wrong.

The correct answer is Truman Capote. So the Os lose Monte's square to the Xs, and Monte almost actually smiles. The review is working, although I didn't realize when I planned this that I'd feel a stab of failure over every question they miss. I mean, really—*Ernest Hemingway?* Schmos.

We're in the final round when, out of the corner of my eye, I notice

David Cohn leave the room. A good sign. He must think it's going pretty well. Then, out of the corner of my other eye, I notice Matt skirting the room in Paige's direction. Nothing new there. Matt's antsy as usual. As long as he doesn't disrupt the class, I let him be. But this time his mouth is also moving, and Paige objects. "Why don't you go back to your seat and shut up," she says to him.

On a good day there's no love lost between these two, except that I suspect there may, in fact, be some attraction, which only intensifies the friction, since he is white and she is black, and Matt hasn't been the same since those boys jumped him early in the year. Now he's seething. "You ain't the teacher." Matt closes in on Paige, jutting his chin.

"Oh yeah?" Paige's voice rises. "I'll teach you something." Next thing I know she's out of her seat and both their fists are clenched. I vault to the back of the room to get between them. Paige is screaming at the top of her lungs, "You ain't so tough, and I'm not one of your little ass-kissing girls."

I try to separate them and quiet the situation, but the trash talk continues from both as I propel Matt back to his seat. "I didn't do nothing, she's a crazy bitch," he says.

"Easy with the language." Anybody can see I'm grasping for straws.

Then Ileana gets involved. "Why don't you grow up," she calls back to Paige, "and stop acting like a fool." These two also have a running feud, so the effect is explosive.

Paige jettisons herself to the front of the room and gets in Ileana's face. "I'll show you who's a fool!"

I leave Matt and try to pull the girls apart, but as soon as I do, he races around from the other side and gets back into the fray, which of course makes things worse. Meanwhile, the rest of the kids are watching, waiting to see what if anything I'm going to do to get this mess under control. *This is pathetic.* I know that's what they're thinking. And they're right.

"Paige, I want you to leave. Get out, and don't come back."

As soon as the words leave my mouth, I know I've hit a trip wire that's way out of bounds. I want to reel them back in, but the damage is done. Paige's look cuts me to the core, and Matt and Ileana are practically high-fiving each other. I stand there, frozen, as the bell rings and everyone makes for the hall. Then I snap back. I shout over the passing noise for the three malefactors to stay put. But Paige is already gone.

"See, it's her," Matt says, and Ileana agrees.

I settle myself on the corner of my desk and am trying to debrief them calmly, find out what was really going on, when Katerina and Chloe burst in. "Al G's been arrested in the cafeteria!"

I'm mystified. Wasn't Al here just a minute ago? I release Ileana and Matt with a plea to find a more constructive way to work out their differences, and head for the basement. Al G is in handcuffs in the holding cell.

One of the policemen tells me, "I asked the young man to put away his phone, and he ignored me. I touched his arm, and we got into a wrestling match."

Al G hears this and yells, "You grabbed me, and you not allowed to touch me."

I remember the expression on this boy's face, the fury of his body language when I touched his arm in New York City. "Al, please," I say under my breath as I approach his cell. "The cop doesn't want to make this a big thing. But if you want him to press charges, I'm sure he'll oblige."

I turn back to the policeman. "Is there any way we could take off the cuffs and talk this out?"

"I'll do it if he apologizes."

That sounds like a long shot, but I give it my best. Losing the handcuffs helps. Al's anything but sorry for his actions, and he's not remotely interested in pretending that he is, but he admits that he's not exactly enjoying himself in lockup. We negotiate an apology that passes muster: "I'm sorry I lost my cool."

That gets us out of the cell, but I can't take him with me. He still has to be written up, and his apology doesn't spare him from suspension. At least there's no assault charge, and before I go, Al promises me he'll be cool. His expression, a cross between sneer and tears, tells me he means it—at least for right now. He doesn't have to say thanks.

I'm pretty well wrecked as I step into the corridor, but not as wrecked as Matt, who's hunched over in a corner, just out of sight of the hundreds of kids in the cafeteria. The blustery young man I left upstairs is now trembling with pent-up emotion.

"You okay?" I ask. Wrong. His face turns tomato red and tears flood down his cheeks. "What is it?"

This big, tough football player stammers through his sobs, "I'm-m-m so angry and I don't know-w-w why."

I hand Matt a tissue and put an arm around his shoulders. We take a back route up to my room, and I shut the door. I use every tool in my kit to get him to talk, but I'd be out of my league even if I weren't exhausted. Since neither our boxing sessions nor school counseling has done the trick for Matt, it's time to kick it up another notch. I promise to talk with his parents about getting him to a professional therapist. Matt not only accepts the suggestion but actually seems grateful for it.

After he leaves, I can't move. I sit staring at the dust, thick as sand, pouring through the afternoon light. I imagine them burying me alive. I've been teaching for eight months, and right now, I feel more incompetent than I did the day I started. How does anyone survive this job, let alone succeed in it?

"Mr. Danza?" Nakiya and Tammy peek in the door. "We're here to help you."

I give them a feeble look. "You are?"

"Yes." Tammy flashes her braces at me. "You have to grow some balls, Mr. Danza."

I wince. They're laughing, but they're not kidding. Nicky says, "It's not just for the bad kids. The good kids need to see you're tough, too."

I know they're right. I let them talk. I even listen. *You don't always have to be so nice. You can be friends with kids and still stand up to them. There's no law against sending the bad kids down to the office.* The girls' pep talk sounds suspiciously like other pep talks I've received from David Cohn.

"Well, thanks for caring," I say at last. "I think."

The girls give me fist bumps on their way out the door. They're just kids. They're all just kids. So why is this job *still* so hard?

ONE REASON it's hard for both teachers and students is that there's so little parental backup. Which is not to say that the parents are always missing in action. Sometimes they're present to a fault.

Whenever I got in trouble as a kid, my parents always supported the teacher. That's not what happens at Northeast in general, and it's not what happens a few days later when Daniel, of all kids, gets in trouble.

The whole incident strikes me as bizarre. It starts with a party, of all things. The half-sandwich crew and a few other teachers and I are having pizza and drinks in the first-floor conference room when the Latin teacher Mr. Smith happens to walk past. Naturally, I invite him in. Smith, as the kids call him, is a good teacher and he cares, though as an old-school educator he has a hard time accepting the behavior of today's American kids. "Where I come from," he told me at the start of school, "students stand and greet the teacher when he enters. 'Good morning, Sir.' " He can be tough on the kids and has high expectations, which doesn't sit well with a lot of them, including my student Daniel, who's standing by the conference table reaching for a slice of pepperoni when Smith comes in. The Latin teacher takes one look at Daniel, and both of them instantly forget about the pizza. It seems that not only is Daniel in danger of flunking Latin but also he cut Smith's class this morning. Smith wheels on the boy and orders him to the principal's office. Daniel puffs up his chest and refuses to move. He also mouths off with a level of disrespect and meanness that's totally unlike the Daniel I know. What is going on?

It strikes me that Smith's out of line, since I'm technically the teacher in charge here, but Daniel's behavior is even more unacceptable. I feel like I have to support the chain of command, so I tell Daniel to go with Mr. Smith. Still, I'm so shocked that my gentle student could act out like this, I can't help tagging along.

Within minutes Daniel's mother has been called. I know her fairly well because she works the concession stand at Northeast football games, and we're on friendly terms, especially since I've told her that her son is one of the sweetest kids I know. Confident that I've got standing, I catch her before she goes into the principal's office and try to explain what's happened.

Immediately she cuts me off. Hands on hips, waving me away, she says, "Daniel has been complaining about this teacher from day one. I want him out of that class. This teacher should be punished."

I'm dumbstruck. She's so intent on protecting her son that she doesn't even want to hear the facts, let alone ask questions. If Daniel says he's in the right, that's good enough for her. And since Daniel shows no remorse about his failing grade or the unexcused absence, as far as his mother is concerned, it's the teacher's fault. Does she

really think she's doing her child a favor? Unfortunately, I have neither the ready argument nor the authority to lecture Daniel's mother.
After she sails on into the principal's office, all I can do is turn to
Glen Dyson, the piano-playing math teacher from our talent show,
who's just been appointed a dean of students.

Glen lifts his hands and drops them. "Because of all this bad press
about bad schools, parents come in predisposed to complain about
the teacher." That empowers the kids to act out whenever a teacher is
strict, Glen explains. The kid gets in trouble, but the parents blame
the teacher. The school's forced to reprimand teachers whose only
crime may be high standards. "It's an exhausting, destructive cycle."

US AGAINST THEM, us against them. *What's wrong with this picture?* If only we could all walk a mile in each other's shoes. The next
day, when I run into the buzz saw of Monte's disapproval, I realize
that, at least in the classroom, we can.

To Kill a Mockingbird, in Monte's opinion, is too easy. The other
students, of course, complain that it's thirty-one chapters and way
too thick. Monte also faults me for taking too long to get through the
book and for constantly losing control of the class. Others say it's not
fair that they have to get their work in on time when some of their
classmates don't, and I agree, but if I come down hard on the problem
kids, I'm afraid they'll stop participating at all. That is my constant
concern, since the last thing I want is for any of my kids to quit. But
Monte's grim expression reminds me that my focus on kids who can't
be bothered is compromising *his* scholarship to Princeton.

If I'd just put him in charge, Monte seems to think, he'd pull us
all into line. So, remembering Crystal Green's strategy with Al G, I
grant Monte his wish. We call it our Student Teacher program. "One
whole period will be yours," I promise him. "You get to make up

your own lesson plan, and the assignments and standards can be just as tough as you like."

Monte's not a kid who shows excitement, but I do believe that, if he were, he'd be rubbing his hands with glee. Certainly, when he moves to the head of the class a week later, he's well prepared. For his do-now, Monte presents everyone with a legal-term work sheet from the trial in *To Kill a Mockingbird*. Then his main lesson focuses on the characters' qualities and interactions during the trial.

Monte aims high, but he's dealing with the same class I have to face every day, and they cut him no slack. Instead, they cut him off. And they cut up. Matt takes his usual stroll around the room, and when Monte tells him to sit down, Matt just laughs. Chloe and Katerina are talking about sandals for spring while Monte's analyzing Atticus Finch and Heck Tate. Erik Choi is corkscrewed upside down in his seat, and Eric Lopez is lost in a love note he's scribbling to his new flame, Ileana.

I'd like to lend Monte a hand, but I'm restricted by the rules of the Student Teacher program, which the other students are more than eager to enforce. When I do tell the others to pipe down and give Monte a chance, Charmaine shouts, "He's the teacher, Mr. Danza. He's gotta make us." As usual, she's got me.

Monte soldiers through to the end of class, but he reminds me of a tire with a slow leak. By the time the bell rings, he's running lopsided and his treads are just about shot. While everybody else shoots off to lunch, Monte sinks into a seat and I debrief him the way David usually does me. We review what he did that worked, and what he would do differently next time. Then I ask him if he's picked up any useful advice for me.

Monte looks down at his copy of *Mockingbird*. He leafs through it until he gets to a scene in which Atticus is explaining to his daughter, Scout, why it's a mistake to judge people on the basis of their appearance. Monte reads, " 'You never really understand a person until you consider things from his point of view . . . until you climb into his skin and walk around in it."

"Would you consider a truce?" I ask.

Monte gives me a sheepish grin, then he stands up and formally extends his hand. We shake on our new understanding.

One kid at a time, I think as I watch him head off to lunch. More and more that seems to me the essence of teaching: one kid at a time. The problem is that there are so many of them, and unlike most of them, Monte actually wants to learn.

ACHIEVING PEACE with Monte makes me feel good, but it hardly proves I'm the boss. Al G has just come back from this week's three-day suspension when I catch him cheating openly on the makeup test I was nice enough to let him take. Even though he sits in the back of the room, I don't need a telescope to see that his book is open on the floor beside his desk. I cannot get over his gall, cheating like that on his first day back, but I don't speak to him until the next day, when I try, try again.

"I could write you up so you get another suspension," I tell him, "or we can make a deal. First, you apologize for cheating. And you mean it. Then you say, 'I want to do the work, and I will do my best the rest of the year.' "

Al G almost sneers in my face, but he manages to contain himself. I keep it up. "It's not that long until summer, and the way you're going isn't working. How about trying something different?"

I think what finally does the trick is my reminder that the year's almost over. Al won't give in right away, but after a few rounds, he apologizes for cheating, and then says after me, "I want to do the work, and I will do my best the rest of the year." I'm not fool enough to think this will be the end of my headaches with him, but at least he acknowledges that another suspension won't benefit either of us.

It just so happens that the next day's lesson plan calls for a conversation about moral education, which helps to seal my deal with Al. I'm working off a model that identifies six stages of moral development. In the most basic, first stage, behavior is motivated only by the desire to avoid pain; in the highest stages, action is motivated by a strong sense of personal principle and concern for the welfare of others. The class generally agrees that Atticus Finch, in our novel, represents the highest stages of moral development, while his daughter, Scout, moves up from the lower stages over the course of the book. Then I ask the kids to decide where they stand in their own moral development. This is just the kind of question somebody should have asked me when I was in tenth grade.

Some of the kids say they behave—or misbehave—to impress their friends (Stage 3). Others say they'd probably misbehave more except that there are rules, and they feel like they have to obey the law (Stage 4). Since everybody loves Atticus in the story (especially as played in an Oscar-winning performance by the late great Gregory Peck in the 1962 film version, which we've screened), the kids agree that they'd like to reach his level of moral development someday, but right now, friends' opinions have more sway over their actions than the common good does. I thank them for their honesty.

Then I pose the question to Al G, who's been frowning in silence at the different stages I've written on the blackboard. "I guess I'm stuck at Stages Two and One," he decides. "I only do things for a reward or to avoid punishment." He seems proud of himself for reaching this conclusion.

"Haven't you ever done something for another reason?"

"Nope, not me."

I don't believe him, and despite his smug comeback, I sense that he's thinking about some possibilities he's never considered before. If you act out of concern for others or because of a code of honor you've created for yourself, you make your own rules. That has a certain appeal for a kid like Al, though at this moment he's not about to let me know it.

I'M ALONE IN MY ROOM a few afternoons later when a sophomore named Brittiny stops in. We've never spoken, but I've been told she's one of Northeast's "older students"—kids who are in danger of aging out of public high school without graduating. Brittiny's uniform shirt is wrinkled and untucked, the sleeves rolled up to her skinny elbows. She looks like a tough fourteen-year-old, but I've heard that she's actually nineteen. "Come on in," I beckon.

Brittiny seems surprised by my welcome. She looks over her shoulder as if I'm talking to someone else and almost disappears, but then sidles in. She stays close to the door as she checks me out, then trains her eyes on the student projects that festoon the walls. After a minute or two she asks, "Did your students do all this stuff?"

I wonder who else she thinks could have done them. "Yes," I say. "Those displays you're looking at there are about *To Kill a Mockingbird*. You ever read that book?"

She shrugs a familiar shrug. It's a gesture of shame and frustration meant to look like indifference. "I can't really read," Brittiny says, as flatly as if she's telling me she doesn't roller skate.

But she doesn't say *don't;* she says *can't.* "What do you mean?" I challenge her. "Sure you can."

I grab a copy of *Mockingbird* from my desk and direct her to take a seat. Dropping next to her, I open to the first page, point to the first line, and read, " 'When he was nearly thirteen, my brother Jem got his arm badly broken at the elbow.' " I check her expression as she tracks the words after me. "Right? What comes next?"

She scrunches up her nose, but her eyes don't leave the page. She reads haltingly, " 'When it healed, and Jem's fears of never being able to play football were ass-ass-yu—' " She halts and shuts her eyes. Her voice turns bitter. "I told you."

"No, no. That's a tricky word. It's pronounces *ah-sway-j'd*. Can you say that?" She repeats *assuaged*. "Can you figure out from the sentence what it means?"

Her whole body is tense, and I can almost feel her holding her breath, but she works through it, glaring at the first paragraph. "Means he's not afraid no more."

"There you go! That's right. *Assuaged* means healed, or made better. He could put those fears behind him and move on. See? The rest of the sentence reads, 'he was seldom self-conscious about his injury' after that. Self-conscious, like you are about reading."

As Brittiny picks up and reads the next sentence without being prompted, I say a silent thank-you to Ms. Harper Lee. But by the second page, I'm biting my tongue. As Brittiny bravely attempts to decode the paragraphs that chronicle the history of Atticus Finch's forebears in Alabama, her breath stutters and her dark eyes flood with frustration. I relieve her by reading the sentences that contain words like *apothecary*, and *stinginess, irritated*, and *descendants*. But she's more familiar than I would expect with *persecution, brethren, chattels*, and *impotent*.

"This boy's granddaddy owned slaves?" Brittiny regards the page suspiciously.

"More like his great-great-granddaddy. The boy's *father* is a white lawyer who defends an innocent black man from his white accusers. That's a lot of what the story's about. How the effects of slavery were passed down in the South, and what personal courage and intelligence it takes to challenge those effects—to fight injustice."

Brittiny will not meet my eyes. She frowns at the book, and I suspect she'd like to throw it across the room. Instead, her lips begin to move as she prepares to continue reading aloud. We trade passages for over half an hour. When the bell rings, a look of panic crosses her face, as if she's just failed a test.

"Want to come back and keep going tomorrow?" I ask.

Brittiny doesn't say anything. She just nods.

That afternoon I visit Brittiny's counselor, a well-intentioned and brutally overworked woman named Ms. Kinney, who does her job with a smile and real concern for the kids and, as best she can, keeps track of their home lives. But like most public school counselors, she can do little more than monitor the hundreds of "problem kids" assigned to her, and she generally intervenes only when emergencies arise.

As we talk I flash back to a heart-wrenching video that was shown to us during orientation at the beginning of the year. The narrator of the video told a story about a student who kept falling asleep in class. The girl's teacher, treating the situation purely as a discipline problem, kept admonishing her to pick her head up and pay attention. No one ever asked why this student was so sleepy. The girl barely managed to graduate and went to work at a fast-food restaurant to support her ailing mother. One day her mother took a turn for the worse. The girl rode with her mother in the ambulance to the hospital, but shortly after they arrived her mother died. Later, the paramedics asked if they could drive the girl home, but she asked instead to be taken back to school. She'd been taking care of her mother night and day for years. That's why she was so tired in class. Nevertheless, school was the only place where she felt hope. The story then took a surprising turn, as the narrator admitted that she had been that young girl. She closed by urging her fellow teachers to find out what's going on in their students' lives, especially when they exhibit unusual behavior.

Now Ms. Kinney tells me that Brittiny has been through the wringer. Like so many of the kids at Northeast, this girl is growing up

without a father, but even worse, her mother passes her around to various relatives and, when that doesn't work, to foster homes. Not only is
Brittiny behind in her studies but her friends are troublemakers and
she's been suspended for fighting. She's tough and always on guard.
"It's not surprising," the counselor tells me. "The way she lives, she
has to be constantly vigilant and ready to defend herself physically."

Brittiny remains on my mind all night. Until this year I took it
as an article of faith that kids belong with their parents and that parents always want what's best for their kids. Our reading of *To Kill
a Mockingbird* has confirmed that ideal. My students identify with
Scout, a young girl whose mother has died and who gets into fights
and doesn't like to go to school, but the character who makes the
greatest impression is Atticus, the ultimate father figure who never
yells at his kids and, instead, reasons with them and respects them.
Every kid *should* have an Atticus. However, I know from experience
how tough it is to be a good father. Few of us can live up to Atticus's
example, no matter how hard we try, and unfortunately, not all dads
actually do try that hard. Fortunately, a lot of the single mothers I've
met more than measure up to Atticus, and I even have a couple of
students whose parents have gone missing but whose grandparents
are totally there for them. Most kids have somebody. I'm not sure if
Brittiny has anybody, and between no parents and only bad parents,
which is worse?

The next day when Brittiny comes by my room, I give her half
of my sandwich to let her know she's a member of our increasingly
crowded club. This afternoon Alex, Courtney, David and Dion, Ar-
turo, Tianna, and Stephanie are all vying for attention. Other kids
come in for a bit, grow frustrated, and leave. Brittiny quietly waits
until I'm free. Determined to improve her reading, I give her my
copy of *Twilight*, from earlier in the year. It's less intimidating than
Mockingbird.

"I can keep this?" Brittiny asks.

"If you promise to read it."

Her face crumples. "I want to read it with you."

Be careful what you wish for. "All right," I say. "Let's do it."

She jumps up, and we each take a desk. She opens the book and starts.

Predictably, the more she reads, the more fun she has. As the days pass and we get deeper into the book, her confidence soars and it becomes fun for us both. I don't know or ask for the details about what Brittiny's been through at home. To be honest, I'm not sure I can handle the truth, and what do I do after I know it? I figure my job is to keep her mind on the positive. And it seems to be working. "I wish I could be in your class just for one day," she tells me. "Not many people believe in me or have faith in me."

"Ah, Brittiny." I give her a hug. "I've got enough faith in you for all of them put together."

The problem is that those other voices are always with her. One day, outside the auditorium, I catch her eye just as she's heating up for a fight with another girl. The issue is the same one that plagues many of the disagreements in school. One kid seems to "disrespect" another. It could be a wrong word or a look; it doesn't take much when you think the whole world is against you. Meanwhile, at the other end of the hall, Ms. DeNaples is heading their way. I speed-walk toward the girls and step between them, pleading, "Stop, Britt, it's me. Brittiny, don't do this."

For an infinite second I'm not sure what she will do. Then she catches herself and backs off just as Ms. DeNaples arrives—a very close call. If she'd gotten into the fight, Brittiny would have been suspended, and a nineteen-year-old sophomore does not need to miss more school.

Unfortunately, this is not the end of it. When she comes to my room the next day, she's beside herself. Some of the kids are saying she punked out because of me, and that has to be corrected. "I'm

done foolin' with her," she explodes. "I'm just gonna hit her the minute I walk into eighth period." This is not for show. She's determined.

I get her to calm down enough to tell me what's really going on.
As it turns out, the problem is not just between her and one other
girl. "Her friends are bitches, and my friends all want me to hit her."

"Are you sure these kids are your friends?"

I realize my mistake even before I notice Brittiny's expression
start to harden. Her friends mean more to her than her family. They
are her family. They're all she's got. I know that many of the kids feel
this way, and I should know better than to attack Brittiny's friends, so
before the words can sink in, I quickly change tactics. "Never mind,"
I say. "What else is going on in your life? Anything besides wanting
to beat up some dumb girl?"

She folds her arms and paces the room a couple of times without
answering. Fortunately, no one else comes in, so she has my full attention. I wait her out. Sometimes I think that's what these kids need
most—just someone to be patient and pay attention.

Finally, as if to appease me, Brittiny says today is her great-
grandmother's birthday.

"Great-grandmother!" I cry. "You have a great-grandmother?"

"Yes," she says.

"How old is she?"

"Ninety-nine," she answers, as if everyone has a ninety-nine-
year-old great-grandmother.

"Wow, do you know how lucky you are?" The irony of calling
Brittiny lucky is not lost on me, but I'd like to think that if she can see
herself as lucky, she can start to change her luck. And if Brittiny cares
enough to remember this birthday in spite of all her anger and hurt,
maybe this is one way to reach her. "Do you ever talk to her about her
life or ask her for advice?" I ask. "She's been around a long time, just
imagine all the things she has seen. I wish I had my grandmother,

let alone my great-grandmother." I mean that, but it's also another attempt to convince Brittiny that she is lucky. I ask, "What are you getting her for her birthday?"

She hesitates and then says, "I don't know, she's kinda hard to buy for."

Speaking of luck, my thought-for-the-day calendar this morning instructed me to make a homemade card for someone's birthday. What an idea! And my classroom is stocked with colored construction paper, colored string, markers, and glue. "Let's make your great-grandma a card," I suggest. "You can write her a birthday poem. And we'll take a picture of you with the Polaroid and put it in the card."

"It's not much of a present," she says.

"Are you kidding? She'll love it, I promise." I know I'm right.

We make a card that looks like a wrapped present—pink with purple string and a bow. It's beautiful, and Brittiny writes a short inscription for the inside: "Happy Birthday, Great-Grandma, we are all lucky to have you." I make her sign it and write how much she loves her great-grandma. "We just need a picture of you for the inside and we're done," I tell her. I pull my trusty Polaroid from my desk.

"I want you in the picture, too," she blurts out.

"No, it should just be you."

But Brittiny won't hear of it. She tells me her great-grandmother is a fan of mine.

I laugh uncertainly. "I know I'm getting old, but your *great*-grandmother's a fan?"

"Uh-huh." Brittiny doesn't see what's so funny. The young can be so cruel.

Nakiya pokes her head in the door to see what's up. "Hey, Nick," I say. "Take a picture of us, will you?"

Brittiny turns out not to be the most willing subject. She folds her arms, hunches, and scowls, but Nakiya's my go-to girl for all things technical and celebratory, and she's a pro with the Polaroid. "Get closer," she directs us. "Hold up the present, Mr. Danza. Look at me and *smile*, Britt."

It's a shy smile, a little crooked, and she's hugging her elbows as if her stomach hurts, but on balance we both look pretty happy. I know I am. We glue the picture inside the card, and Brittiny still has that smile on as she heads for eighth period, where once again, she squeaks through without fighting.

The next day she comes in beaming for real. "My great-grandma thought it was the best present she got," she tells me proudly.

This small victory gives me a new tool. I'll use this card trick again with Alex when his aunt has a birthday and he's trying to get on her good side. More immediately, though, it gives me a positive base to try something different with Brittiny. I've been using *To Kill a Mockingbird* to direct my students to think about their own life lessons. Since the book is written from the point of view of a young child, I started by asking the kids what they remember from second grade. Did they like school? What games did they enjoy? Did they get into trouble? What adults did they like and dislike? As we've progressed through the book, I've pushed the questions toward their current life. When do they have to compromise? Where do they turn for justice? In class, I usually post these questions on the board as do-nows. Today's question is still on the board, and I point Brittiny to it now: "What do you think it means to have courage?"

I explain that the students in my class have ten minutes to write their responses. Some write stories, and some write their thoughts, and some write in the form of letters. "There's no right or wrong way to do it, and no right or wrong answer," I assure her.

Brittiny bites her lip and hugs her arms. I slide her a piece of paper and a pencil. "I'll bet you have something to say about courage." Her smile dims. I tell her, "You don't have to show me what you write if you don't want to."

She takes the pencil and gives the page a hard stare. Then she curls over the desk and begins to write this letter in her perfect, careful print:

Momma

> *Why are you always cryin?*
>
> *Im sorry if I made you cry, Momma you wasn't there for me when I needed you the most. Momma I remember crying to you on the phone late at night while in foster care, Cause I was scared of the dark, Scared to sleep in a stranger house.*
>
> *Momma I remember waking up at night Screaming your name but there wasn't an answer.*
>
> *Momma I remember crying everyday, all night because I was being sexually abused you didn't care cause you let those different men take control of me. Momma do you remember the last words you said to me? I remember Momma you said Everythings gonna be okay but it wasn't my innocents were taken away from me and I felt like I wasn't worth it. Momma Im letting go of my past and living on with a fresh and new improve life. Momma I forgive you, even though you don't have the heart to say you're sorry for all the pain you put me through. Momma I still love you but I will never trust you*

> *Sign—*
>
> *Brittiny*

She finishes writing, folds the paper twice, and hands it to me. "I have to meet somebody. I'll see you tomorrow," she says quickly and gathers up her things.

I watch her scurry out the door, allowing her to escape. Then I sit at my desk and look at the paper she's given me. I take a deep breath, not knowing what to expect but worried about what I will read. When I finish, all I can think is how much easier it was not to know. Now I have to report this to her counselor. I do, and as a result, Brittiny is moved to yet another foster home.

I want to think that she knew I'd have to report this and that that's what she wanted me to do. But I don't ask. In fact, even though we continue to spend time together, we never discuss any of this. She doesn't seem to need to, and I figure, or rationalize, that she just needed me to know what she's up against. She doesn't bring it up with me, and I have to admit I'm happy with that arrangement. Call it taking the easy way out or letting well enough alone; I chicken out.

This is all still rolling around my mind several days later when the head of my SLC, Ms. Dixon, asks if I'm going to come back to teach again next year. I tell her honestly, "At my age, I'm not sure I want to care this much about anything."

Ms. Dixon just smiles and sighs. "That's what it takes, baby. That's what it takes."

Adequate Yearly Progress

Most afternoons on my way home from school now I stop by the gym for a workout. It's strange lifting weights in a shirt and tie, but the grunting and groaning in the gym sounds like cheers after the moaning and groaning of my students, and the resistance of iron weights is a relief after the heavy lifting of classwork.

One day as I'm doing bench presses, a woman across the room recognizes me from the media coverage about the show and comes over to introduce herself. She's been a teacher for several years and wants to know what I think of her profession. When I turn it around and ask her what she thinks, she's ready and willing to tell me.

"I have a hundred and fifty students," she vents, "five classes a day. Some are trying to get out of gangs, or have brothers who've been shot or killed by gangs, or fathers in prison. Some have no one—and are actually homeless." She gets more agitated. "I try to be there for them, but it's impossible. There just aren't enough hours in the day. Paperwork alone! I give a quiz every week. If I spent one minute grading each one, that would be one hundred and fifty minutes, and believe me, you never spend just one minute on anything in school. So what's left over? Does anybody ever think about that? If I don't give kids the extra attention, they take it the wrong way. They think I don't care. But where is all that energy supposed to come from?"

When she pauses for breath, I tell her I understand. I tell her about Alex and Phil and Gwen and Paige and Brittiny. This dilemma has to be a constant in any caring teacher's life. How much do you get involved? How far do you probe? Can your involvement do more harm than good? What does the child really want, and what is best for him or her?

She nods. "The grunt work is overwhelming, but the hardest part of teaching is definitely the emotional grind."

"My problem," I confide, "is that being there not only means paying attention and extending yourself to give or get them the help they need, but it also means putting aside your own personal life to make room for their stuff. I can't even imagine the toll this must take over a thirty-year career."

She puts her hands on her hips. "What teacher has time for a life, let alone a salary to support one? And yet, to hear the politicians and parents scream about us, you'd think we were all running off to the Caribbean, destroying our students' futures, and stealing the public blind."

We finish commiserating and return to our workouts, but the issues we discussed follow me home. Some veteran teachers, who seem better able to pace themselves, have advised me to set clearer boundaries. Without limits, they say, some students will take everything out of you, and then some. Unfortunately, no matter how much training they receive, few first-year teachers seem to have this boundary thing under control. More than one hundred of the new teachers who went through orientation with me in August quit before we even got to Christmas. There has to be a better solution.

And then it comes to me. Three classes per teacher, instead of five. Teachers would have more time to prepare for their classes and follow through with each student. Their schedules would be less chaotic. Call it my own "Three-Fifths Solution."

Expensive? Definitely. A pipe dream, sure. But nothing that money and public awareness couldn't buy if education were truly the national priority that it needs to be.

Instead, the educational priority seems to be test scores. The sun is finally shining after the meanest, snowiest winter in Philadelphia's history—and Philadelphia has one serious history—but a whole new

storm is looming over the annual Pennsylvania System of School As-
sessment test.

The statewide PSSA is the standardized test that measures students' proficiency in reading, writing, math, and science in their junior
year. Even though the PSSA is given to only one grade level, the state
uses the results to assess each school's overall Adequate Yearly Progress. Unfortunately, Northeast High did not make its all-important
AYP target in 2009, so the pressure to excel in 2010 is intense. Every
class will have an important role to play as the school prepares first
for the practice test and, a few weeks later, for the real deal.

As if the administration weren't jumpy enough about test results,
one of the teachers sets off a tempest by telling his students, "Maybe
we should all just not do well, and then the administration would be
fired." It's an offhand remark, probably meant as a joke, but when it
gets back to Principal Carroll, she is not amused. She orders every
teacher in the school to a special meeting in the auditorium.

"It won't just be the administration that's fired if your students
don't demonstrate progress," she warns us. "All our jobs are at risk.
If we fail to achieve AYP, Northeast could become a Renaissance
School. Anybody here not know what that means?" Everyone knows,
but she tells us anyway. "It means we go down as a failed school. It
means the superintendent takes over, everyone here gets fired, and
the school starts over under a private contractor. They might even
turn Northeast into a charter school."

Fortunately, it turns out that the person who made the offending remark was a first-year teacher. When this gets around, it lowers
the temperature a bit; what does a first-year teacher know, after all?
He hasn't invested years—decades—in this often thankless career.
He hasn't been through the union and contract battles, and he has no
idea what a truly bad principal even looks like.

But the next day in every teacher's mailbox sits an anonymous letter deriding the principal and urging the faculty to speak out against the administration. This time my number one suspect is an older teacher who's always gassing off in the teachers' lounge and in the hallways about how many times he's sued the administration and the district. This guy strikes me as someone with a persecution complex, and I cannot figure out what he's doing here. He'll loudly tell anyone that he'd never consider sending his own kids to Northeast, and in fact he homeschooled them. "This principal and the one before her are criminal and worse," he declares. Whenever I see him, he's filling the air with plenty of sound and fury, but he never seems to notice that nobody's listening.

Ms. Carroll calls another meeting, and most of the experienced teachers speak up in support of her. Job security is one of the few benefits a teaching career promises, and they'd like to hang on to theirs. For everyone's sake, we all agree to make sure our junior class does as well as possible on the PSSAs. Even though the real exam won't be given until next month, the practice test is a critical dry run, and the whole school will take it as seriously as if it were the real thing. To minimize distractions as much as possible for the eleventh graders taking the test, kids in ninth, tenth, and twelfth grades will have to stay in their homerooms while the exam is administered. My job, since I have no official homeroom, is to proctor a test room.

The morning of the practice test I arrive at school early and go to the office for my room assignment and to pick up the sample test forms. The head of the Math Department, Chuck Carr, is in charge of administering the exam. Mr. Carr is large and sturdy, with white hair combed along a precise part. Ordinarily he trudges through the halls with a look of resignation, but today he seems energized as he sets the teachers up with their testing materials and directs them where to get calculators and anything else the students might need. This is serious business.

Mr. Carr and I have an interesting relationship. At the beginning of the year, he wasn't too sure about me. Actually, he was sure. He shuffled into my classroom one day early on, sat down, and peered at me through his glasses. "Are you here to be a teacher," he asked, "or to act the part of a teacher?" When I failed to answer immediately, he continued, "Is this something you choose to do because you want to make a difference and you know you can, or is this just another acting job?"

I'd been sitting at my desk working on a lesson plan. "I'm here to try to make a difference," I said, "and I know I can't do that if I'm just acting the part. I'm scared stiff, but I want to do this and I do realize the responsibility I am assuming."

Then Mr. Carr shot back the tough question, "Will you be back next year?"

I hadn't been teaching for more than a few days. "I want to see how this year goes before I commit to another," I stalled. Then I tried to lighten it up. "And heck, you might not want me back."

Chuck Carr pushed his glasses up the bridge of his nose with careful deliberation. "What I want you to understand, Mr. Danza, is that teaching is my life's work and the life's work for many of us here. Whether you're here for two weeks, two months, or two years, make sure you keep that in mind." And with that he gathered up his books and folders and made his way to the door, where he stopped and looked back over his broad shoulder. "I wish you luck, Mr. Danza."

Well, I've made it through eight months, anyway. And today I'm also armed with a bag of Lynn Dixon's lucky test pencils. "They have a spell on them," she said as she gave them to me first thing this morning, "and they say 'Superstar'!"

At first the test seems to go well. Attendance is good, which is the initial hurdle, since kids can't do well if they're not in school. The students in my room stay with it, and most complete each of the sections. Only two boys have some math problems left at the end. When they ask to go back and finish them after completing the English section, I don't see any problem. I figure, we still have time and every little bit of extra effort will help us meet our AYP.

However, the boys need their calculators, which have already been collected, and to retrieve them I have to go to the storeroom next to Chuck Carr's office. I sneak in and grab a couple of calculators. Coming out, I try to be inconspicuous, but Mr. Carr spots me.

"What the hell are you doing?" he demands.

"I have two boys who didn't complete the math section and I was going to give them some extra time to—" That's as far as I get.

Mr. Carr unloads on me. "Are you trying to sabotage these results, Mr. Danza?"

"I was just trying to be helpful," I say weakly.

"If this were the real PSSA and someone were to report you, Mr. Danza, the whole test could be nullified. Do you have any idea what that would mean?" He snatches the calculators from my hand and storms back into his office.

After a moment, I follow and try to apologize. "Mr. Carr, I thought I was helping, but I should have known better. I am so sorry."

He collects himself, and then lets his guard down. This test, he admits, has everybody a little unhinged, but he feels personally responsible for the results. "I work my butt off to make it run smooth so we're in a position to do well. Any impropriety, no matter how innocuous, could be disastrous. Do you remember what was going on last week with the principal and the letters in the mailboxes?"

I nod sheepishly.

"To tell you the truth," he continues, "I'm not sure what the PSSA tells us about the school's performance, but it's the policy and my job is to get it done without a hitch."

I push my luck. "Do you oppose the testing, then?"

His expression flickers, as if he wants to be honest but knows better. "Let's just say it's not like the old days."

After the PSSAs are administered for real, I'll come to share Mr. Carr's doubts. Despite gains in every category except writing, we fail yet again to make our AYP target. Now called an Empowerment School—talk about a euphemism!—Northeast moves a step closer to Renaissance School status and receives even tighter scrutiny from the district and the state. Under "corrective action" we get more professional development meetings, more "walk-throughs" by district auditors, more student assessments in reading and math, and more pressure to "perform." All of our parents are notified that the school did not make Adequate Yearly Progress and that they have the opportunity to move their children elsewhere. The other teachers tell me they're constantly under the microscope, which is both exhausting and counterproductive. Kids learn better when classes are fun, and how can teachers make education fun when they feel humiliated and have the district constantly breathing down their necks?

The kicker is that our scores may be pulled down by kids who don't even go to the school. When Linda Carroll addresses the staff, she says we've made AYP as far as she's concerned. Without coming right out and complaining, she alludes to an unfair process that "credits" Northeast for all the kids in our designated region, even if they're not enrolled in our school.

It turns out that there are two ways students are attributed to a school: participation and performance. We're always able to meet the participation requirement because Chuck Carr identifies and locates all the kids living within Northeast's boundaries who've been reassigned to disciplinary schools or programs like the one Phil, my Wanderer, went to. Mr. Carr also tracks down any IEP (Individualized Education Program) students in our area who've been placed in other schools to accommodate their needs. And he makes sure all these subgroup kids take the PSSA.

The trouble is that these kids' performance also affects Northeast's AYP. These students might never have walked through our doors, but their scores are attributed to our school. Other teachers tell me that the attributed students' performance always has a negative impact on our scores. No wonder inner-city schools can't win.

Ten

Spring Fever

OUR FIRST DAY BACK after spring vacation, I greet the class with a do-now assignment to write about something that happened to them over the break. When they get up to read their work, most of the kids describe family outings, or parties that were "raging." But then Daniel, my varsity defensive tackle, volunteers to tell us his story.

" 'The first day of vacation it was raining,' " he reads. " 'I thought I heard a cry from out in our backyard. It was raining hard so I didn't investigate, but next morning it was nice out, so I went into the backyard and had a look around. I heard the cry again and next to the fence I found a tiny little kitten. It was all wet, it was crying and it looked so hungry.' " As he describes the kitten, Daniel gently cups his huge hands under his chin and pretends to hold the creature he rescued. His mouth curls into a meow. His sad, dark eyes plead with the ceiling. Daniel is pushing two forty and the sight of him playing this imaginary kitten defines incongruity. " 'I named it Fluffy.' " He sighs.

We're all watching this, mesmerized, when big Howard, of all people, calls out, "Hey, Mr. Danza, doesn't Daniel remind you of that Lenny guy with the dead mouse from *Of Mice and Men*?"

Yeah!

He really does!

Hey, Lenny, don't let the cat get your mouse!

Daniel lowers his hands and smiles, but I'm the one who's grinning. They read Steinbeck *months* ago. That's a lifetime in kid years. I cannot believe they remember. Is it possible that I'm actually doing something right?

Leave it to Charmaine to bring me back to earth. For the umpteenth time, she strides into class late, and when I ask what's kept her, she tosses her head and mutters, "I had to talk to somebody."

It's her attitude that does it. She won't look at me. She juts out her chin and slams down her backpack, then drops into her seat as if she's doing us all a favor. Nakiya and Tammy have seen enough. They lean toward me, fists clenched the way mine are when I'm watching a boxing match. I can feel them thinking, *Do it, Mr. Danza!*

All right, then. "Charmaine, that's a pink slip," I say to the silent approval of the Greek chorus.

For just a moment Charmaine's mouth falls open in surprise, but then she catches herself and puts back on her tough face. "I was right outside the door. I wasn't even that late."

"This isn't the first time, Charmaine, and I've warned you." I'm trying to be authoritative, but she shuts down and won't give me anything else.

This is the first pink slip I've ever given, and I don't really know how it works, so I go on with my class and afterward take the slip down to my SLC office. Lynn Dixon informs me, "Charmaine's dean is Ms. Karpinski. I'll get it to Ms. K., but watch yourself." Ms. Karpinski is famous in the school as a teacher and dean who's as tough as her name. She brooks no nonsense from either students or faculty, and she's one of the more skeptical about my being at Northeast. The prospect of mixing with her unnerves me, but I tell myself I'm only doing what I'm supposed to.

The next day a student I don't know brings my pink slip back to me with a note from Ms. Karpinski: "Mr. Danza, please list the consequences for this student's actions. Are you assigning a detention?"

It's news to me that I have to decide the punishment, but detention sounds about right. In my day, kids who got in trouble routinely went to detention hall after school; the teacher on duty handled whatever was supposed to happen to kids in detention. Assuming the same deal applies at Northeast, I return the slip with Charmaine's assignment—my first detention.

The first rule of teaching should be, Never assume. I'm well on my way to a major dressing-down from Ms. Karpinski when Lynn Dixon saves me. "What did you do about Charmaine?" she asks when we meet for SLC.

"Detention!" I say, sounding like a kid who's just gotten his driver's license.

"When are you doing it?"

"What do you mean when am I doing it? I sent the pink slip back to Ms. Karpinski."

Ms. Dixon shakes her head. "Tony, Ms. Karpinski has nothing to do with administering the punishment. That's your job. Every teacher handles his or her own detentions."

"You mean if I give a detention, I have to be there? Don't the kids just go to some detention place?" I'm picturing the portable classroom where I found Al G doing his in-school suspension at the beginning of the year. I'd have been (selfishly) better off giving Charmaine an in-school suspension! Talk about a backward policy.

But the realization that detention penalizes the teacher as much as the student is quickly overshadowed by my relief at not having to deal with Ms. Karpinski. I thank Lynn profusely and track down Charmaine.

We arrange to hold her detention in my classroom before school the next day. She arrives at 7:15 exactly, plunks herself in a seat, and glowers at me through her black-rimmed glasses. She's a mix of contradictions, this girl, and they all show up in her wardrobe. Those glasses make her look like the smart, serious student she could be, but her ruffled blouse and black jumper suggest a little girl. Her hair is slicked back and held down with pink barrettes, and around the hem of her dress she's stuck pins with sayings like I ♥ ICE CREAM and EYE CARE ABOUT YOU. And finally, there are those mismatched socks. It's no accident, I think, that Charmaine read Michael Jackson's "Child of Innocence" for the poetry contest.

I pull a seat around to face her, and after a little small talk I ask, "How long do you think you're going to be in school?"

She answers with sullen emphasis, "Forever!"

"No, you're not." I stretch my arms out wide, hands pointing forward. "Here is your life." Now I bring my right hand in close to the left. "This is the time you spend in school. In the scheme of your whole life, it's not really very much, right?" Charmaine gives a shrug. "The catch," I continue, "is that what you do here in this one little piece of your life can make a really big difference in everything else that happens." I open my arms again and wave at her with my right hand. "And you don't want to be over here later in your life, looking back, saying, 'Why didn't I make the most of it back when everything was possible?' " Then I add, "Like somebody else we know."

Charmaine plays with one of her pins and tries to hide her smile, but I'm pretty much in her face. "You and I both know that you can be a good student," I tell her. "What you need to understand is that you can also have fun. It's not one or the other. You don't have to choose between learning and being a kid. You have the time and the opportunity now to find your passion. But you've got to set your priorities and budget your time. Before you know it, you'll be on your own. You'll need the knowledge and skills that your teachers are trying to help you learn. Why can't you be the one in your family that everyone is proud of and looks up to?"

I'm lecturing now, and she's not really liking it, but she can't help but hear me. "Remember what I told you guys way back at the beginning of the year?" I ask her. "Most people don't aim too high and miss . . ."

It takes a minute, but grudgingly she finishes the line. "They aim too low and hit."

"See that? You *do* pay attention! And I know you know your Michael Jackson. What's that last line of 'Child of Innocence'?"

She scrunches up her face as she runs the whole poem through her mind. "Um, 'To change this world is my deepest desire.' "

I give her a second before asking, "Do you agree with that? Is it your deepest desire to change this world?"

"I don't know."

I sit back and fold my arms. "You know what, Charmaine? I think you do know. You chose that poem for a reason, and I think that line there is the reason. Why wouldn't you want to change the world? Why shouldn't it be you? If you just give yourself the chance, I know you can do it."

The first bell rings, and the building hums with movement. As Charmaine starts to gather up her backpack, I put out my hand and point to the pin that reads EYE CARE ABOUT YOU. "*I* really do care about you, you know."

She smiles and says, "Yes, Mr. Danza."

OVER THE NEXT few days, the tenor of the class shifts. I nod approvingly as everyone, Charmaine included, arrives more or less on time. They find their seats, and stay in them. Everyone participates. One day after the break between our two periods, Ben-Kyle looks around and exclaims, "Hey, we're all here!" The kids applaud themselves. This can't last, I think.

How right I am. By the end of the week, my young boxing pal Matt gets into a wrestling match with a school guard and winds up in handcuffs. And spring fever seems to be kicking the romance between Ileana and Eric Lopez into overdrive. They're always together now, hand in hand, and cannot take their eyes off each other. The whole class starts mimicking their passionate sighs, and they don't even notice, much less care. Every once in a while, when the romance flares in class, Nakiya, who proudly wears her own abstinence ring, will lead us in a loud chorus of *"Abstinence!"* I move the young lovers to opposite ends of the room, but even if he can't see Ileana, Eric still spends the whole class writing notes to her. The good news is that they tend to be poems—even sonnets. A sample:

I savor it when she smiles all day.
I love it when she uses a soft touch.
My brain never wants her to go away.
Her kisses are a fiery torch.

If angels can sing then man she is one.
She is beautiful as the star above.
I know our love will never be undone.
She's as delicate as a little dove.

I love my lover's body with a kiss.
She's the only one for me on earth.
I dream of one day calling her my miss.
We were destined to be since birth.

I now know I will never kiss another.
I know we will be loving each other.

This would all be pretty sweet except that Eric has unwittingly gotten in the middle of a spat between Ileana and her former best friend Stephanie. The girls' feud erupts in class when Ileana refuses to read from the same handout as Stephanie. Not realizing what a hornets' nest I'm stirring up, I give my mini-lecture about our class being like a family and needing to share. Eric pipes up from the back of the class and tries to give his copy to Ileana so the girls won't have to work together. I tell him to mind his own business, and the next thing I know, Stephanie is in tears.

After class I sit her down and ask what's going on. These two girls have been best friends for three years. Now Stephanie says, "I hate her. She used to be all colors and always happy and always got along with everybody. Now she's all dark and mean."

I have to admit that Ileana is challenging. Some days, just getting her to pick her head up off her desk is a struggle. It's difficult for me to imagine her wearing bright colors because, this year, black pretty much defines her. She lines her eyes with heavy black makeup and arranges her black hair into extreme styles—cornrows, or a massive Afro, or straightened flat over her eyes. She has a piercing in her lip, and she's been known to go into moods so dark they threaten to take the whole class down. Ileana's tough exterior flies in the face of Stephanie, who's soft and pale and never wears any makeup.

"Let me ask you something," I say to Stephanie. "Do you think it's wise to let Ileana control *your* emotions?"

Stephanie tugs on the end of her sandy brown ponytail. "I didn't do anything to her. If you ask me for help and I give it to you, you don't start cursing me for no reason and calling me names."

Her anger borders on irrational, but I remind myself that these things are life and death to sixteen-year-olds. "Okay, right," I tell her. "You've got to be able to count on your friends. So what are you going to do? Right now, I'm just concerned with Stephanie. I want Stephanie to take care of Stephanie. I want Stephanie to be okay and get her work done and make it happen for Stephanie. Forget about everybody else."

After ten minutes she's calmed down enough to go to her next class, but we haven't solved anything. The next day after lunch she shows up sobbing. "Ileana just spit on me. That's the highest level of disrespect. I swear to God if I see her, I'm going to kill her."

I give her a cup of water and tissues and try again. "You can't be this upset. It's not good for you!" True, but not helpful. She ignores me. So I try the let's-think-this-through approach. "What do you think is the best solution here?"

"She's dead."

I take a deep breath. "All right, let's set that aside for one second. Let's put *dead* over here." I motion to the left and struggle to keep a straight face. Clueless though I may be, even I know that smiling while a teenage girl is crying will not get us anywhere good. "Okay," I say after a pause. "What else?"

"I'm gonna leave school."

"Oh, we're not going to do that, cause I can't let you go. I'm sorry, but I'm not giving you up." I keep my voice calm and cheerful, as if we're solving a math problem together. "So *dead* and *getting out of school*, over here. What else?"

She shrugs at the chalkboard. "I can't think of anything else. I can't forget that she just spit in my face for no reason."

"Who said you have to forget about it?"

"You want me to ignore her!"

"No, I do not."

"It doesn't matter what I do. I talk to her, she gets mad at me. I don't talk to her, she gets mad at me. She don't care about anybody but herself."

"Then why do you care, Stephanie?"

"We were best friends, like family. You don't do that to your friends."

I have an idea. "I think you're judging her the same way you judge yourself, Steph, and you can't do that. You know why not? Because she's not like you."

She takes that onboard, and once again, she calms down enough to go to class, but a few minutes later Eric pays me a call, solo. He's worried about Ileana. It seems that Ileana also feels betrayed, and maybe this betrayal has roots that stretch back before he even entered the picture. At the beginning of the year, he tells me, Stephanie became friends with another girl in our class, Crystal, and that made Ileana feel left out. By this time my head is spinning. Round and round we go, I think. It's not easy for me to take any of this seriously, but it's deadly serious to the kids, and anything that gets in the way of their education is something I have to try to handle.

Poor innocent Eric. I thank him for clueing me in and warn him not to get sucked into the drama. He made the honor roll last marking period, and I want to encourage him. "You're an honor student now," I remind him. "You've got to take care of yourself."

There's only one solution. We've got to get the two girls together to talk this out. But for that, I need some professional help, so I arrange for us all to meet in a school counselor's office. Ms. Morton lays out the ground rules. One girl talks at a time, and the other person listens. Everybody will have her say.

Ileana opens it up. "You said that I spit on you yesterday. I never spit on you. I didn't even have any water—"

"So water just flew into my face," Stephanie interrupts her, "and you just happened to be right next to me."

I stop them. "This is a momentary misunderstanding. Why can't we move past it?"

That pushes Stephanie to the real issue. "I just want to know why she said in class she won't talk to me and we're not friends."

"All right," I say. "Ileana?"

"Ever since you been friends with Crystal you've been acting different. You always been dissin' me. You always act different when you're around other people."

"What do I do that's different?"

Ileana rolls her eyes and starts to sputter until Ms. Morton tells her to stop and breathe.

"How 'bout this?" I turn to Ileana. "How about if you say, 'I'm sorry you thought I did this when you walked by.' " I turn to Stephanie. "And how about you say, 'I'm sorry you took it that way.' And then we can move on. Because otherwise it's like beating our heads against the wall, girls. We're not getting anywhere."

In the middle of this Rob Caroselli, the dean of students, has joined us. Rob's a young guy, good looking and a natural peacemaker. "No one's going to force you girls to be friends," he tells them now. "You don't want to be friends, that's fine. But you are going to coexist, within the school and within your classrooms."

"But I want to be her friend," Stephanie says.

"All right." I jump in before the cycle can start again. "How about we try to focus on the positive, the things you know about each other that you like, the reasons you were friends in the first place. Think of all the things that are great about each other and all the fun you've had together. Put aside the things that are bothering you, and give yourselves a cooling-off period. You both say 'I'm sorry,' and we see how it works out, okay?"

The girls glance at the counselor and Mr. Caroselli, who both nod. It's not perfect, but it's the best we can manage today. "You know," I tell them, "I'm always around if you need to talk."

For the first time all week the girls exchange a look. Yeah, they seem to be saying, we know about Mr. Danza and talk.

It's something. It may be at my expense, but if it brings peace to the classroom, I'm always ready to take the fall.

As IF THE STUDENTS aren't giving me enough to worry about, the next day the TV show comes back snapping its jaws. Because the network has not yet scheduled an airdate for *Teach*, we've been prohibited from talking about the project to anyone in the press. The network's fear is that the media might lose interest in our story if we get too much coverage too early, and this would undermine their efforts to launch the show when they finally decide to broadcast it. But the policy has backfired. A small local newspaper, the *Northeast Times*, is writing stories that paint our silence as some sort of sinister conspiracy. One in a series of headlines asked, WHY WON'T TONY DANZA TALK? Not surprisingly, this has prompted the network to rethink its position. To punish the upstart paper, the network and production company have invited the city's big gun, *The Philadelphia Inquirer*, to send their education reporter to interview me and observe my class.

When Leslie Grief calls with this news, I feel whipsawed. We're switching overnight from a total blackout to full-on classroom invasion? Unfortunately, Les reminds me, if I resist, the newspaper will conclude I have something to hide. So when the *Inquirer* reporter arrives the next day with her photographer in tow, I'm all smiles.

As luck would have it, a big PowerPoint project is due this morning. I wanted to deepen my students' understanding of the history behind *To Kill a Mockingbird* and give them practice doing research on the Internet, so I divided them into groups and assigned each group one of seven topics: (1) The Jim Crow Laws, (2) Harper Lee, (3) A Trial in the U.S. Legal System, (4) The Great Depression in Alabama, (5) The Effect of the Depression on the Black Community, (6) Capital Punishment, or (7) The Scottsboro Boys. The kids were to visit preassigned websites for information and then create PowerPoint presentations. Of course, since you can't assume that public school kids have access to computers, I had to bring in a COW—computers on wheels. This cart of thirty Apple laptops shuttles around the school, which makes the process cumbersome and progress on projects slow, so I expect one or two presentations to come in late, but since there are seven groups and this creative stuff is what the kids love, I'm not worried. In fact, I'm almost looking forward to showing off to this reporter their talent and my classroom management skills.

As we wait for the students, I hook up my computer to the projector. The presentations were to be emailed to me before class, and of course, my in-box was empty last night, but the kids always wait until the last possible second. I fiddle with the cables and ask this not unattractive young woman what section of the paper she usually writes for. She reminds me that she's the education reporter—as requested by my network. Extracting my foot from my mouth, I mutter something brilliant like "How nice of you to be here" and direct her and her photographer to seats at the side of the room opposite David Cohn.

The kids have been told about our guests and file in on their best behavior. I open my email, and as they settle down, I tell them we're skipping today's do-now exercise so we can get right down to their presentations. The class grows eerily quiet, and a second later I understand why.

Exactly one project has been submitted. One!

I lose focus for a second, and when I look up, the excuses start to fly. More than Carter has pills, as my father used to say, but I put my hand up to silence them. The reporter is having a fine old time scribbling all of this on her pad. I know I must not panic, but I have no backup plan. Zip. As an actor, I'd call this "dead air." As a teacher I call it "death."

Stalling for time and scrambling for ideas, I happen to look down at my desk. There in my physical in-box lies a printout my daughter Emily sent for my birthday a few days ago. It's a short story with an accompanying lesson plan that she found online. Unrelated to anything I've been teaching, "Frank Sinatra's Gum" is a story about a high school girl in 1945 who poses as a reporter for her school paper so she could interview Frank Sinatra, who at the time was the biggest star in the world. The kicker is that somehow she winds up with Sinatra's chewed gum in her mouth—without kissing him. My daughter grew up listening to my own Frank Sinatra stories—about the time he yelled at me on national TV for trying to take his arm when I thought he might fall, or the time I introduced him to my former bobby-soxer mother, who used to say after I'd been on TV for a few years, "Big shot, when you introduce me to Sinatra, *then* you're a star" (Frank Sinatra treated her like a queen). I was lucky in Hollywood to become part of a social circle that included Sinatra and other maestros such as Dean Martin, Sammy Davis Jr., Gregory Peck (yes, I actually knew Atticus), and the great director Billy Wilder. My daughter hasn't met many of them, but she knows her father. "Happy Birthday Dad," she wrote on the printout. "You'll like this."

The sight of Emmie's handwriting calms me down. It occurs to me that this short story is all about the character's quick thinking and improvisation just as she starts to panic. It's filled with figurative language and imagery. And it comes with a list of questions to prime students' critical thinking. I pick up the story, turn to the class, and begin to read.

The kids nearly gag when the girl in the story reaches under the table to pry off Sinatra's just-chewed gum and then pops it into her own mouth, but they can identify with a kid who'll do almost anything to impress her more popular classmates. They also notice that she gets the better of Sinatra because she's done her homework on him.

After finishing the story, I ask, "How many of you know who Sinatra is?"

They give me blank stares. Then Al G mutters, "He's that old guy P. Diddy likes."

All right. Whatever it takes. "Who's the Sinatra of today?"

Jay-Z! Beyoncé! Eminem! Other rappers they name I've never heard of. Not for the first time this year, I'm struck by just how unfamiliar I am with my students' culture—and not only because I'm older.

"Okay, say you were interviewing that person for your school paper. What questions would you like to ask?" That one's for the *Inquirer* reporter, who's still busily writing. But there's also something serious that I've been wanting to discuss with the kids all year, and the short story sets it up beautifully. "Why do you think some people wind up as superstars?"

They all jump at once. *They just got it! It's a gift. Nah, it takes talent! You got to be beautiful. No, man, you just gotta know people.*

Many kids are fame-crazy. How could they not be? Our society celebrates and venerates celebrity, and the rise of reality TV has only stoked the idea that anyone and everyone can "get famous," regardless of smarts or talent. This is a particularly thorny issue for me as a teacher because reality TV brought me here, and although my students were not paid to be on the show, when it airs they will undoubtedly have a small taste of celebrity. So throughout the year I've pushed the kids to think about true success and what that really means. Whenever they answer, *I just wanna be famous,* I stop them. "What are you going to be famous for?"

Some will say they want to be movie stars and athletes. Emmanuel wants to be a real estate entrepreneur. Chloe wants to be a model— and/or ambassador to China or France. And Monte wants to be a pediatrician. But reality TV is an unmistakable magnet. "That *Jersey Shore* gang is making big bucks," one boy told me. Unfortunately, he's not wrong, and this represents a huge and barely acknowledged obstacle to education. I tell my students that good behavior will pay off, but then they go home and watch television and tell me I'm wrong. "Bad behavior pays off, Mr. Danza." Where's the motivation to pay attention in school when you can get rich just by letting a camera crew into your living room and acting out?

Now I try to help the kids see that there are actually two types of fame. "Reality TV fame is *meaningless* because it requires no skill, talent, or accomplishment. *Meaningful* fame, on the other hand, shows that you've done something truly special and good." I reference Malcolm Gladwell's book *Outliers*, which shows that many of the successful people we think are just gifted or lucky actually had to work very hard. "If you're going to be famous, be famous for something you're willing to work for. You'll feel better about yourself."

Next we consider the actual experience of fame. "What are the pluses and minuses of life as a celebrity?" I ask.

They start with the assumption that fame is all about money, attention, and freedom, but the more I draw them back to the story "Frank Sinatra's Gum," the more they have to admit that it's not always so great to have fans constantly after you for autographs—or your gum—and maybe the paparazzi could be pretty annoying, and maybe sometimes you just want to hang out and not get all dressed up for the camera. Maybe there are even some responsibilities that come with fame. "When you're famous," I suggest, "you have influence. But how do you handle that influence? What happens if you don't work hard or perform well?" We talk about the pressure—and opportunity—that comes with fame, especially the opportunity to share your good luck with people who are not so fortunate. I'm not sure everyone is convinced that celebrity is a mixed bag, but it turns into a spirited discussion, and I feel like a real teacher.

After the bell rings and the students leave, the reporter and photographer thank me for an entertaining class. When they, too, are gone, David Cohn throws an arm around my shoulders. "Mr. Danza, you sure pulled that one out of your ass."

I grin. "Emmie came through for me, Mr. Cohn."

The next morning I open the *Inquirer* to read:

> *Mr. Danza was having a bad day. The laptop acted up. Few students were ready to present their projects and the group was restless, giggly, and distracted. A few snickers and moans erupted when the new reading assignment was announced.*

In other words, a typical day in a typical high school class—with a typical teacher. And all the groups eventually do turn in their PowerPoint presentations.

Fight Night

Petey Pop, the manager at the gym, gives me tickets to a boxing show that Joe Hand is promoting Friday night at Philadelphia's legendary fight club the Blue Horizon. There's nothing more fun than a local fight club. It's the type of club where I had most of my fights. Even if the fighters aren't world class, there's an immediacy and excitement that you just can't duplicate in a big arena or on-screen. In a small club, you can actually smell the sweat and feel the heat from the ring. Since neither Joe Connelly nor Rob Caroselli has ever been to the Horizon, I invite them to make a night of it.

After some great Philadelphia Italian food, we arrive at the Blue Horizon. It's already packed to the rafters, with people hanging over the balcony railings, but with Petey taking care of us, we're in luck. Our seats are ringside. A referee and judge I know from my own fighting days, Frank Cappuccino, comes over to say hello. And sitting next to us is Tex Cobb, who fought Larry Holmes in 1982 for the heavyweight title. He took quite a beating. In fact, that bout was such a brutal mismatch that Howard Cosell, who was calling the fight, quit in disgust and never returned to cover boxing. Fortunately, Tex can now laugh about it. "I'm your man if you need someone to come to school and straighten out the kids," he jokes with Joe and Rob.

"Yeah, some days we could use your kind of help," Joe says.

Rob smiles but shakes his head. Though as young as Joe, Rob has a privileged view of the kids who most need straightening out at school. It's his job to find ways of dealing with them that do not involve fists. A cheer goes up over the action in the ring, so I can't hear what Rob and Joe are now saying, but their conversation has their full attention. Then I catch the name of another Northeast teacher, Mr. Grant.

Joe smiles. "Well, sure. That's why we need Tex here, to save us from ourselves."

"Hey," I interrupt. "What are you guys talking about?"

Joe asks me if I know the teacher Rob just mentioned, but I know only that Grant's another first-year hire. "Well, he's a hothead." Joe glances at Rob to see if he's talking out of turn, but Rob motions him on. "Frankly, I'll be surprised if he makes it through the year."

"Why?" I ask. "What happened?"

Joe says, "I passed him and a student in the hallway a couple of weeks ago and heard the kid mouthing off. Next thing I knew they were yelling at each other." Joe stopped and turned back just as Mr. Grant stepped toward the kid. "You get in some of these kids' faces, and they feel they have to respond."

I shudder, remembering my own near dustup with Pepper's personal bully, Elvis Jones.

"Fortunately," Rob says, "Joe suggested a different solution. Otherwise, Mr. Grant wouldn't have made it through the day, let alone the year."

That makes Tex laugh hard. Everything makes Tex laugh hard. But it doesn't sound funny to me.

After the fights, we stop for a nightcap at Nick's Roast Beef. We want to celebrate Joe's wins on five of the six bets of the night, but all we can talk about, as usual, is school.

"Hey," Joe says, "something happened this week that really made me feel good. My sixth period is crazy. There are too many big personalities in that class and they see me right after lunch. So during sixth period on Monday some of these kids banged on my door and ran away. With help from security I got them back into the classroom, but after security left, I was asking for their IDs to write them up when one of the kids ran his mouth. He refused to give up his ID and walked out of the room."

"I'm waiting for the part that made you feel good." Rob rolls his eyes at me.

Joe waves his hand for us to listen. "The great part is that two of my more difficult students—I suspended both of them earlier this year—they went into the hall and squared off with the kid and told him he can't speak to Mr. Connelly like that. They were my enforcers! Of course, I was glowing with pride, but I chased all three back into the room, and now the holdout handed me his ID. It made me feel like sixth period might be going better than I thought." He grins as if the payoff of this story were a badge of honor.

"You're a good guy, Joe," I say.

"Small victories." Joe shrugs.

A common refrain, I think. In fact, I've heard it, or something like it, almost every day lately. I've taken to using the bathroom in the teachers' lounge on the second floor—not much of a lounge, really, just a cubicle with a table and chairs and a bathroom, but space enough for a handful of teachers to hold a private conversation—and the most frequent concern I hear there is teachers' doubt about whether they're still making a difference. Unlike the gung-ho first-year teachers I met at the start of the year, many in the lounge are discouraged veterans, including retirees who've come back to substitute. Some blame the administration, district, or superintendent. A few blame the current culture of violence and disrespect. But most blame parents for checking out and expecting teachers to do the family's work.

"How many parents did you get for parent-teacher conferences?" I ask Joe.

"Me?" Joe lets out a grunt and shakes his head at Rob. "Not many. I'm not sure they care whether their kids learn math. But, Tony, you must have had them eating out of your hand, coming in to check out the Boss."

"One," I tell him. "I counted. One." In fact, the school was like a ghost town on the afternoon of the conferences.

"In the parents' defense," Rob says, "most have to work, sometimes more than one job, and it's tough to get off during the day. We do schedule conferences at night, and we see more parents then, but not that many more."

"I hate to say it," I say, "but in private schools the teachers practically have to fight the parents off with a stick. I remember cooling my heels out in the hall more than once while the parents ahead of us monopolized the teacher. It's not just that you get what you pay for. There's a whole different attitude."

"Dream on," Rob says. "Did you see the article in the paper the other day about the public middle school where the teachers made gift baskets to entice parents to come in for parent-teacher conferences?"

I start to laugh until I realize Rob's not joking. "You mean the teachers are bribing the parents to come in and talk about their own children's education?"

"Afraid so."

I nurse my beer. "Maybe Dinh's right."

"Dinh?" Joe asks.

"He's that Vietnamese math teacher who hangs out in the teachers' lounge on the second floor. He's always talking about how much better schools are in Asia, where the students respect the teacher and the parents make sure the children know they have to learn."

Rob nods. "He's got a point. Most of the students on our honor roll are ESL students." English as a second language. "Many of them have recently arrived from Asia. And unfortunately, the longer the kids are in this country the more their grades tend to drop. What's wrong with *that* picture?"

All three of us stare glumly up at the television above the bar. Sarah Palin is pumping her fist and winking at her supporters in front of a huge red, white, and blue banner. When Anderson Cooper cuts to a commercial, the bartender changes the channel to a fight on ESPN.

"Which do you think is tougher," Joe asks me, "boxing or teaching?"

No contest. "Admittedly," I say, "boxing is a tough way to make a living, but I honestly think teaching is harder."

"Mentally, anyway." Joe glances up at the two welterweights dancing around the screen. The fighters are mixing it up pretty good.

Rob grunts. "The real difference is that you can't fight back, you have to stand there and take the punches."

"Like I said," I say, picking up the tab, "teaching's a tough way to make a living."

Rob finishes his beer and smiles.

Eleven

Finals

IN MAY, we enter countdown mode. I have just six weeks to wrap up the curriculum and get my class through finals—which seems like plenty of time until David clues me in to the year-end realities at Northeast. He says that attendance typically plummets during the last month of school, and in the last two weeks, most classes are more than half empty. To counter this trend, the administration is planning to drop the school uniform requirement in June, but I don't really see how this will help with attendance—and I know, based on the beginning of the year, that free dress will make the place crazier. Suddenly, the pressure to wrap early just got a lot more intense.

Strangely, nobody else seems to feel this pressure. When I ask other teachers what they're doing for year-end reviews, they shrug or tell me they don't bother. I don't get it. How do the kids survive finals if they don't review?

Then David informs me that Northeast has no finals week. "Graduating seniors have to present a final multimedia project to a panel of their teachers, but in the lower classes, most teachers base grades on work done throughout the quarter." Finals aren't required by the district, he explains, and since they're not required, most teachers don't give them.

I'm still confused. "I've assumed from Day One that I have to give a comprehensive exam covering everything we've learned all year."

David sighs. "Nope."

It's true, I realize; no one ever said a word to me about finals. "But why not?"

He points to the stacks of printouts and academic assessments in the corner of his office. "Because the system only cares about standardized tests."

"Aah." By *standardized tests*, David means those PSSAs that dominated the collective consciousness of the entire school back in March and April—the general proficiency tests that determine whether the school "succeeds" or "fails." But only eleventh graders take the PSSAs! Also, the tests bear little, if any, relation to a teacher's individual curriculum. "What about all the books and debates and projects we've done this year? Doesn't anybody care how much actual knowledge the kids have retained?" I sound plaintive, I know, but it seems as if a year's worth of work is about to vanish into quicksand. Without a final, how can I gauge my effectiveness as a teacher?

David assures me that no one will stop me if I want to give a final exam. "Go for it."

JUST A FEW DAYS later, Katerina informs me that she's going to spend the summer in Russia. "We will be with my family in Moscow," she tells me in her breathless, little-girl way. "I cannot wait to see them."

I try to imagine summer in Moscow. Russia's a place I've always wanted to see—I guess because of the Cold War. "You're lucky," I say. "I envy you." Then, without giving the question much thought, I ask, "When are you leaving?"

She answers, also without appearing to give it much thought, "The Friday before Memorial Day."

The banter goes right out of me. *"Memorial* Day? That's two weeks from now! You're going to miss the whole last month of school?" *What is her mother thinking?* I manage, just barely, not to say that last part.

Katerina seems surprised that I'm upset. "I don't mind." She giggles. Then she says something about cheaper airfares and family commitments. I don't get it, but I also can't do anything about it. In this case as in so many others, parents call the shots, and teachers just have to work around them. If we get through our comprehensive review, maybe I can give the final exam before Katerina leaves.

We spend the third week of May reviewing with handouts and a PowerPoint presentation, to be followed by another scavenger hunt like the one that prepped the class for their *Mice and Men* final. But this hunt will cover much more material, take more time, and be more challenging—ultimate, in more ways than one.

I use the same design as the first hunt, starting and finishing on the baseball diamond behind school, with stations all over campus. I enlist many of the same teachers and school workers who served as monitors before and tap my unofficial advisory kids to help set up the stations. Teachers need helpers. And there's a buzz; word has gotten around that Mr. Danza's scavenger hunt is fun. Other kids who aren't even in my class offer to field a team. Ms. Carroll and Ms. DeNaples wish me luck. It's all much easier than the first time, when I set up everything myself, though I still work up a good teacher sweat.

As before, the teams will have to get their passports stamped at each station. But there are a lot more stations. There's one where the kids have to tap out the rhythm of a sonnet, and another, titled "Five-Paragraph BFF (Best Friend Forever)," dedicated to our neme-sis, the five-paragraph essay. In the gym, the station requires the team to make a human pyramid, the levels from base to top mirroring the class system of Maycomb, Alabama, in *To Kill a Mockingbird*. The monitor there will take Polaroids of the kids' pyramids and tape them to their passports. And at my favorite station, the kids in tandem have to recite "If," the poem by Rudyard Kipling. Each kid will recite a line, and the monitor will judge if it's correct and understandable. If not, the team has to do it again.

The final challenge is Nakiya's idea, based on a race she ran at summer camp. "It's a scream, Mr. Danza," she assures me. The game is to take a baseball bat, put one end on the ground and place your forehead on the other end, then circle the bat five times before dizzily running to a marker on the field and back to the finish line. I agree, with one special educational wrinkle: each team member must wear the costume of one of the characters from our reading. I pull together a toga for *Julius Caesar*; a sheriff's outfit for Heck Tate from *Mockingbird*; overalls for Lenny from *Of Mice and Men*; a silver sweat suit for the pig in *Animal Farm*, which we've just finished reading in class. The first member of each team will pick a costume, put it on, race to the finish line, and then run it back to the next team member in the relay. First team to get everyone to the finish line and out of costume wins.

THE DAY OF THE HUNT dawns hot—and *hot* in Philadelphia means blistering. We've set up as many stations as possible indoors or in the shade and made sure to have water at every station, but I caution everyone that there's to be no running, especially because of the heat. Good luck. The kids are excited. There's extra credit on the final at stake, and once again, competition works. When I say, "Go!" they're off like a shot—every one of them running.

I spend a few minutes setting up the final challenge and laying out the costumes, then walk around to the stations to see how it's going.

The kids are so fast, it's as if they studied for the scavenger hunt. They help their teammates when they get stumped, and I'm feeling so proud of us all that my doubts about my final actually slip away for a time. In the gym the human pyramids have even Monte and Eric Choi laughing. Unfortunately, the station monitor there doesn't use the right setting on the camera, and the pictures all look like shadows, but I figure if that's all we get wrong, we'll have done all right. Listening to my students trying to quickly recite "If" puts me over the moon.

I get back down to the field just as the teams are closing in on the final challenge. It's a tight race and the costumes are even tighter—tough to get on over shirts and shoes. The kids are still running, bearing down, and Al G really makes quite a sight in his toga. In second place, Ben-Kyle Whatever Your Name Is pulls on Lenny's overalls and spins the bat around one, two, three, four, five times.

He starts to run and halfway to the finish goes down so fast I'm sure he's fooling around. Great pratfall, I think and turn to make sure there's a costume for the next incoming team. But when I glance back, Ben-Kyle hasn't moved.

Time suddenly slows down. He's got to be faking it. *Smart to cover your face with your hair so I can't see you laughing.* But his chest isn't moving, and I'm holding my own breath as I sprint to reach him. Seconds split. *Stop goofing around.* The thought sticks in my throat. I'm close enough now to see his feet splayed sideways, dead still.

I've seen my share of guys knocked out. I've gone down more than once myself. *This kid is not moving.*

This cannot be happening. Kids don't die on teachers. Sixteen-year-olds don't just drop for no reason. I cannot lose this student.

Confusion is scrambling my brain. Everything is happening in slow motion and high velocity. I drop to my knees beside Ben-Kyle and brush his hair off his face. He's out cold. I search for a pulse. I think I feel it.

He's out . . . but breathing, a little.

Everybody on the field has converged as I kneel beside Ben-Kyle. I say what I've always heard you say in a situation like this: "Stay back, give him some air." I sound ridiculous. All I know is what I've seen on TV. What would a real teacher do?

One of the kids hands me a bottle of water while the rest just stand and stare. I wet a towel and lay one end across Ben-Kyle's forehead, wipe his face with the other. It seems like a lifetime passes before he slowly starts to come to. I finally exhale.

"Hey, buddy." I try to cover my terror with a smile. "You all right?" Stupid question.

He seems to know where he is, but not what happened. I tell him he fainted as I give him a sip of water. We get him to sit up and drink some more, and eventually we help him to his feet.

I have a déjà vu memory of being knocked out in a boxing match in my twenties. What we're doing is just how they revived me. The memory jars me even as the kids cheer Ben-Kyle, the way they would a football player who walks off the field on his own after being hurt. Only Ben-Kyle still isn't walking on his own.

Daniel and I sling his arms over our shoulders and walk him unsteadily into the building. In the nurse's office, Ben-Kyle lies down. While the nurse calls his parents, I stay with him and ask dumb questions to make sure he's fully conscious. How am I going to face this boy's parents?

Ben-Kyle's father arrives in a panic. My own pulse still is racing so hard that I can't fully take this man in, but he's older than I expected and has rushed from work wearing some kind of uniform. The main thing, though, is that once he sees his son he calms down.

I tell him what happened and apologize profusely. He's more understanding and gracious than I probably deserve, and Ben-Kyle seems to feel better as well, now that his dad is here.

The nurse suggests that Ben-Kyle should be checked out at the hospital, just to be safe. But his father came on foot; the family has no car.

Finally I can do something to actually help. I get clearance from the office and drive them to the hospital, where Ben-Kyle is examined and tested. I'm not sure who's more relieved when he's released with a clean bill of health—Ben-Kyle, his father . . . or me. On second thought, I'm sure, it's me.

AFTER THIS NEAR-DEATH experience—or what felt to *me* like a near-death experience—the final exam looks like a cakewalk. It's eleven pages, including essay as well as multiple-choice and fill-in-the-blank questions. The test is long, but fair and comprehensive. When I show it to some of the other teachers in my SLC, most commend me. Only one has reservations.

Vanessa Detolla is a veteran English teacher, and I respect her opinion immensely. She's also helped me throughout the year, which is why it throws me when she glances up from my examination and says, "Pretty risky."

I can't help asking, "What do you mean?"

"What if you're reaching too high? There's no time for second chances."

I know Ms. Detolla has a point, but I've reviewed everything with the kids backward and forward. And I need hard evidence that the knowledge has stuck. "They're going to do well," I declare, more out of hope and bravado than out of conviction.

Silently, I decide to spend more time on review. Katerina will just have to take the exam in cyberspace from Russia.

IT HAD TO HAPPEN. Eric Lopez finds me alone in my room, and one look tells me all I need to know. Gone is the ebullient kid who demonstrated his break dancing on the first day of class. Actually, he stopped dancing and broke up with his Renegade Break-Dancing Crew as soon as he started spending all his time with Ileana, but first love kept him fired up in other ways. Now the light's gone out. His face is ashen, and he leans against the doorframe as if it's all that's holding him up. He's been dumped.

"Come on in, Eric." I coach him into the room. "Park it."

How well I remember what it feels like to be fifteen years old and in love for the first time. You can't think of anything else. You can't imagine life without her. In my case, her name was Millie Zizzo, and she was as delicate as Ileana is tough, but she broke me just the same. With Eric, I've been expecting this for days now. He's been lethargic, ignoring his classwork, and hiding behind his long hair. And Ileana acts as if she doesn't even know his name.

"I just saw her with another guy," he blurts, sounding as if he's been stabbed. Then comes the killer: "He's a senior!"

It's the end of his world. I assure him that first love always feels this bad when it ends. In fact, all love feels this bad when it ends. I don't tell him just how well I know this, but I try to sound consoling and encouraging. "It gets better, Eric. It really does." Unfortunately, I don't really believe that, and it's not making a bit of difference.

Eric's not a scary kid, but broken hearts can make boys desperate. His pain turns into obsession. During the next couple of days, Eric starts following Ileana, showing up at her house uninvited. After the episode with Stephanie, I'm impressed by the power Ileana seems to exert over her friends, especially when she turns on them, but Eric's only going to hurt himself if this keeps up. I call his father.

Eric's dad and I double-team him. His father pleads with him to open up and talk. I stop pulling punches. My love life is in a shambles, too, and if misery loves company, I have more than enough to share.

I sit Eric down and level with him. "You think when you fall in love it's going to last forever, and if you're very lucky and really work at it, sometimes it does. But there are a million things that can go wrong, and a lot of them are out of your control." I take a deep breath. "I'm actually in worse shape than you, pal. If you think it's bad breaking up with your girlfriend, try it with your wife and kids."

Eric pushes a hand through his hair, getting it out of his eyes. His head is tilted like a parrot's. I wonder if there's a rule against teachers sharing personal information with their students. I decide I don't care since I have his attention for the first time since his breakup.

"You know I'm living three thousand miles from home, right?" I ask, and he nods. "Well, this isn't the first year I've done that. I had a TV show that I did for two years in Manhattan, and while I was there, my family got used to living without me. After that show ended, I tried to put it all back together, but I couldn't seem to make my family understand how much I needed their help. The more I didn't feel I was getting that help, the more I demanded and begged for it. That's never good. I was way too needy."

I let that sink in. No need to point out that Eric now knows a little something about demanding attention, too.

"My wife and I have been married over twenty years," I tell him. "We've had lots of ups and downs, and we should be able to weather this stretch, but this time I don't know."

Suddenly Eric is worried about me. "But you're going back, Mr. Danza. You're not getting a divorce or anything."

"That's what I'm trying to tell you, Eric. Whenever you have two people, there are a lot of variables. Like they say, it takes two to tango, and if one person refuses to dance, the other person eventually has to make the decision . . . and it's that decision that's the hard part."

I notice that Eric's gaze has dropped to the decal on his notebook for Breaksk8, an MTV break-dancing crew. "The choice is yours, Eric," I say. "At a certain point, you just have to decide this is not good for you. Once you've made that decision, you can move on with your life."

I wish I knew how to take my own advice, but amazingly, Eric needs no further encouragement. The next day he walks into class with a new short, very sharp haircut and a kick to his step. Ileana is clearly miffed, but I'm elated to have the old Eric back.

KATERINA'S LAST DAY sneaks up on me. When we say goodbye, I tell her I'm going to miss her, and I mean it. But after she's gone, I feel guilty. I worry that I didn't show Katerina how much I truly appreciated her, or how much I hope she does well in life, or how badly I want her to stay safe and healthy and happy despite all the unknowns in her future. I realize, I'm not anywhere near ready to say goodbye to my kids.

After Memorial Day, however, guilt is the last thing on my mind. The kids go wild. On June 2, Paige blows me off, Charmaine chews me out, and Russian Playboy and Pepper waste the whole class swapping stupid jokes. Worse, I can't even ride them for it, since the entire school acts as if the year is already over. What's my leverage? I can stage a walkout.

Knowing that there's only four minutes left before the end of class, I get up and make a scene of leaving. "All right, that's it. I've had it. You don't want to listen? I'm not fighting this battle anymore. You're on your own. You want this class, you can have it."

I shut the door hard behind me. Not a slam, but hard. I'm really just acting to make a point. But they don't know what to think.

Out across the hall, I stand against the lockers and wait for the bell to ring. When it does, instead of the usual rush, they peek out the door to see if I'm there.

I play it cool. Say nothing. They edge toward me, still trying to figure out what's going on. *We're sorry, Mr. D. We didn't mean nothing.*

But then, as they close in, everything shifts. *We love you, Mr. Danza. Don't be mad at us. Are your eyes watering?* And then, boom. I'm dissolving in the middle of a twenty-five-person group hug, and the emotion is so overwhelming, there's nothing I can do to stop it. I weep. I sob. I hiccup.

Now everybody else is laughing. Of course, they're laughing at me.

Count on it: just when you think you can't stand the sight of them, your students will do a one eighty and suddenly you're in love again. The next night is Senior Prom. With some trepidation, I volunteer again to chaperone, but this dance is nothing like the Winter Formal. Instead of dirty dancing, Northeast's young men and women waltz through the lobby of the Bellevue Hotel in tuxedos and evening dresses. Chloe, Tammy, and several other sophomores in my class turn up looking radiant and sophisticated on the arms of seniors. I breathe in the perfume and aftershave, dance to the beat of oldies that I actually can dance to, and wonder what I've done to luck into a night like this. When Katerina's boyfriend videotapes us for her, I feel like we're sending her a digital valentine from a high school prom paradise.

THE DAY OF OUR FINAL, I wake up at 4:00 A.M. The sunrise through my magic window seems to coat the city in gold, and I can't help but view this breathtaking dawn as an omen. I've done everything in my power to prepare my students. They know the work. They're good kids. They're smart. I tell myself they'll do fine.

For the first time all year, every single student, minus Katerina, is present for the test. When I hand out the final, the kids are less indignant than I thought they would be at the sight of eleven pages. They have both periods to complete the test, and nobody but me seems nervous.

Those ninety minutes simultaneously crawl and speed by. I walk around the room to see what they're writing, and try to help without actually helping. I tell Matt to bear down when he wants to give up, and Daniel to think before he writes, but generally I just encourage them to stay on task. I may not be able to tell what they're getting right or wrong, but I take it as an excellent sign that they're hard at work.

Monte naturally finishes early, but most of the others still are at it when the bell rings. I have to restrain myself not to give them another fifteen minutes; the whole point of a final exam is that there is no more time. And no makeups.

As they hand in their tests, some kids smile, and some grimace. Al G wears his usual smirk, and Charmaine and Paige flip their tests onto my desk, then start trash-talking about who did better. But basically everybody seems okay. No one appears upset with me, and that alone seems like a huge triumph.

Nakiya's the last to leave. "See you tomorrow, Mr. Danza. Nice test." She gives me two thumbs-up. The instant she's gone, I sit at my desk and get to work.

With every other test all year I've stalled, taking the papers home to grade later and then stalling some more for fear of seeing the results. This time's different. I can barely wait to stack the exams in front of me before tearing into them.

I start with Daniel's test because he's usually my bellwether. A good student, he pays attention, but at times he struggles. If he does well, I can maybe breathe. If he does well, there's a good chance I've actually done my job.

I race through Daniel's eleven pages, red pen working the margins. The test seems to have lengthened since I wrote it. Maybe Ms. Detolla was right and I have overreached. But then I reach the end. Danny's grade is good. I exhale.

Another fear strikes. Is it too good? In my eagerness for a positive result, did I go too easy on him? I take it from the top and double-check my work. No, there's no question, Daniel has a solid B. I shut my eyes and say a little prayer of thanks, then plunge ahead.

Two hours later I can say with certainty that no one has failed my class. Matt's grade is not what it should be, but many of the others, including all three of my IEP students, have done better than I dared hope. My relief leaves me dazed. I didn't even realize how much I had riding on this thing. Now I'm spinning between exhilaration and exhaustion.

The final essay question asked, "What was the most important lesson you learned in class this year?" I go back now and flip through the answers again. It shouldn't amaze me that the students all used correct essay form, but it does. It shouldn't surprise me to see some of my own phrases in their handwriting, but it does. And it certainly shouldn't touch me to know that the lessons many of my students consider most powerful were not scripted in any book, but this in particular shakes me to the core.

"Make the best of a baaaad situation," Nakiya wrote.

"Take part in your own education" appears in Al G's loopy cursive.

And for Ben-Kyle, the most important lesson was that "books are more than books. They are stories, too."

In almost every essay, I find advice that I've given them, almost verbatim. This is why people teach, I think. This is how you make a difference. They heard me and they remembered. That is one thrilling accomplishment.

Another is the sweetness of silence. The next afternoon, after I've given the finals back to the kids and we've all danced and traded high fives, I'm starting in on end-of-year paperwork when who should shuffle into my room but Al G. He lifts his chin in greeting and plunks down in a chair, as always with his backpack on. I wait, but he doesn't seem to be particularly agitated. He heaves a sigh and lets his body settle. I get on with my paperwork. It's taken the whole year, but I've finally learned to hold my tongue with Al, let him initiate. I'm here if he needs me. He never says a word.

Occasionally I look up. He's twisted around and is gazing out the window. The air conditioner is droning. It's sweltering outside and cool in here. If that's the only reason he's here, it's enough. Forty-five minutes pass. The bell rings. Al G gets up and nods at me on his way out.

"I'm wearing him down," I tell David Cohn when he stops by a few minutes later.

"Sounds more like you've worn each other down," David says with a rueful smile. "But in a good way." He hesitates, and I realize the same could be said about David and me. He's been there every step of the way this year, putting up with my angst and patiently saving me from myself on more occasions than I want to admit. And now he's leaving before I am.

David's moving to a school in Vermont. Tomorrow is his last day. "I can't believe you're not going to see this thing through to the finish," I tease him.

He tips his head. "I never thought I'd live to say this, Mr. Danza. But you don't need me anymore."

I grin. "I never thought you would, either."

"Keep it up and maybe one day we'll open a charter school together."

That is a compliment of such a high order that, for once in my life, I'm speechless.

THE NEXT WEEK is reserved for celebration, as far as I'm concerned, but everyone else is way ahead of me. My prediction that free dress would make Northeast crazy has more than come to pass, and not in a good way.

On Thursday, all the eleventh- and twelfth-grade students assemble in the auditorium for the ceremonial passing of school leadership from seniors to juniors. The two classes are seated on opposite sides of the audience. First the senior football players hand over a ceremonial torch to the junior players, then the other senior sports teams, cheerleaders, band members, choirs, academic and social clubs follow suit. The ceremony takes place on the stage, and with each passing there is a tremendous ovation of cheers and calls of "One Six Nine" and "One Seven O," the numbers of the graduating and rising senior classes.

The glow is good until someone from the senior side of the auditorium throws a water balloon at the junior side. War must have been declared in advance, because one second later all hell breaks loose. Both classes have come to assembly armed, and the balloons fly fast and furious, drenching everything and everyone in sight. When the supply of missiles is exhausted, the kids start spraying from water bottles. Then the battle escalates. One person throws a bottle, then another, and pretty soon the air is filled with plastic projectiles. Kids start screaming and running for the exits. From water balloons to stampede inside of three minutes.

Standing in the back, I try to slow them down, but the crush of students quickly overwhelms me. I grab another teacher out of the aisle and pull her to safety. The kids are piling up on each other, yelling. Panic is rising. Then Ms. Carroll's voice bellows from the stage. "That's enough! You will sit down and be quiet, or I will cancel everything planned for the rest of the year—including graduation!"

I've seen this principal handle all sorts of situations this year, and there were times when I thought she was a pretty good actor. There's no faking it this time. She's on fire. The kids stop in their tracks, seniors especially.

Luckily no one is hurt. Soaking wet, yes, but not hurt. The kids sheepishly return to their drenched seats. Later, Ms. Carroll chooses not to cancel graduation.

The Sons of Happiness

The next to last week of school, Rob Caroselli approaches me with the news that I've been tapped to join the Sons of Happiness, a fraternal society for men at Northeast High. The concept of a fraternal society of high school elders is a new one to me, so I ask Joe Connelly about it. He says they tapped him, too, but he knows no more about it than I do. We're both surprised that Rob never mentioned this group before. Maybe it's secret. We decide to just take it as an honor and try not to think about what the induction ritual might involve. At least Joe and I will go through the hazing together.

On Saturday, Joe drives us to the designated address, a trim white house with a big yard in a pleasant neighborhood. The home belongs to one of the Sons and looks anything but threatening. Still, it feels a little creepy when we're greeted by two teachers who usher us into the garage and tell us to put on the caps and gowns provided and stay there until we're called.

Two other inductees are already waiting. Both are slight middle-aged math teachers who seem even more nervous than we are. They also know enough to fill us in on this fraternity's brief history. The group was formed a few years ago by a small cadre of veteran teachers and retirees who'd noticed that camaraderie among men who work at Northeast—especially male teachers—was sorely lacking. Their idea was to provide an outlet for guys to let off steam outside of school. Now, members get together for dinner every few weeks, and at the end of every school year they induct a handful of new victims. Mentioning the society at school is strictly forbidden.

A voice outside summons one of the other novitiates, then a few minutes later Joe. I put my ear to the door, but we're too far away to hear what's happening. I can make out what sound like cheers, but that's it. The other math teacher is quaking now. He asks if I've ever been through a fraternity hazing. I say yes, when I was in high school. He hasn't but now starts reciting a litany of news reports about young men who've drowned, suffocated, or died of alcohol poisoning during fraternal inductions. I tell him I don't think there will be anything like that today. Still, he has me spooked enough that when my name is called, I practically leap out of there.

In the yard behind the garage stand some twenty men, including Joe and the other new member—who both appear to be just fine. I relax. Mr. Smith is here, and Rob Caroselli. Most of the others are guys I've seen around school all year.

The group speaks together in a kind of chant, instructing me to stand and state my name. Then they ask if I'm sure. Okay, they're messing with me. "Yes, that's my name," I reply, trying to catch Joe's eye, but he's now one of them and playing it totally cool.

Then it's one crazy question after another. Some are vulgar frat-boy jokes, but there are also a couple of serious questions about being a teacher. *Why are you here? What can you offer to students that someone else can't?* I answer as best I can, attempting to be clever and impress the club, but after a while it becomes a real grilling, with a free-for-all of follow-up questions. Mostly they're silly, but I can't help feeling as if I'm on trial for the crime of impersonating a teacher all year. Even here and now, trying to have fun, I still feel the need to prove myself to this group of veterans. The questions continue until finally the men seem satisfied with my answers. It's time for the open vote.

"Should Mr. Danza be admitted to the Sons?"

To my relief, everyone yells, "Aye!" Joe and Rob clap me on the back, and I scramble out of my induction costume as fast as humanly possible, then grab for a beer like a drowning man.

Seconds later, I'm one of them, hazing the last candidate, who somehow makes it out of the garage without needing to be carried. I have substantially more sympathy for him now.

Afterward we have a barbecue and sit around talking about—what else?—teaching. To these guys, their profession is both a calling and a way of life. The mood is good and bad. The retired teachers all seem to miss the classroom and look back on their careers fondly. The current teachers love their work, but everybody's concerned about the way teachers are portrayed in the media and in our culture.

One retired teacher, a tall man with a mustache, waves his cigarette and reminds me about the letter he sent me at the beginning of the year. I remember! This is Harry Gilbert, who retired three years ago after over three decades in the classroom. How can I forget the suggestion in his letter to always carry a shield in case of an unwanted woody—or his more heartfelt advice never to embarrass a student? It's good to finally put a face to his words.

"I voted to tap you for the Sons," Harry tells me. "Figured you deserved that much for sticking it out all year. Wasn't sure you would." I thank him for his vote and for his letter.

But they're not done with me yet. After Joe has a few drinks in him, he lets me know what he and the other teachers really thought when they first heard I was coming to their school. It turns out Harry wasn't alone in his predictions. I've climbed an even steeper hill than I realized. Back in September, not one of them would have called me a future Son of Happiness.

Then Joe asks the fateful question. "So, Tony," he says. "You coming back next year?"

"I don't know," I tell him, but even as I say it I know I do.

I need to go home. I need to work on being a husband and a father. Also, I have to admit it, teaching is awfully hard work.

Twelve

If . . .

ALL OF A SUDDEN it's the last week of school. I wake up on Monday fuming. Mondays annoy me anyway, what with the whole week of work and uncertainty bearing down, but today I'm radioactive. I don't really know why, though the TV production is one logical scapegoat.

The camera crew needs to film the end of the year, just in case the network orders additional shows, so I have to go back on camera for two more days. They'll shoot commencement, which is Friday, but Leslie also wants a goodbye in the classroom, and because the vast majority of students skip the last couple of days, he wants me to pretend to say goodbye today. All the old arguments about cooking reality come back to haunt me as I drive to school.

What I'm feeling is out of proportion to my anger over the shoot, and I'd do well to figure out what's really bugging me. When I get like this, I can be unpleasant. But I can't figure it out, and when I arrive at my room, the crew bear the brunt of my mood as they set up and mike me. Then I start in on the kids, who turn up behaving like their usual rowdy selves. I actually drag Eric Choi's chair out into the hall with him in it.

But it's when Les Grief appears and takes me aside that I really snap. "Ready to shoot your goodbyes?" he says, as if inviting me to dance. And that does it.

"No," I tell him, under my breath but coldly and right in front of everyone. "School's not over. We've still got this week. I'm not going to say goodbye now. And I'm not going to fake it."

"Then what are we here for?" he challenges me.

"I don't know, and I don't care."

The kids are watching this family feud with their mouths gaping, loving it even though they're not sure who to root for. When Les storms out, there's dead silence. The cameras are rolling.

I really don't care. I turn my attention back to controlling my unruly class.

Charmaine asks, "Mr. Danza, what's wrong with you? Why are you so crabby?"

Two other kids chime in, "Yeah, what's up with that? School's practically over."

I glare at them. "Because for some unknown reason, I'm going to miss—"

That's as far as I get. Out of nowhere and yet again, I break down. The sobs come up in great choking waves, the tears worse than ever. How can I not return to these kids next year? What's *wrong* with me?

My waterworks get them up out of their seats, and before I even know what's happening, we're locked in another huddle—even Al G is hovering close. Some of them are crying with me, this time. I sputter how much I love them, how much I'm going to miss them, how they've changed my life. They pat my back and squeeze me tight. They take all the anger out, and Leslie gets his goodbye.

THE REST OF THE WEEK only a handful of kids come to class, and most aren't even my students. The air-conditioning is on strike again, and I'm pretty much resigned to just shooting the breeze with the kids. Two of my girls, Paige and Tianna, show up with a DVD and ask if we can watch a movie. They've been nagging me to watch this film all year. "It's so good, Mr. Danza."

What I know about *Freedom Writers* is that it chronicles the true story of a young teacher, played by Hilary Swank, who goes to an inner-city school and tries to make a difference. It's a by-the-numbers tale of rough kids and a caring teacher who refuses to give up on them. "I don't want to see some sappy movie," I say over and over.

"No, Mr. Danza," Paige insists. "It's real good. You'll like it."

Finally, they wear me down. "Okay, put it on."

They jump up, put it in the computer, turn on the projector, and then take seats directly in front of me. For the next two hours I sit at my desk and sob as the movie plays on the front wall screen and Paige and Tianna watch me as if I'm the show. They love that it gets to me. That's just what they hoped would happen.

Afterward, they hand me Kleenex and pat me on the back. I seem to have passed some kind of challenge. Belatedly, I get it. That movie was their final test for me. If the story touched me as it did them, that would mean I really do care and they're right about me. They *are* right about me.

There is one moment in the film, though, that resonates with me in a way I cannot explain to the girls. Swank's character, Erin, is arguing with her husband, who just does not understand her all-consuming zeal for teaching.

Erin turns to him and says, "I don't know, but in that classroom my life makes sense."

BLINK TWICE, and it's graduation day. Technically, it's a regular school day for the few underclassmen who deign to show up, but all the energy on campus swirls around commencement. At noon I head down to the football field, excited and honored to be the commencement speaker.

The mood is electric. Philly has pulled out all the stops, weatherwise, and the stadium shines under a bright blue sky. The stands are full to bursting with proud parents, relatives, and friends, and chairs have been set up across the field, waiting for the graduates to file in. Self-conscious in my cap, gown, and even a turquoise blue cowl, I share the dais with Ms. Carroll, the district officials, the senior faculty adviser, and the senior class president.

I've sweated over my speech as if it were the State of the Union address. When I read it to my teacher friend Bobby G., he thought I was worrying so much about it because I wanted to say something that the students would always remember. I bought that for a minute, but then realized this past year has made me enough of a realist to know that *always remember* is way too high a bar. I told Bobby, "What I want is just for them to listen and not let the words go in one ear and out the other." Just hear it for one day, I think now, because that's how we learn: one day at a time.

"Pomp and Circumstance" begins to play over the loudspeakers. It takes more than an hour for Mr. Flaherty to announce each and every name of the nearly seven hundred graduates as they take their seats in the sun. The young women are gowned in Viking red, the guys in classic black—with red ties. They are a diverse and beautiful bunch, and their beaming faces make a powerful sight.

Finally everyone's settled and Ms. Carroll welcomes the graduates, family, and friends to the commencement of Northeast's Class 169. She is followed by one of my unofficial advisory kids, Dion, who happens to also be president of the student body. In his speech Dion singles me out for "all the stories [I] so unreluctantly told" him. I shoot him a peace sign; he's got my number, but he did pick up the ukulele from me.

Now it's my turn. I gaze out over the throng, clear my throat, and take it from the top. "For those of you who don't know, I am Tony Danza, a.k.a. Mr. Danza. *Mr. Danza.* Boy, do I like that."

It's a little tricky addressing this class, since I didn't officially teach any of them, but I did get to know many of the seniors through the half-sandwich club, talent shows, dances, and my coaching duties. "My first week," I tell them, "before you kids came to school, a couple of football-playing seniors helped me set up and decorate my room. They were so tall I didn't need a ladder. They helped me put up my fadeless paper. *Fadeless paper,* that's teacher talk. Like *graphic organizer, model it,* or *collaborative learning.* Watch out; don't make me say *Venn diagram.*" At least the teachers chuckle at that.

I turn the talk to the graduates. "By finishing high school and getting your diploma, you have done something that nearly fifty percent of kids your age don't do. That's right, one out of two kids that start high school in America do not finish. So you beat the odds. You've set the table for a good life. Now, as you go forward, make sure you continue to put the work in to make yourself good at whatever you choose to do.

"You have the time and the opportunity to find your passion," I assure the graduates, "but remember that time is finite. Don't waste it. Remember that if the time you have now is well spent, your whole life will be enhanced. As Shakespeare says, 'There is a tide in the affairs of men which, taken at the flood, leads on to fortune; omitted, all the voyage of their life is bound in shallows and in miseries.'"

I expect I've lost more than a few in the audience with that quote, but I figure I earned it. "And now for some general *after* high school tips." They'd enjoy this next part more if I played it for laughs, but I can't do that. I've seen too many Northeast kids—or their older brothers and sisters—crash and burn this year. So I tell them straight, "Take care of yourselves. That means, don't abuse your bodies. And *take your time with love.* Don't be in such a rush. Girls, know that the guys are up to no good. And, guys, be responsible. Understand that the choices you make are pivotal. One wrong move and *your* life is very different, so get your own lives in order before you have to think about taking care of someone else."

I thank the parents and families, and I make a plea. "As a teacher, I appreciate parents who stress the importance of education, because the schools and teachers can't do it alone. We need your support. We need a culture that celebrates education and holds it up high, where it belongs. You have stood by your children, and it has, so far, paid off, but we all know your work is not done. Please don't stop having high expectations for your children." That said, I know from experience that some of these parents are supportive to a fault, so I remind them that the kids are now officially not kids anymore. "Call on them to start being adults. Not all the way, but get them started. Sorry, graduates, it's time."

Finally, I have to acknowledge my colleagues. It's a little presumptuous for Mr. Danza to speak for the students, but that's the prerogative of the podium. "Thank you to the teachers who were there every day, the teachers who put up with your moods, told you to put away your phones or take out your earbuds. Thank you to the teachers who agonized over your grades and tried as hard as they could to give you what you will need as you continue on in life."

By this time I can feel Ms. Carroll behind me calling for the hook, but I have to get in my own thanks. "This has been the greatest year of my life. I learned more and worked harder than I ever have. I met people I will always look up to and students I will never forget. I am a different and better person because of all of you, and I thank you for that."

I finish, once more in English teacher mode, with the Kipling poem "If," which might as well have been written for commencement addresses. It concludes:

If you can talk with crowds and keep your virtue,
Or walk with kings—nor lose the common touch,
If neither foes nor loving friends can hurt you,
If all men count with you, but none too much;
If you can fill the unforgiving minute
With sixty seconds' worth of distance run,
Yours is the Earth and everything that's in it,
And—which is more—you'll be a Man, my son!

"Make your lives count!" I urge the Class of 2010, and then, "One last thing." I raise my hand up like a visor and peer back and forth across the stadium. "Any Vikings in the house?"

The place fills with a roar that I sense is fueled half by delight and half by relief that I've finally stopped talking. Even I have to admit that poem was pushing my luck. But the others on the dais are polite, and afterward a few of the teachers compliment me for putting poetry into my commencement speech.

AFTER ALL THE PICTURES are taken and hugs shared all around, I head up to my classroom, where the last of my die-hard students are waiting. The camera crew tags along for a final wrap-up. The kids have filled an album with photographs and notes commemorating our year together, and now they'll present the album to me on-camera.

Fortunately, these are my kids, and there's nothing reverent about their album entries. "Danza's Top Ten Dumb, Annoying Habits," for example, cites my inability to say the word *idea* without it sounding like *idear;* my drenching sweat; my overuse of the word *schmo;* and my constant refrain, "You can do it, you can do it." Maybe I come off looking like a schmo, but they've put so much heart, cheek, and effort into this book that I'm not sure whether to laugh or cry, so I do a little of both.

There is one particular page that I really can't get over and definitely can't live up to. It's a full-page picture of me at a football game wearing a Northeast High School sweatshirt. Underneath, my class has written, "Our Atticus."

I cry again for good measure. And that's before we say goodbye for real.

First, everyone pitches in to help me strip the room of their work, which they'll take home. Then one by one they all leave, except for Daniel and Alex, who's been hovering around my room all day. Alex's home life has recently spiraled downhill. A couple of weeks ago he was moved to yet another foster home, separated from his sister. I began reaching out to everyone I could think of who might be able to help, and my assistant Kelly Gould, the angel on our crew who saved Courtney from failing physics earlier in the year, stepped to the rescue again. Kelly is a native of Philadelphia, and her family owns and operates a summer camp in the Poconos. She's gotten them to offer Alex a free stay at the camp. Now, after much effort, all the paperwork is in and he's looking at four weeks in the mountains, a world away from foster care. This boy is one of those kids who's more at home at school than he is at the place that others call his home, and now, thanks to Kelly, he'll have another school away from home for the summer. Except that it will be a whole lot more fun than school. I tell him to make sure he sends me a poem from the Poconos.

Daniel proudly holds his portraits of Shakespeare and of the old man from his poetry contest recital. "You know, Daniel," I say, "I really did mean it all the times this year I told you that you're talented. Seriously talented."

Instead of acknowledging what I've just said, Daniel gazes at the walls. "The room looks different, Mr. D.," he says.

Alex agrees. "There sure was a lot of stuff on these walls." He whistles for emphasis.

I can't resist one more parting shot. "Daniel," I say, "I expect you to keep up the kind of work you did this year. You make your mom proud."

"I have no choice," he answers. "She's bigger than me."

Alex laughs, but I jump on him. "Hey you, don't laugh. You made a deal with me, too, and I will be checking."

"I can see you in L.A. right?" he asks.

I nod. "That's our deal, but you have to do well for your own sake, not just for this or any trip." I'm starting to hate the sound of my voice.

The guys walk me outside and help me load my rental car. We fist-bump. We bear-hug. I get in the car. Suddenly, they're gone.

I feel about as alone as I've ever felt in my life. I'm still on a high from the thrill of the day, but I'm also bereft. It's gotten late, and the sky's clouded over. A work crew has already taken in half the chairs from the commencement ceremony. The school has that vacant, blank-windowed look that schools always get during summers, when their sole purpose for being—the students—is gone. And what exactly is my purpose now?

Refusing to go there, I turn the ignition, shift into reverse, and head for the exit. As I reach the intersection, I spot Danny and Alex waiting to cross at the corner. I beep my horn and wave. They shoot me two radiant grins and both pretend to tap-dance.

Saving Starfish

The final day of the school year for teachers is June 21. No kids, just teachers. The district wants every last second of those snow days credited back. The good news: only one day is left to make up after graduation. The bad news: it's a Monday, which means that all the teachers have to adjust their summer plans to come in.

By this point, no one has any real work to do. I say goodbye to Ms. Carroll and to my fellow Son of Happiness, Joe, who promises to come out to L.A. one day and take in another fight with me. Both of these goodbyes are pretty tough, but I even get teary-eyed bidding farewell to Ms. DeNaples, who despite our rocky start has indeed wound up being one of my best friends in the school.

Then, coming out of the office, I bump into Chuck Carr, my old PSSA partner. I've heard the rumor that Mr. Carr has put in his papers to retire at the end of the year. I can't help thinking what losing a teacher like this will do to the school. He's one of so many of those great baby boomer educators who have given their lives to the cause of education and will be so hard to replace. He's loaded down with books and doesn't seem to want to talk, but I have to ask if it's true that he's throwing in the towel. "Changed my mind," he says gruffly, not stopping.

I walk along with him. "What do you mean?"

"One more year."

After a few more feet I ask, "How many years has it been?"

"Thirty-six."

"And you're *not* ready to be done?" Right now I find that impossible to imagine. "Why one more year?"

Mr. Carr looks down the length of the empty corridor. He sighs. "Maybe next year I'll get it right."

I shake his hand and let him go and feel a tidal wave of guilt that only multiplies when a few of the teachers in my SLC present me with a farewell video. They went around the school asking for good-bye sound bites, which they've edited together. The tribute is wonderful, but by this time I can't take any more. I feel like a deserter. I don't want to leave these people, and I especially don't want another reminder that I'm not coming back to my kids in September.

I have a train to catch for New York City, and I badly need to be on my way, but just when I reach the front door, Lynn Dixon catches me. She has a present for me. Another piece of kitsch from Ms. Dixon, I think, and accept the plaque without even reading it. One last quick hug, and I stuff the gift into my tote bag. "I'm late," I tell her. "I have to go. I'll miss you."

As the train pulls out of 30th Street Station, I think back over the strange turns this year has taken, and I wonder whether I've been successful in my mission—or even exactly what my mission was. Between the show and the class and my own uncertainty, I'm still not sure. Maybe because I had only the one class I became too attached. I inserted myself into my students' lives, and now I'm gone. That seems wrong, and yet I remind myself that teachers and students have been coming and going from each other's lives forever. It's what students take with them and keep that matters. They'll get along fine without me, I think. I'll stay in touch with them. In emails I can still drive them crazy with advice and aphorisms.

As the train nears Trenton, I'm rummaging in my bag when I notice the box from Ms. Dixon. Figuring now it's safe to open it, I find a polished wood rectangle embellished with a metal scroll. The inscription on the scroll tells the story of a huge storm that roils the sea and washes thousands of starfish up onto the beach. The clouds break, and the sun comes out and begins to bake the starfish. A man wanders by and sees the thousands of stranded stars. He doesn't know what to do at first, but then he starts to throw them back in the water one by one. Another man comes by and says to him, "What are you doing? There are so many, you're not making much of a difference." The first man bends and picks up another starfish, throws it in the water, and says, "Made a difference to that one!"

I love Ms. Dixon for giving me this story. I did try to make a difference. Maybe I didn't get them all in the water, but I think I got most of them closer to it. Maybe that's all any teacher can do.

Epilogue

ON OCTOBER 1, 2010, A&E finally premiered *Teach*. The show lasted six weeks, buried in a late Friday-night time slot, where we were virtually guaranteed to fail. Even so, I received many encouraging letters from a few of the stalwart teachers who were actually home and awake on a Friday night. One wrote that he identified with my struggles, having experienced similar moments in his teaching career. Unfortunately, he added that his wife, a psychiatrist by trade, thought I might be having a nervous breakdown in the first episode. That's not how it seemed to me in the moment, but in hindsight the diagnosis could be a little close for comfort. Instead of taking it personally, I chose to view her observation as proof that this profession requires a highly specialized and valuable mix of personality, perspective, and skills for success, and that it's emotionally grueling. If our viewers took one thing away from the show, I hope it was a profound appreciation for the challenge that teachers across this country face each and every day. If my meltdowns in class helped dramatize that challenge, then maybe we did some good after all. Still, after the show ended, I kept feeling as if a golden opportunity had been missed. The series was taken off the air so abruptly, our story seemed to have no conclusion. Those great shots of our group hug at the end of the year never even aired.

Some time after the show was officially canceled, I met with the head of the A&E network, Bob DeBitetto, and he told me, "You did a great job. I'm really proud of *Teach*. But, you know, when I first bought the show, I never thought people would watch it."

"Really!" I was taken aback. "Why not?"

"I've been doing this for a while now," he said. "I'm a pretty good judge of the market, and this is not the kind of stuff audiences want to watch."

That seemed to beg the question "Well then, why did you buy it and put it on?"

He was matter-of-fact. "It was a good cause, topical, and you never know, with you, I might get lucky."

A good cause, topical, and you never know, I might get lucky. I came away from that meeting thinking, Well, there you have it. That's America's attitude toward education in a nutshell. We all know that America's children—and future—are a "good cause" and "topical," but as a country we'd rather take a shot at "getting lucky" than invest the effort, money, time, and attention it takes to *guarantee* their success. Our show suddenly seemed like a metaphor for the overwhelming problem of education in America. And a big contributor to that problem is the attitude that Bob DiBitetto echoed. Learning, most of this country seems to think, is like medicine that we know we need but refuse to take unless somebody makes it so entertaining that we forget to think it tastes bad.

Whether or not our show could have changed attitudes about teaching, it never really had a chance. And whether or not the educators who are trying to raise up America's students can actually set and meet higher academic standards, our cultural values make their job next to impossible. It's so much easier for pundits and politicians to point fingers and blame the people who are in the trenches every day than it is to get in there with them, or even to find out what actually goes on in those trenches. It's so much easier for parents to blame teachers when their kids get in trouble than to do the heavy lifting required at home to keep those kids on track. And it's so much easier for us as a nation to cross our fingers and hope that we'll "get lucky" with the innovative "solutions" being tested on America's schools today than it is for us to roll up our sleeves and invest our own time, talent, and money in the schools that are even now—with or without us—shaping our nation's future.

If I learned anything during my year at Northeast, it's that the blame game serves no purpose in our educational system. Sure, there are some bad teachers, and some bad administrators, just as there are failing corporate CEOs and lousy actors, but the vast majority of educators I met at Northeast were not bad so much as they were discouraged and overwhelmed. The rising numbers of low-income and immigrant children, the underwhelming involvement of parents, and the impact of a culture that sneers at knowledge instead of treasuring it all make the classroom a very tough place to work. Beyond that, the sheer logistics of teaching, counseling, comforting, coaching, and inspiring 150 students each and every day are beyond the capability of most normal human beings. Yet public school teachers are expected to perform these tasks calmly and brilliantly while simultaneously documenting and evaluating every move they and their students make. Oh, and don't forget staying up-to-the-minute and responsive to those constantly changing district mandates and national policy shifts. All for less money than the average plumber, real estate agent, or sales manager makes. Shouldn't we value the job of expanding our children's minds more than we value the job of Roto-Rooting our pipes? We say we do, but we never seem to put our money where our mouths are.

Teachers and students need help, not accusations and pay cuts.

They need to be a national priority, not an experiment stuck into a late time slot and then canceled for underperforming. But just when our schools need more support than ever, they're getting less than ever. Why can't everybody see what's wrong with this picture? Because, like the A&E audience, most people don't want to see it.

But I do. I see the problem of education now like I never did before. Since I left Northeast, many of my students and fellow teachers have become my email BFFs, and they keep me up-to-date on the latest changes at school, of which there have been many. Budget cuts have loomed over the district as they have across America. Any teacher with less than three years' seniority is in danger of being laid off, and many of those who went through orientation with me have already left the profession because of cutbacks, frustration, and/or their own economic necessity. Joe Connelly, I'm happy to report, is still hanging on, but at the other end of the spectrum, many of the most seasoned teachers are now gone. The list of Northeast veterans who retired the year after I left includes Chuck Carr, Lynn Dixon, and more than twenty others. Although they've more than earned their pensions and some R & R, their absence represents a colossal loss for the school. I hate to think how my year would have gone if these pros hadn't been there to set me straight, and I can't imagine the place going forward without them.

The deepest impact on me, however, was made by the kids. Every few days I get a bulletin from another one—Paige, Nakiya, Eric, Brittiny, Daniel, even occasionally Charmaine and Al G. Their lives, like those of most teenagers, are roller coasters of highs and lows. But some of them have to survive more hairpin turns than anybody should. I'm still struggling to keep up with the twists and turns in Alex's life.

When I last saw him at school, he was dancing off to that summer camp in the Poconos, which represented a highlight in his rough life. At camp he met a boy his age who became his best friend. Both poets, they wrote poems together, videotaping their work and posting it on YouTube. They grew so close that when this boy's parents came to visit, they, too, fell in love with Alex—and agreed to become his foster parents. After camp was over, he moved into their home in Bucks County, outside Philly. In the fall, they enrolled him in the same terrific school that his new brother attended, and everything seemed to be playing out like a fairy tale.

A few months later I returned to Philadelphia to take part in an education conference headed by Arne Duncan, the secretary of education. While I was in town, I met Alex's new family, and seeing him with them was one of the happiest moments of my life. I tried to impress on Alex, though, that he'd have to make an effort to prove to the family that taking him in was the right move for them, too. The decision to take a sixteen-year-old boy into their lives was major, and I didn't want them to regret it. I didn't want Alex to be moved again. So I counseled him that what he gives, he will get back. He seemed to get that.

As we were saying goodbye, I mentioned a line that the singer Suzanne Vega wrote for an old boyfriend: "I am bound to you forever." True to form, Alex immediately knocked out a poem:

I'm bound to you forever,
Like the sky is to the sea.
We'll be together always,
how lucky can two guys be.

Sweet. I could not have been prouder if he were my own son.

I wish that were the happy ending. Unfortunately, life—like teaching—is not so simple, and any time I need a reality check, I look to Alex.

It seems to me that his foster mother had only good intentions and hopes for Alex. The problem was that the arrangement hinged on the friendship between the two boys. After a few months, that friendship soured, and there was also some strife in the family that had nothing to do with Alex. I became aware of the problems and tried to help smooth things out long distance, but after talking to him on the phone a few times, I began to think that maybe this wasn't the best spot for Alex after all. He missed Northeast, he wasn't speaking to his friend now, and I could hear how distressed he was. Then the foster mother called to tell me they were making a change. They'd spoken to Alex's social worker and all decided to move Alex to live with his brother, who was twenty-three, married, and had an apartment near Northeast.

Alex later told me he was happy to be back at his old school, but I had a tough time not acting on my own adoption fantasy during this transition, especially when he said things like "I wish I lived with you." I settled for becoming his unofficial mentor. He seemed to be doing well back in Philly, but then he finished his junior year with a C average. And he got himself a girlfriend, which excited him but concerned me. We persuaded the camp in the Poconos where we'd set him up in 2010 to have him back the next summer, and I check in with him every Sunday, but I can only do so much. Where does teaching stop, and start? Where should it?

I still don't really know. To engage my students, I found that I had to become engaged in their lives, their problems, and their futures. That connection was what made the job most rewarding. Yet it was also the intensity of that involvement that, by the end of the year, had made the job of teaching so much tougher than I'd ever expected.

After walking a mile in their shoes, I now see America's educators as heroes who deserve our wholehearted respect and support. At this point in my life, I may not be cut out for a career *in* the classroom, but I am committed to making education a priority in all the other ways I can make a difference. That, too, is an important lesson. It's not an all-or-nothing proposition. You don't have to be a full-time teacher to be an education activist. You can read to kids at the local library. You can volunteer in your neighborhood school. And you can contribute to programs that promote teaching excellence. Teach for America, DonorsChoose, the Freedom Writers Foundation, the EnCorps teachers program, and the Fulfillment Fund are just a few of the many terrific organizations that support public education in a variety of ways, from counseling and mentoring students and teachers to providing scholarships and grants for educational innovation.

The bottom line is that every one of us has a stake in getting education back on track in America. Even if we can't all be great teachers ourselves, we should be rooting for those who do go into this profession. We may not all choose to send our kids to public schools, but we all still need to support the public school system, because our country's future depends on its success. And on a personal level, there's one very simple thing we all can do—especially those of us who used to be the kids who made teaching even harder than it needed to be. So let me do that right now:

I would like to apologize to every teacher I ever had.

Acknowledgments

Writing a book, I have learned, is a difficult, almost monumental task. My only experience writing any kind of book before was *Don't Fill Up on the Antipasto,* a cookbook and memoir of our family that my son, Marc, and I wrote together. I am proud of that project, but this book was a completely different experience. First, I didn't have my son to help me, and second, the issue of education in America is so much more important even than my father's meatball recipe (although his meatballs really are the best!). My year at Northeast was one of the hardest and best years I have had in my adult life, and I struggled mightily at times to do justice to the experience in these pages. Now that the book is completed, the list of people I need to thank is long.

First and foremost, I must thank the kids in my class and my unofficial advisory, who in the end not only were easy to write about but also gave me so much hope—hope that we all should share and support.

For putting up with the production, and me, I'm grateful to the rest of the student body at Northeast and the administration, with special thanks to our principal, Linda Carroll, and to Peggy DeNaples,

Sharon McCloskey, Rob Caroselli, Byron Ryan, and Andrew Lukov. Thanks to the teachers of Northeast, who not only accepted and encouraged me but also inspired me with their commitment and dedication. I owe them. Thanks to my coteacher, mentor, and main cheerleader, David Cohn, and to my close colleagues Crystal Green, Tim Flaherty, Bill Winglicki, Coach Chris Riley, Theresa Bramwell, Harry Gilbert, Lynn Dixon, Lynn Keiner, Glen Dyson, and Matt Callahan. My pal Joe Connelly not only inspires me but also is the model of what I'm hoping this book will highlight. Kelly Gould, my assistant, was a big reason I was able to make it through the year. Every teacher should have an assistant.

.I also want to thank the staff, guards, and janitorial department of the school—the staff for putting up with all my procedural mistakes; the guards for being there and also manning my scavenger hunt stations; and the janitorial staff for the support they gave me whenever I needed it.

The A&E network, particularly Bob DiBitetto, Neil Cohen, and Rob Sharnow, deserves credit for getting me to *Teach*! Thanks to my dear friend Leslie Grief and Adam Reed, who I know I drove crazy. I also want to thank Mayor Michael Nutter for his amazing support of my efforts and commitment to the children of his city; Philadelphia's film and TV chief, Sharon Pinkenson; the Philadelphia School District; and the people and the city of Philadelphia. Thanks to Patsy's.

I'd also like to acknowledge my editor, Rick Horgan, and his colleagues Tina Constable, Sarah Breivogel, Tammy Blake, and Christina Foxley at Crown; my manager, Dan Farah; my book agent, Peter McGuigan, who really made this book happen, and his colleague Stephanie Abou at Foundry Literary; my publicist Jill Fritzo and her colleague Gabe Walker; and Aimee Liu, who pulled it all together and dragged me over the finish line. I couldn't have done it without her. Thank you, all. I am eternally grateful.

About the Author

Born and raised in Brooklyn, Tony Danza attended the University of Dubuque in Iowa, where he earned a bachelor's degree in history. Discovered at a boxing gymnasium in New York, Danza was ultimately cast in the critically acclaimed series *Taxi*, earning him a place in television history. He followed *Taxi* with a starring role in the classic ABC comedy series *Who's the Boss?*, which ran for eight seasons.

Eventually Danza explored his love for the stage, and among his many stage credits is his exciting run on Broadway in Mel Brooks's hit musical *The Producers*, playing Max Bialystock (2006–2007), and his reprise of the role in the Las Vegas production at Paris Las Vegas (2007). For his theatrical debut in *Wrong Turn at Lungfish* (1993) he earned an Outer Critic's Circle Award nomination. Other stage credits include the critically acclaimed *Iceman Cometh* opposite Kevin Spacey, Arthur Miller's Tony Award–winning play *A View from the Bridge*, and *I Remember You*. In 2008, Danza and his son, Marc, saw their father-son cookbook, *Don't Fill Up on the Antipasto*, released to great success.

Among Danza's other television experiences is his role as attorney Joe Celano on the CBS dramatic series *Family Law* (2000–2002); his Emmy-nominated performance on David E. Kelley's award-winning series *The Practice* (1998); and ABC's *The Tony Danza Show*, a talk show that blended celebrity interviews, human-interest stories, cooking, and audience participation, and was broadcast live from New York (2004–2006). He also starred in and executive produced the ABC comedy series *Hudson Street* and NBC's *The Tony Danza Show*, and hosted the 2001 Miss America Pageant, the 2003 People's Choice Awards, and the 2008 season of *The Contender*, produced by Mark Burnett Productions and Dreamworks Televison.

Among Danza's big-screen credits are his roles in Walt Disney's *Angels in the Outfield* with Danny Glover, *She's Out of Control*, *The Hollywood Knights*, and *A Brooklyn State of Mind*.

Danza is currently developing several projects for the stage and television. He resides in New York City.